SEPECAT

JAGUAR

The Jaguars' Finest Hour, Gulf War 1991. These Desert Cats are armed with overwing AIM-9L Sidewinders and a CRV-7 rocket pod under the starboard wing. (Mike_Rondot)

SEPECAT

JAGUAR

Tactical Support & Maritime Strike Fighter

Martin W. Bowman

Pen & Sword
AVIATION

First published in Great Britain in 2007 by
Pen & Sword Aviation
An imprint of
Pen & Sword Books Ltd
47 Church Street
Barnsley
South Yorkshire
S70 2AS

ISBN 978 1 84415 545 3

Printed and bound in England
By CPI UK

Pen & Sword Books Ltd incorporates the Imprints of Pen & Sword Aviation, Pen &
Sword Maritime, Pen & Sword Military, Wharncliffe Local History, Pen & Sword
Select, Pen & Sword Military Classics and Leo Cooper.

For a complete list of Pen & Sword titles please contact
PEN & SWORD BOOKS LIMITED
47 Church Street, Barnsley, South Yorkshire, S70 2AS, England
E-mail: enquiries@pen-and-sword.co.uk
Website: www.pen-and-sword.co.uk

Acknowledgements

I am most grateful to the following, all of whom very kindly supplied photos and/or information for this book: Squadron Leader Dave Bagshaw, AFC; Chris Bennett; Squadron Leader Ed Bulpett; Mick Cartwright; Roger Cook; Mick Jennings MBE, who for many years opened many doors for a series of memorable visits to RAF Coltishall and who supplied many photos for this book; Dick Jeeves, Steve Jefferson; Bill Johns; Steven Hill; Colonel Bruno Maurice, *Minstère de la Défense, Republic Française*; Bernard Noble and his son Kevin Noble who very graciously allowed me to quote freely from their family 'bible' *Noble Endeavours*; Gary Parsons; Group Captain William Pixton DFC AFC; Rolls-Royce; Mike Rondot; Air Chief Marshal Sir Jock Stirrup GCB AFC ADC BSc FRAeS FCMI; Group Captain Edward Stringer BSc; Squadron Leader Johnny Stringer; the late Tom Trower and Denis Calvert.

Time to Reflect. GR.3A XZ117/FB after a downpour at Coltishall on 1 April 2006. (Author)

Contents

Jaguars on the production line at BAC's Military Aircraft Division at Warton near Blackpool, Lancashire, in March 1973. On the left is XX111 with a partially camouflaged rear fuselage, with XX112 and XX113/PS606 behind. On the right a Model B can be seen on the line. On 30 May 1973 Squadron Leader John Preece delivered XX111 to the Jaguar Operational Conversion Unit (JOCU) at RAF Lossiemouth on the Moray Firth in Scotland for ground crew training. The aircraft was also used later by the Indian Air Force. Eighteen years later XX112 formed part of the initial deployment to Oman. XX113 was issued to 226 OCU and was lost in a crash on 17 July 1981. (BAC)

CHAPTER ONE

Entente Cordiale?

The six Jaguars of 6 Squadron are cruising east to their target at 500 mph, 190 ft above the undulating ground of central Bulgaria. The formation is in card, each pair of aircraft two miles line abreast and thirty seconds spaced from the other pairs. Five minutes ago Number 2 had defeated an SA-8 surface-to-air missile system that had attempted to engage him; his Radar Warning Receiver had alerted him to the danger and he had kicked the rest of the formation away from the threat. Suddenly, an urgent voice breaks the silence on the Jaguars' 'chat' frequency: 'Boxer, duck! Single MiG, Black's 6, two miles, high to low.' The jets descend to 100 ft and accelerate to 550 mph. Even so, the MiG continues to close towards the front pair of Jaguars; the pilot of the front left jet pulls the throttles back, and breaks hard into the MiG, closing the range rapidly and simultaneously putting out flares to defeat any infra-red missile shot. Meanwhile, unsighted to the MiG, one of the middle pair of Jags has closed to missile range and has locked the 'Bandit' up with his AIM 9L Sidewinder air-to-air missile. Slew . . . good tone . . . uncage valid track . . . 'Fox 2, MiG, Bull 120, 37 . . .'

Squadron Leader Johnny Stringer

Although the above 'belongs to a (very) distant element of the Clancey school of military writing,' says Stringer, 'the events described definitely belong in the realm of fact.' The only difference is that when these words were written they referred not to an undeclared Cold War combat by NATO forces but to a visit in August 2002 to Graf Ignatievo Air Base, Bulgaria, by RAF Jaguars. The 'Flying Canopeners' were thus the first RAF fast-jet squadron to operate with the *Bulgarski Voenno-Vazdushni Sili* (Bulgarian Air Force, or *BVVS*) since the end of the Cold War.

The first steps that ultimately led to this scenario occurred some fifty years earlier, when the document creating the North Atlantic Treaty Organization (NATO) was signed in Washington DC on 4 April 1949 by ten European countries, including Great Britain, France, Canada and the United States of America. From 1939 to 1945 Europe was ravaged by six years of war, and the Soviet Union was fast emerging as a threat to the uneasy post-war peace after strengthening its hold over the eastern European states liberated from Nazi Germany. The first steps to words establishing an alliance of free nations occurred in January 1948, when the British Foreign Secretary, Ernest Bevin, proposed a Western European Union. Just two months later, on 17 March, Britain, France, and the Benelux countries signed an agreement in Brussels, and then in June the Soviets began their blockade of West Berlin. General Dwight D. Eisenhower was appointed the

XX110, the third production Jaguar, on the assembly line at Warton at the mating of the wing and fuselage. The nose, fuselage centre sections and undercarriage were made by Breguet, and the wings, tail unit, rear fuselage and engine air-intakes by BAC. These assemblies were then mated together on identical production lines at Warton and at Colomiers at Toulouse-Blagnac airport in France. (BAC)

first Supreme Allied Commander Europe (SACEUR) in December 1950, and his headquarters at Rocquencourt near Paris became operational on 2 April 1951, designated Supreme HQ Allied Powers Europe (SHAPE). Enormous numbers of American ground and air forces began arriving in Europe to strengthen those of the Western democracies, and on 5 May 1955 West Germany became the thirteenth NATO member.

One of the biggest dividends received by America was the supply of American-built military jets to the European air arms. Republic fighter-bombers, Northrop F-5 Freedom Fighters and collaborative projects such as the Lockheed F-104 Starfighter (and much later, the General Dynamics F-16), were built in huge numbers and used to equip several NATO air forces. The one exception was France, which had never purchased American military hardware to any great degree and on 10 March 1966 announced its intention to leave the military structure of NATO at the end of the year. All Allied units were forced to withdraw from French soil and SACEUR moved its HQ to Belgium. France was put into cold storage, and in 1968 a British initiative resulted in the creation of the Eurogroup, which was composed of all European members except France and Iceland. Eurogroup's aim was to strengthen members' contributions to NATO by collective policies and efforts. Despite national ambitions and divisions and lingering political differences, NATO successfully prevented all-out war in Europe during the remaining fifty years of the twentieth century and afterwards. Politically, Britain and France were poles apart, and relations were not helped by President Charles de Gaulle's decision to block Britain's entry into the Common Market (now the European Union). However, before the swinging sixties had passed into history the two countries had reached agreement on two highly successful collaborative projects that resulted in the supersonic passenger transport and the Jaguar combat aircraft being built in France and Britain.

On 29 November 1962 two important agreements were signed. One was between the French and British governments, which would provide development funding. The other was between the four companies (the British Aircraft Corporation, engine manufacturers Rolls-Royce and Sud-Aviation and the *Société Nationale d'Étude et de Construction des Moteurs d'Aviation*) that would collaborate on airframe and engine development, for the aircraft later to become known as Concorde. Three years later, on 28 February 1965, the

Entente Cordiale seemed alive and well, not only in the corridors of power but in aviation circles also. The British Minister of Defence, Denis Healey, publicly revealed that an agreement in principle had been forged between the UK and French governments. On 17 May an accord known as the Memorandum of Understanding was signed by the British and French governments to participate in a joint venture to build a supersonic advanced trainer to replace the Folland Gnat in RAF service and the Fouga Magister in the *Armée de l'Air* inventory by 1970. A new supersonic design would also bridge the gap that had opened up since the introduction of more advanced first-line combat aircraft like the Dassault Mirage III in France, while the RAF

Sir Freddie Page congratulates Jimmy Dell at Warton, Lancashire, after the first flight of S-06 XW560, the first BAC-assembled prototype, on 12 October 1969, when Dell flew S-06 supersonic at the first attempt. Former chief test pilot with English Electric, Roland 'Bee' Beamont, Director, Flight Operations at BAC, Preston (left), looks suitably pleased. On 11 August 1972 the port engine exploded during the run-up for take-off from Boscombe Down, Wiltshire, owing to the disintegration of the third-stage disc on the high-pressure compressor. The pilot evacuated the aircraft, which was soon engulfed in flames after a fuel pipe was severed by the explosion. It was subsequently used for ground instruction at Lossiemouth. (BAe)

would need a replacement for the Hawker Hunter by about 1975. In Britain there was a perceived need among aviation concerns for a two-seat trainer aircraft between the Jet Provost and the TSR.2, P.1154 and the Phantom, but the British Labour government was not interested. In the main it believed that American aircraft could be 'bought off the shelf' more cheaply and/or an agreement on a collaborative project with another nation could be reached with equally perceived savings in expenditure.

Finding funds can often make for strange bedfellows. In the case of Concorde it was born of necessity, and as far as the joint military project was concerned it was desirable,

Jimmy Dell points out some of the features of the SEPECAT Jaguar to Roland 'Bee' Beamont. Although outwardly the aircraft differed little from the French prototypes, the avionics fit, together with several other internal changes, made it a different aircraft altogether, and it was the first RAF aircraft to have a head-up display (HUD). (BAe)

Bee Beamont makes a point about the Jaguar to HRH Prince Charles at Farnborough. Jimmy Dell (right) looks on. (BAe)

especially since the successful design was expected to incorporate some attack capability, which on paper would result in further savings. Eventually, the attack role became the more important consideration in both France and Britain, while the training requirement could perhaps be addressed by a two-seat version of the same aircraft. As in the case of Concorde, a new company would be formed to administer the project. (The outcome of co-operation on this scale would ultimately result in future collaborative projects such as the Tornado and the Eurofighter 2000).

A committee is rarely the best method of achieving a successful outcome, and where aircraft are concerned this usually proves to be the case. The search for a successful combat-trainer design with increasingly high strike ambitions not only had to meet an internal French requirement – known as the ECAT (*École de Combat et d'Appui Tactique*, or Tactical Combat Support Trainer) – but it also had to conform to Air Staff Target AST 362 laid down by the Ministry of Defence in London. In effect, the French were looking for a small, relatively simple, cost-effective, subsonic front-line trainer, while the RAF requirement (and to a certain extent, the Royal Navy's) was for a supersonic advanced trainer. France also wanted the aircraft to fulfil an additional light strike role

Bernard Witt and Jimmy Dell pose before a Jaguar at Istres in 1968. The Jaguar was the last aircraft that 46-year-old Jimmy Dell test flew, for in October 1970 a routine six-monthly medical revealed a minor heart problem, and after two test flights in the Jaguar one Saturday he was told to cease flying at once. (SEPECAT)

and be able to operate not only from permanent runways but also from unprepared grass strips. Not unnaturally, competition was fierce, on both sides of the Channel. In France no fewer than five companies were invited to submit designs to meet the requirement, and all of their submissions had a fixed wing, whereas British companies on the whole favoured using variable-geometry, or swing-wing. English Electric (later BAC – the British Aircraft Corporation) was one company which saw a requirement for a variable-geometry multi-role combat aircraft for operation in overseas theatres operating from short runways. The BAC concept became the P.45 strike/trainer/interceptor aircraft powered either by a Spey RB.168 or two RB.172 engines, and it could have flown before the end of 1968. Hunting proposed the H.155, Hawker Siddeley the P.1173 and Folland the Fo 147. Hawker Siddeley, having acquired Folland Aircraft Ltd, was in the process of designing a supersonic single- or two-seat version of the Gnat trainer, which was in service with the RAF. The Gnat 5, as it was known, would be a fixed-wing design powered by either two RB.153R or a pair of Viper 20 engines. It was estimated to have a maximum speed of Mach 2 plus and a sustained flight

The first three Jaguar prototypes airborne from Istres. Nearest the camera is A-03 'D' flown by Paul Millet, next is E-01 'B' with Bernard Witt in the front of the two-seater and to his left is Jimmy Dell in E-02 'C'. (SEPECAT)

E-01 'B' F-ZWRB, a French two-seater powered by an early Adour Mk 101, was the first of the eight Jaguar prototypes, and was rolled out at Toulouse-Blagnac on 17 April 1968, making its first flight on 8 September. E-01 was lost in a flying accident on 26 March 1970 when the prototype suffered a catastrophic fire in the No. 2 engine and it crashed on approach to Istres. (SEPECAT)

ceiling of 60,000 ft. Hawker Siddeley decided to take the design a stage further and introduce a variable-geometry wing in place of the fixed wing, and either tailless or with a tailplane. The new design, called the Fo 147, would be capable of supersonic interception at 50,000 ft.

As a precursor of what lay ahead, in May 1964 Nord and Marcel Dassault, obviously under the impression that his company's design would prove ultimately successful, signed a confidential common accord, declaring that if either company won the ECAT contract

Jimmy Dell flew A-04 'E' F-ZWRE, the second French single-seat prototype, at Little Rissington in July 1979 when the Royal family attended the 57th Anniversary celebrations at the Central Flying School. This was the first time that the Jaguar had been positioned outside France. Walking alongside the aircraft is Len Dean, the chief ground engineer. (BAe)

On 14 November 1969 M (for marin – maritime) *-05 F-ZWRJ, a single-seat prototype used to evaluate* Aéronavale *compatibility, flew for the first time. Early in July 1970 M-05 was flown from Lann-Bihoue to the aircraft carrier* Clemenceau *as it sailed off Lorient to complete sea-going trials, and the first real deck landing took place on 8 July. During 10–13 July 1970 M-05 made twelve full-reheat catapult-assisted launches and arrested landings, as well as carrying out deck handling assessments and compatibility tests with the ship's deck lifts, and once again they were completely successful. M-05 made twenty more launches and landings from* Clemenceau *during 20–27 October 1971, but in the end the* Aéronavale *was unhappy about the single-engine recovery characteristics caused by thrust problems associated with the Adour Mk 101 engines, and eventually opted for the Dassault Super Etendard. (BAe)*

then the other would become an equal partner in the project. On 30 June Dassault offered the Cavalier (the first flight of which was planned for April 1965), Breguet the Br.121, which used the Br.1001 *Taon* (Gadfly) single-seat light attack fighter as the basis of the design, Nord the 3600 Harpoon, Potez the P.92 and Sud-Aviation the SA-12. The French government announced that the Breguet Br.121 was the winner of the ECAT competition. One of the reasons for this choice was to prevent the Dassault company from having a monopoly on combat aircraft. Marcel Dassault, who believed his company's entry was far superior to all the rest, was furious at the outcome. Breguet had not been a major force in French aircraft design over the previous twenty years, and in many areas was not thought capable of being able to meet the requirement, which is exactly what did happen subsequently. Nevertheless, Breguet proposed no fewer than five variants of the Br.121 – the Br.121A tactical fighter-bomber; the Br.121B two-seat fighter-bomber; the Br.121C interceptor; the Br.121D advanced trainer and the Br.121P tactical reconnaissance

A-03 'D', the first of the single-seat aircraft, was used to test navigation and attack systems for the French tactical aircraft, and flew for the first time on 29 March 1969. It is seen here at the 1969 SBAC show at Farnborough carrying an AS.37 Martel missile. This aircraft was later written off after a heavy landing at Tarnos on 14 February 1972. (SEPECAT)

aircraft. The French and British governments agreed that their aircraft industries should join forces and jointly develop a single aircraft type, which would meet the needs of both the RAF and the *Armée de l'Air*. The Wilson government believed that a joint project might enhance Britain's chances of Common Market entry, and furthermore, it had single-handedly ensured that there was no prospect of a suitable British design being able to meet the needs of the RAF. On 2 February 1965 the Labour government had announced that the supersonic P.1154 vertical take-off fighter (and the HS 681 V/STOL transport) would be cancelled (and that McDonnell Phantoms to replace the naval P.1154 and Lockheed C-130 Hercules aircraft would be purchased). Development of the P.1154 was aimed at providing a replacement for the RAF Hunter and possibly also the Royal Navy Sea Vixen, and it was hoped that it might meet the NATO requirements for a new tactical strike fighter. While the Prime Minister, Harold Wilson, also stated that development of the TSR-2 would continue for the time being vis-à-vis performance evaluation with the F-111 bomber, he drove the final nails into the supersonic strike aircraft's coffin by announcing that the eventual cost for the development and production of 150 TSR-2s would probably be as high as £750 million. He added ominously that a saving of £300 million could be effected if F-111 aircraft were purchased instead of TSR-2. The TSR-2 prototype flew supersonically on 21 February, but on 6 April it was announced that TSR-2 was to be scrapped 'forthwith'. The £125 million already spent would be written off, another £70 million would be paid in compensation and the supposedly cheaper option of

S-07 XW563, the second British 'S' prototype, was rolled out at Warton on 25 March 1970 and flew for the first time in June 1970. (BAC)

B-08 XW566, the first British two-seat aircraft, which was built to evaluate training options and take part in navigation and attack trials, was the final prototype Jaguar, and it was flown from Warton by Paul Millett on 30 August 1971. XW566 was put into store at Farnborough in 1985. (BAC)

S-07 XW563 with the Elliott digital inertial navigation and weapons-aiming system now installed (the first of its kind to be produced in Europe) in the 'chisel nose' that was a distinguishing feature of all RAF Jaguar aircraft, though the LRMTS windows were faired over. The aircraft is carrying four cluster-bombs on the inboard pylons and 1,000 lb (454 kg) bombs outboard and beneath the fuselage. XW563 was flown to RAF Brüggen in January 1978 for use as an instructional airframe. (BAC)

purchasing fifty F-111s would be made instead. The British government wasted £46.4 million on the F-111 before Harold Wilson announced in January 1968 that Britain would pull out of the Far East and the Persian Gulf by the end of 1971 and therefore the RAF had no further need for the F-111. As it turned out, this supposedly cheaper option would have cost the taxpayer almost £450 million because of delays and development problems, which resulted in rising costs.

The Memorandum of Understanding signed in London on 17 May agreeing to the selection of the Br.121 also covered a variable-geometry air force/naval strike/intercept/reconnaissance aircraft to be known as the Anglo-French Variable Geometry Aircraft (AFVG). This would be developed jointly by Dassault and BAC, and would be based on the English Electric P.45 variable-geometry, or 'swing-wing', supersonic fighter design. By June 1966 it was agreed that Dassault would take the lead in the airframe selection, the British acting as partner. Engine power would initially be provided by the SNECMA/Bristol Siddeley M45G (in October 1966 Rolls-Royce absorbed Bristol Siddeley, and it was agreed that the RB 153 turbofan would be used). However, it soon became apparent that France, and Dassault in particular, had little appetite for the AFVG project, and on 29 June 1967 at a meeting between Dennis Healey and his opposite number Pierre Messmer, the French Defence Minister, France's withdrawal from the project was announced.[1]

In May 1966 SEPECAT (*Société Européenne de Production de l'Avion d'École de Combat et d'Appui Tactique*), combining Breguet and BAC, was created and registered in France. The heads of both companies, Sir Frederick W. Page of BAC Preston and M. Benno Claude Vallières of Breguet, chaired the management committee, which included officials from the Ministry of Defence, the Ministry of Technology, the *Delegation Ministérielle pour l'Armament* and the *État-Major de l'Armée de l'Air et Aéronavale*. The

S1 XX108, the first production single-seater for the RAF, taking off from Warton with twin Matra rocket launchers on both inboard pylons and a 264-gallon (1,200-litre) fuel tank beneath the fuselage. S1 first flew on 12 October 1972 when Tim Ferguson flew the aircraft for 1 hour 11 minutes. (BAC)

S2 XX109/PS602, the second British production aircraft and the first to have the LRMTS and full avionics package. (BAC)

nose, fuselage, centre sections and undercarriage were to be made by Breguet, and the wings, tail unit, rear fuselage and engine air-intakes by BAC. These assemblies would then be mated together on identical production lines at BAC's Military Aircraft Division at Warton near Blackpool, Lancashire, and at Colomiers at Toulouse-Blagnac airport in France, where all eight prototypes would be built. (In 1967 Breguet was 'merged' with Dassault and the company became known as Dassault-Breguet, until in 1992 the Breguet name was deleted. In 1971 the British government nationalized BAC and it formed part of the new British Aerospace (BAe). Airframe contracts were issued by the DTCA

Jaguars of the Armée de l'Air *off the French coast. The French Air Force was the first to receive the Jaguar production aircraft. At St Dizer, the new base for* 7ième Escadre de Chasse, *the Jaguar was officially welcomed into* Armée de l'Air *service on 19 June 1973. (Breguet)*

In 1973 XX109 was used in field trials on the as yet unopened M55 motorway near Blackpool. BAC test pilot Tim Ferguson made a landing run of only 450 yards (410 m), using the brake parachute, and after four cluster bombs and a 264-gallon (1,200 litre) fuel tank had been attached he took off again in full afterburner, and was airborne in about 600 yards (550 m) without causing any damage to the road surface. In September 1977 four Jaguars of 31 Squadron practised similar landings and take-offs from an autobahn between Bremen and Bremerhaven. That same year the UK Aeroplane and Armament Evaluation Establishment (A&AEE) at Boscombe Down successfully conducted further STOL experiments from a specially prepared surface interspersed with ditches and other obstacles. (BAe)

(*Direction Technique de Construction Aéronautique*). By the same token the French and British governments stipulated that the power plant had to be a collaborative effort also.

In 1966 Rolls-Royce/Turboméca Limited was registered in the UK as a prelude to the two companies developing an all-new power plant common to both the Br.121 and AFVGA aircraft. The Turboméca T-260 Tourmalet turbofan had been proposed for the original Breguet Br.121 design as part of the ECAT submission, but it had proved unsuccessful, Breguet preferring the Rolls-Royce RB.172 power plant instead. The RB.172 would include parts from the Tourmalet T-260 and was specifically sized to fit the Jaguar airframe. Twin-engine safety was paramount as it improved survivability over a single-engined aircraft, and ease of maintenance was another important consideration for the design teams. Their target was an engine change achievable in less than thirty minutes. Rolls-Royce would be responsible for the combustion chamber, turbine, mixer and other components, and Turboméca would produce the low- and high-pressure compressors, the intermediate casing, the gearbox, afterburner and jet nozzle assemblies. The new RT.172 engine was named the Adour, after a French river, which was in keeping

Jaguars of 54 (F) Squadron at RAF Coltishall in July 1976.
Markings consisted of a heraldic blue-coloured lion rampant superimposed
on a yellow shield on the aircraft's nose, with blue and yellow chequers applied to the
engine intake walls and repeated across the RWR fairing on the tail. (MoD)

with the Rolls-Royce tradition of naming its engines after British rivers. Production would be centred on Derby in England and Tarnos in France. The new engine had to have good specific fuel consumption, a high by-pass ratio and be capable of developing high thrust for take-off and supersonic operations, as well as a low-level 'dash'. The first Adour was successfully bench tested on 9 May 1967 at Derby, but there were problems when reheat was selected, and the problem manifested itself again later during air tests. A major problem occurred on 4 February 1971 when it announced to a stunned nation that Rolls-Royce had gone into receivership. The government had to step in and nationalize Britain's premier aircraft engine manufacturer. Never one to miss a commercial opportunity, French engine manufacturers saw a chance to replace the Adour with the SNECMA Atar power plant, which had twice the thrust at half the cost of the Adour, but which would have proved unsuitable in meeting the Jaguar's low-level performance needs. Adour Mk 101 turbofan development progressed slowly but satisfactorily. Fuel efficiency was good, but the Mk 101 had been designed with the Jaguar's cruising flight in mind, and it required a powerful afterburner if it was to meet take-off and supersonic requirements. A 'part-throttle reheat system' (PTR) was introduced on the production Adour Mk 102, which allowed operations to be continued within the dry-thrust range and permitted continuous power without extinguishing or having to relight the engine to maximum, thereby making single-engine recoveries possible at higher weights. All the RAF Jaguars would be powered by the Mk 102, and the power plant was introduced to the eleventh French Jaguar onwards. The Adour has since been used to power the very successful BAe Hawk T.Mk 1/Mk 100/Mk 200 and Boeing/BAe T-45 Goshawk derivative.[2]

Britain and France initially agreed to each procure 150 aircraft, the *Armée de l'Air* receiving seventy-five single-seat 'A' (*appui* – support) strike versions and seventy-five two-seat 'E' (*école* – school) trainers, while the MoD requirement was solely for 150 'B' (British) trainers. Even so, the RAF still desired a much more sophisticated aircraft with supersonic performance and a far superior avionics fit than was required by the *Armée de l'Air*. After the cancellation of the TSR.2, P.1154 and F-111K and the abandonment of the AFVGA project, the Br.121 was the only viable strike aircraft design available to the

GR.1 XZ357 of 41 Squadron taxiing out at RAF Coltishall on 18 March 1975. Sixteen years later the same aircraft was one of those en route *to Oman in the build-up to the Gulf War. No. 41 (F) Squadron had been a specialist tactical reconnaissance unit since 1 April 1972, when the unit re-formed as a fighter squadron with 38 Group, Air Support Command, operating Phantom FGR.2 aircraft from Coningsby. In those days a pilot had to be on his second Phantom tour in order to be posted to 41 (F) since the role was considered to be too challenging for an inexperienced pilot. Aircraft assigned to the squadron began arriving at RAF Coltishall on 27 April 1976. On 1 October 41 (Designate) Squadron was formed to become the first Jaguar tactical reconnaissance squadron, with the Phantoms being re-roled for ground attack, a function they flew for six months when the two squadrons operated independently. On 1 April 1977, following the disbandment of the Phantom Squadron, the standard was handed over to the Jaguar squadron and the 'Designate' caveat was abandoned when the squadron was declared combat ready in a reconnaissance role, a role it retained until April 2006. (Dick Jeeves)*

GR.1 landing at Coltishall at dusk in March 1975. (Dick Jeeves)

RAF, and to meet its requirements would involve considerable redesign. It would need a thinner wing, an area-ruled fuselage cross-section, an increased weapon load and the sightline for the rear seat instructor's view improved, which in turn would involve reshaping the forward fuselage. Another RAF requirement was a ferry range of 2,600 miles (4,200 km), which would mean an increase in engine power. Fortunately for the RAF, all of this could be achieved with relative ease (though with an increase in all-up weight). In 1965, just in time to be advertised at the Paris Air Show, the aircraft received the official name 'Jaguar' after several other names, including Star, were rejected. The MoD order for 150 trainers was increased to 200 aircraft by amending the MU to ninety 'S' (strike) examples and 110 'B' trainers. In early 1967 the French requirement was also increased to 200 aircraft, with forty of these being a new 'M' (*maritime*) single-seat strike reconnaissance version to meet a carrier-based requirement for the *Aéronavale* (*Aéronautique Navale*, or French Navy Aviation) of ten two-seat trainers. The French Navy sought an aircraft to replace its Etendard IV, and it therefore had to be

GR.1 on finals at Coltishall in March 1975. No. 41 (F) Squadron was the declared Arctic specialist in the Jaguar wing, although 6 and 54 Squadrons also regularly deployed to the inhospitable snowy wastes as part of their rapid deployment capability. (Dick Jeeves)

Jaguars of 6 Squadron at RAF Coltishall in July 1976. The only RAF squadron to have an uninterrupted history, having never been disbanded and re-formed in its 91-year history, 6 Squadron formed at Farnborough on 31 January 1914 and operated throughout the First World War. In July 1915 Lanoe Hawker, flying a Bristol Scout, was awarded the first-ever Victoria Cross for aerial combat. Close co-operation with the Army earned the squadron its red 'Gunner's stripe', which is still applied to the squadron's aircraft. It was in 1941/2, during anti-tank duties in the North African campaign equipped with Hurricanes, that 6 Squadron gained its nickname 'The Flying Canopeners', of which the symbol is painted on the engine intakes. (MoD)

one that possessed excellent attack capabilities and twin engines for operational safety. On 9 January 1968 an agreement to cover the production of the first 400 aircraft was signed in London by the Secretary of State for Defence, Denis Healey, the Secretary of State for Technology, John Stonehouse, and the French *Ministre des Armées*, Pierre Messmer. In October 1970, the RAF having been forced to reconsider its requirement, the order was reduced to 165 single-seat strike versions and thirty-five two-seat trainers. Withal, the latter aircraft were no longer to be used as advanced trainers but purely as operational trainers for *ab initio* pilots destined for a single operational conversion unit (OCU) and the Jaguar front-line squadrons.

The first of the eight Jaguar prototypes was E-01 F-ZWRB, a French two-seater powered by an early Adour Mk 101, which was to be used for general systems tests, handling and control evaluation and flutter trials. In 1967 Breguet's chief test pilot, 42-year-old Bernard Witt, and BAC Preston's chief test pilot, 45-year-old Jimmy Dell, gave presentations and briefings to the world's press and invited visitors. Over the next year the two pilots familiarized themselves with the prototype at Warton using the simulator, and defined the flight commands and finalized the engines, which had never been used in the air prior to the first flight of the prototype. E-01 was rolled out at Toulouse-Blagnac on 17 April 1968 and then sent to the Breguet factory at Velizy-Villacoublay near Paris to begin static ground tests and engine-running trials. After this it was dismantled and shipped by road to the Centre d'Bassais et Vol (the French Flight Test Centre) at Istres near Marseilles. Preliminary taxiing trials were carried out late in August 1968, but minor technical problems prevented E-01's appearance at the Farnborough Air Show. Finally, on 8 September E-01 made its first flight with Bernard Witt at the controls. In France it was the first time that a prototype had been flown with engines not tested beforehand, either on another aircraft in the same flight programme or flying test systems. Jimmy Dell accompanied the Jaguar in a Hunter chase aircraft. Witt flew the prototype to 17,000 ft and successfully completed twenty-five minutes of flight without reporting any problems, but further trials revealed teething troubles with the Adour engines' fuel consumption and the afterburner. On the third flight E-01 flew supersonic and was then flown successively by Witt and Dell to investigate the aerodynamics and handling qualities of the aircraft. E-01 was lost in a flying accident on 26 March 1970 when the prototype suffered a catastrophic fire in the No. 2 engine and crashed on approach to Istres. The French pilot, who successfully ejected, said that an engine-bay fire warning light had come on and he had shut down the engine and selected the fire-suppression system,

GR.1 XZ111/A of II (AC) over Germany in July 1976. XZ111 was stored at St Athan and issued to Coltishall in September 1997, where it joined 54 Squadron as XZ111/GO. On 27 October 2000 it suffered a bird strike and crashed five miles north-east of Dumfries, on open hillside between the town and Lockerbie, after Flight Lieutenant 'Torch' Clarke RNZAF, the pilot, ejected. Another Jaguar circled the crash site until a rescue helicopter arrived to pick up the pilot, who was not seriously injured. (MoD)

A pair of Jaguar GR.1s and two FGR.2 Phantoms of II (AC) of RAF Germany in 1976. II (AC) Squadron was equipped with Jaguars XZ101-XZ120 and XZ355-XZ367, which were specially modified batches for reconnaissance operation. Markings consist of a white disc on the engine intake, flanked by white triangles on a black rectangle, the disc containing the 'Hereward's Wake Knot' (MoD)

A Jaguar being 'armed up' with 1,000 lb bombs and cluster bombs during a MINEVAL exercise at RAF Brüggen in August 1976, which was carried out under nuclear, biological and chemical (NBC) warfare conditions. (RAFG)

which in the process shut down one of the two main hydraulic systems. As E-01 came in to land the pilot then shut down the 'good' engine to reduce thrust, and in so doing lost all hydraulic power. He did not select manual emergency power, and with no automatic system available to operate the hydraulics the controls froze and he had to eject. This incident led to the installation of an automated electrical power system, which cuts in if a double engine failure occurs.

E-02 F-ZWRC, the second prototype and also a French two-seater, which was used for engine optimization trials and flight performance tests, was first flown on 11 February 1969 from Istres, with Witt at the controls again. Along with the first and fourth prototypes E-02 made an appearance at the 1969 Paris Air Show (although a month before the show only two Jaguars were flying), Marcel Dassault having insisted that all three Jaguars be shown. On 9 September 1971 BAC Preston's deputy chief test pilot, Paul Millett, with Brian McCann as his navigator in the back seat, flew E-02 the 600 miles (965 km) from the Breguet airfield at Cazaux, near Bordeaux, to Warton, where it joined the three British prototype Jaguars S-06, S-07 and B-08. E-02 undertook engine development trials and remained in the UK until 1980, when it was returned to France. E-02 flew for the last time on 28 February 1989, before being air-freighted inside a Transall C.160F to the Technical Training School at Rochefort on 7 June for use as an instructional airframe. Meanwhile, A-03, the first of the single-seat aircraft, which was used to test navigation and attack systems for the French tactical aircraft, flew for the first time on 29 March 1969 with Witt at the controls once again. This aircraft was later written off after a heavy landing at Tarnos on 14 February 1972. The second French single-seat prototype, A-04 F-ZWRE, which was used for weapons and stores carriage and weapon-firing trials, flew on 27 May 1969 from Istres, with Jimmy Dell at the controls this time. Marcel Dassault had decreed that A-04, together with the first and fourth prototypes, were all to be shown at the Paris Air Show. Jimmy Dell was to carry out the initial flight trials on A-04, and once they had been completed successfully he was to fly the prototype to the show, whereupon the three aircraft would carry out a synchronized display. Flight rules for the 1969 show stipulated that all the aircraft taking part had to take off from Runway 03, which ran parallel with the crowd line, but land on the far side of the airfield far from the public view. Jimmy Dell had intended to demonstrate the short field-landing characteristics of the Jaguar, but using the far runway would mean that the effect would be lost on the public. However, Bernard Witt assured Dell that they would all land back on Runway 03, and they did! A-04 was retired in 1979 and put on display at the Musée de l'Air at Paris-Le Bourget.

On 14 November 1969 M (for *'marin'* – maritime) -05 F-ZWRJ, a single-seat prototype used to evaluate *Aéronavale* compatibility, flew for the first time from the airfield at Melun Villanoche just south of Paris with Breguet Avions test pilot Jacques Jesberger at the controls. The main external differences from the Jaguar A was an arrestor hook and a smaller undercarriage, with a twin nosewheel and larger single main-wheel arrangement for catapult launches and arrested recoveries. (The land-based version had a single nosewheel and twin main wheels for rough field operations.) Internally it differed in having general structural strengthening to help withstand catapult forces. A retractable in-flight refuelling probe was fitted beneath the windshield, and provision was made to carry a 'buddy-buddy' aerial refuelling pack on its centreline. The airbrakes had four rows of perforations instead of the two rows of the other Jaguar prototypes. M-05 was transferred to Istres on 21 November 1969 and spent the following months being flown on practise deck-landings at Istres and Nimes/Garons naval base before being ferried to the Royal Aircraft Establishment at Thurleigh near Bedford on 20 April 1970 for initial carrier deck-landing trials, using the land-based dummy deck. This fully equipped catapult track built on raised steel girders was used to simulate 'cat-shots' from a carrier at sea. These tests and a further series of trials were very successful, and early in July M-05 was flown from Lann-Bihoué to the aircraft carrier *Clemenceau* as it sailed off Lorient to complete sea-going trials. On 8 July a French naval pilot, Capitaine Yves Goupil, made the first real deck landing of the Jaguar on the *Clemenceau*, M-05's 71st flight. From 10 to 13 July M-05 made twelve full-reheat catapult-assisted launches and arrested landings, as well as carrying out deck handling assessments and compatibility tests with the ship's deck lifts, and once again they were completely successful. M-05 returned to Bedford before returning to sea to make twenty more launches and landings from *Clemenceau* during 20–27 October 1971.

The outlook looked promising, but the *Aéronavale* was unhappy about the single-engine recovery characteristics caused by thrust problems associated with the Adour Mk 101 engines, and these signalled the end to any plans to operate the Jaguar M at sea. On one occasion the arrestor hook failed to trap a 'wire', and the throttle response was not sufficient to prevent the M-05 sinking dangerously close to the sea. Even so the Jaguar M was considered far superior to its rivals in the race to find a replacement for the Etendard IV, but the Jaguar's high cost meant that the *Aéronavale* could only budget for sixty aircraft rather than the hundred it needed. In January 1973 the French government cancelled the Jaguar M, and after considering the McDonnell Douglas A-4 Skyhawk and the LTV Corsair, opted for sixty examples of the Dassault Super Etendard, powered by a single 11,023 lb st SNECMA Atar turbojet, as the Etendard IV replacement. The allocation of fifty naval Jaguars was transferred to the *Armée de l'Air*. Dassault, already in a win-win situation with the *Aéronavale*, would also reap further dividends selling the Super Etendard to countries such as Brazil and Argentina, whose navies were also in the market to replace the Etendard. A 100% export value was much better than 50%, and this equation was always to the fore when potential Jaguar versus indigenous Dassault exports occurred in the future. After its cancellation the

GR.1 XZ374/CA in formation with a laser-nosed Harrier GR.3 during the re-equipment of 20 Squadron in Germany in January 1978. XZ374 was the first of the squadron's Jaguars to arrive, on 1 March 1977. No. 20 Squadron disbanded on the Jaguar on 24 June 1984, to re-form on the Tornado before disbanding again and reappearing as 20 (Reserve) Squadron, the Harrier OCU, at RAF Wittering. (MoD)

M-05 was used for test flying, and it made its last flight on 12 December 1975 before being consigned to technical training at Rochefort.

Meanwhile, S-06 XW560, the first BAC-assembled prototype, which was to be used for weapons trials and IFR studies, was rolled out at the BAC factory at Warton on 18 August 1969 and flew for the first time on 12 October, when Jimmy Dell flew it supersonic at the first attempt. Although outwardly the aircraft differed little from the French prototypes, the avionics fit, together with several other internal changes, made it a different aircraft altogether, and it was the first RAF aircraft to have a head-up display (HUD). (The Jaguar was the last aircraft that 46-year-old Jimmy Dell test flew, for in October 1970 a routine six-monthly medical revealed a minor heart problem, and after two test flights in the Jaguar one Saturday he was told to cease flying at once.) On 23 February 1971 Paul Millett flew S-06 to Istres on a direct flight from Preston – a distance of 738 nm (1,366 km) – in 1 hour 25 minutes. XW560 was destroyed in a ground fire at Boscombe Down on 11 August 1972. S-07 XW563, the second British prototype, which undertook RAF navigation and attack system tests and ground handling trials, did not fly until June 1970. This aircraft later had the Elliott digital inertial navigation and weapons-aiming system installed (the first of its kind to be produced in Europe) in the 'chisel nose', which was a distinguishing feature of all RAF Jaguar aircraft, though the LRMTS windows were faired over. S-07 made its 200th flight on 17 March 1971, and it was used to trial the Matra Magic AAM before being flown to RAF Brüggen in January 1978 for use as an instructional airframe. The nose and centre fuselage were later mated with parts from other Jaguars, and as XX822 the aircraft was placed on static display on 25 October 1985. B-08 XW566, the first British two-seat aircraft, which was built to evaluate training options and take part in navigation and attack trials, was the final prototype Jaguar, and it was flown from Warton by Paul Millett on 30 August 1971. XW566 was put into store at Farnborough in 1985. The trials undertaken by the prototypes led to changes and improvements to the airframe. The short nosewheel door, with its unique twin landing-light array, was extended to full length, the intake splitter plates were deleted and perforations were added to the airbrakes, while the original 'short tail' was extended on two of the British prototypes to provide additional stability during manoeuvring. Starting with prototype B-08, the original one-piece starboard-hinging nosewheel door was split into a three-door unit.

The Jaguar collaboration project had been put in place to reduce each nation's overall costs, and at the same time permit France and Britain to produce an inexpensive combat aircraft that could still meet each other's widely exacting requirements. As far as costs and export orders were concerned, in hindsight it might have been better for each country to have continued with indigenous designs such as the Supersonic Harrier and Dassault Cavalier. In 1971 the French concluded that the Jaguar had cost roughly twice as much to produce when compared to the Mirage IV and the Mirage F1. In France alone the spending on the design and prototype stage had increased sevenfold, a situation that is not uncommon where aircraft development is concerned. The Jaguar was also late arriving in service, in 1973, after being deemed an urgent requirement in 1964, but then one has only

GR.1 XX122 of 54 (F) Squadron carrying four inert bombs passing Happisburgh lighthouse (now disused, while cliff erosion has now reached to within yards of the houses in the foreground) on the Norfolk coast in March 1978. XX122/GA crashed on 2 April 1982 into the Wash off the Holbeach range, killing the Norwegian pilot, who had become disorientated in the hazy weather. (MoD)

to consider just about every other military and commercial undertaking since the sixties to realize that this is not unusual. Even in the aviation industry some clouds, if not every one, have a silver lining, as was ultimately proved with the F-86 Sabre, Lockheed F-104 Starfighter and F-5 Freedom Fighter, where export orders and/or sub-manufacture balanced the books and even produced a profit into the bargain. As far as the Jaguar was concerned, neither was the case, though none of these aircraft began life as a common advanced training aircraft for two disparate nations' air forces. The Jaguar's service history, though, has since proved that it was an exceptional design.

The *Armée de l'Air* was the first to receive the Jaguar production aircraft. On 4 May 1972 the first A single-seater model rolled off the assembly line at Mont-de-Marsan, near Bordeaux. Here the pilots and ground crew of *7ème Escadre de Chasse* completed their basic and advanced training on the prototype Jaguars and initial production Jaguar E two-seaters being used by the CEAM (*Centre d'Experiences Aériennes Militaires*) in preparation for forming the first operational unit at Nancy-Ochey. E1, the first of forty Jaguar Es, had flown on 2 November 1971, and deliveries were completed in early 1976. A1, the first of 160 Jaguar As, flew on 20 April 1972, and the last was handed over on 14 December 1981. On 19 June 1973 at St Dizer, the new base for *7ème Escadre de Chasse*, the Jaguar was officially welcomed into *Armée de l'Air* service by the Armed Forces Minister, Robert Galley, and General Claude, Chief of the French Air Staff, among the invited throng. The three Jaguar wings that were formed were incorporated in the *Force Aérienne Tactique* (FATac), the tactical air arm of the *Armée de l'Air*, the majority of units coming under the *1er Commandement Aérienne Tactique* (CATac). Jaguar pilot conversion began with EC 2/7, and consisted of two weeks of ground school and sixteen simulator sessions, followed by a flight conversion phase. This consisted of forty sorties over a two-month period for new pilots, fifteen missions over one month for existing pilots, or ten sorties for experienced pilots with at least 1,500 hours' flying time. New pilots were allowed to go solo after ten flights. In its final phases training included tactical work and weaponeering before the pilot was ready to go to an operational unit.

The first of the production aircraft for the RAF was XX108, which flew for the first time at Warton on 12 October that same year, with Tim Ferguson, BAC's deputy chief test pilot, at the controls. The RAF's first production two-seat Jaguar, T.2 XX136, flew on 28 March 1972. The first batch of production aircraft was dispatched to Boscombe Down for type proving before the aircraft was released for RAF service. A total of eight front-line RAF squadrons and an OCU were to be equipped with the Jaguar. On 30 May 1973 Squadron Leader John Preece delivered XX111 to the Jaguar operational conversion unit (JOCU) at RAF Lossiemouth on the Moray Firth in Scotland for ground crew training. The JOCU had been established at Lossiemouth in March 1973 under the command of Wing Commander Clive Walker. RAF Lossiemouth lies in the middle of the finest low-flying areas in the UK, with two air-to-ground weapons ranges at Tain and Rosehearty only five minutes' flying time away.

The first single-seat deliveries to the JOCU were XX114 and XX115, which arrived on 13 September 1973, when they were flown in by Squadron Leader Preece and BAC test pilot Jerry Lee. The JOCU had a staff of ten instructors who had initially been trained at BAC Warton, and went on to train pilots of 54 Squadron, the first operational Jaguar unit, followed by 6 Squadron and the OCU staff. On 30 September 1974 the JOCU was redesignated 226 OCU, taking its identity from the former Lightning OCU, which disbanded at Coltishall on 17 June 1974. The new OCU began life with fourteen GR.1 and eleven T.2 aircraft and a total strength of 259 personnel. Students arrived in large courses of ten to fill places on the eight operational squadrons, which were based predominantly in West Germany. The OCU's primary role was providing seventy-hour courses to pilots with little air time and including those straight from flying training. On 11 November 1974 the OCU split into Nos 1 and 2 Squadrons. (On 24 June 1994 226 OCU gained the numberplate of 16 (Reserve) Squadron following the disbandment of four of RAF Germany's Tornado GR.1 squadrons.)

During the time that the OCU was responsible for Jaguar pilot training, no fewer than seventeen Jaguars were lost in accidents. Seven of these were two-seaters, including one on 18 September 1996, which involved Flight Lieutenant Jon Witte, a student on his third solo.

It was only my second formation flight on type, and it was a beautiful day over Lossiemouth. The lead pilot commented during the outbrief that it was a lovely day for parachuting. The irony of what was to happen was not lost on me. I was flying my third solo; the third time I had been up alone in the Jag, and I remember the lead had an air squadron cadet in his 'boot'. With pre-take-off checks completed on taxi we got to the end of the runway. As we lined up on the threshold I ran through my personal 'last chance' checks where you basically make sure you've got everything you need to get airborne! We were both happy and my lead gave the signal to go. We released brakes and I counted two banana before hitting full reheat. A quick glance inside confirmed all was okay and from there my chief concern was not to hoover past the lead (again!).

I hit the go/no-go speed for our fit – just two underwing tanks, so a speed of 165 knots – and everything was okay. It was go. I was just sitting back watching my lead and he started his rotate. It was a three banana count and then a matching rotate to around 15 alpha [angle of attack] for me, and then I would try to get airborne.

Just after I started my rotate, things started to go pear shaped. I heard a sound from the back, like a mute cat trying to get out of a cardboard box. I started to fall behind the leader so I gave it max throttle, then looked inside and saw that one engine was well over temperature with a turbine gas temperature knocking on 9,000 C. I simply thought, 'Fuck, I've lost an engine.' The immediate actions for engine failure on take-off (EFATO) are clear cut. I had the mantra clear in my mind – was I 'V safe at 20 flap'? No, so I hit the 'clear aircraft' button, which dropped both underwing tanks. Weighing one tonne each, they both broke up in the airflow, and sprayed the end of the runway – and I later discovered the broken parts of the plane set the vapour alight, producing huge black clouds on the runway.

Drill required me to reduce to 7 to 8 alpha but I soon realized that that meant I was pointing at the floor, so I settled for a little more. I remember going feet wet – getting out over the water – and tootling along with the world coming up around my ears. The sea was dead calm, and I lost all visual cues to my height, thinking I had loads of time before having to punch out. I dropped the engine into idle to try and clear the surge, and then saw the leader miles above me, which with the poor climb rate of the Jag is not a good sign. I had a moving cone of attention around each instrument and it felt like minutes rather than seconds but when I heard the leader,

Wildcat One, call, 'Wildcat Two engine failure, Mayday, Mayday, Mayday' I snapped out of it, thought, 'Fuck this, the bag's gone bad, time to go', made a quick RT call and prepared to eject. I didn't realize how close I was to ditching until I saw the film.

As I pulled the handle and the charges fired, I remember hearing the canopy going, and almost instantly being hit by an indescribable kick. Ouch! My head was forced between my knees as the 38 g of ejection rammed me home, and although I am always quite religious with locking my harness on take-off, there was absolutely nothing I could do to stop my head going down to my knees. I kept my eyes shut – a throwback to my Hawk days – and as I was about to try sitting up the rocket pack fired and pushed me down again. Then there was the clunk-clunk-click-whirr as the barostatic time release unit released the main chute. The drogue pulled the chute out of the headbox, which in turn pulled me out of the seat. When I opened my eyes, I was surrounded by a wall of water – the splash from my downed T-bird. I went straight into drill – mask, visor, LSJ, splosh, dinghy. I felt totally detached from everything but I could tell my back was knackered.

A helicopter had been hovering nearby, holding while we took off. It had a grandstand view and popped back to Lossie, got the winchman, and came to pick me up. They flew me via the station to get the SMO and then flew me on to Elgin where an ambulance met us in a sports field. I noticed that the pilot and copilot were both female – the first time I've been picked up by two girls! As I had been flying a two-seater the ambulance crew tried to admit the winchman as well, who was also in flying suit and wet. I suffered compression fractures of the T7 and T8 vertebrae, bruises on shins and feet, and the obligatory chin scar which all Jag ejectors get – from hitting the chin on the oxygen regulator.

GR.1 XX971/DE and others of 31 Squadron from Brüggen on a German autobahn during an exercise in the 1970s. XX971/DE crashed during take-off from Lahr on 21 March 1978 when the No. 2 engine failed. The pilot jettisoned the external stores and attempted an emergency landing on one engine. He allowed speed and height to decay, and ejected when he considered that he would not reach the airfield. (MoD)

When the Jaguar turned 25 in 1998 the OCU had completed over 118 long courses and 135 short courses, which makes a total intake of approximately 888 students for flying courses. In addition the OCU trained pilots for Oman, Ecuador, India and Nigeria, as well as many exchange officers who have flown the Jaguar for the RAF during this time. They all have one thing in common – each one past and present is justifiably proud of the traditionally high standard of instruction and friendly reputation that the Jaguar OCU has earned over the years, and also of its links with both the front-line squadrons and the local Lossiemouth community. In July 2000 16 (Reserve) Squadron moved south to Coltishall in a move, part of the Strategic Defence Review, that made the station the last operating base for the Jaguar in RAF service. The arrival of 16 Squadron, under the command of Wing Commander Andy Sudlow, also saw an additional 100 personnel and their families take up residence on the Norfolk station.

RAF Germany (RAFG) was the largest user of the Jaguar, with four squadrons in the strike role and a fifth in the reconnaissance role. RAFG formed part of the 2nd Allied Tactical Air Force (2ATAF), and was responsible for interdiction, battlefield support and reconnaissance. At its peak RAFG operated four squadrons of Jaguars in the strike role and one for reconnaissance after conversion in stages from the Phantom FGR.2. The first of the Jaguar units, 14 Squadron, re-formed at Brüggen on 7 April 1975, when the Boss, Wing Commander Anthony Mumford, flew the first Jaguar (a two-seater) into the station. GR.1s followed from 16 April, and the Jaguar element was operational by the end of 1975, when the last Phantom was withdrawn on 1 December. In 1975 and 1976 14 Squadron took the prizes in RAF Germany's annual navigation and bombing competition for the Salmond Trophy, flying against Harriers, Buccaneers and Phantoms. It was followed by 17, 31 and 20 Squadrons, all of which were declared combat-ready at Brüggen by 1978 with sixteen aircraft each, including one T.2.

With the exception of 20 Squadron, the Jaguar units had previously operated the Phantom in the strike/attack role, 20 Squadron being a former Harrier close air support unit. After operating the Phantom FGR.2, 17 Squadron began converting to the Jaguar as RAF Germany's second Jaguar squadron in June 1975. The Jaguar element formed on 1 September, and the last of the Phantoms left in February 1976. No. 31 Squadron began conversion from the Phantom in January 1976 to become the third Jaguar squadron at Brüggen. The last Phantoms were withdrawn on 1 July, and the Jaguar element became operational with twelve single-seat GR.1 and a T.2 aircraft. During the 1980 Tactical Air Meet at Ramstein AFB in Germany, 31 Squadron won the Canberra Trophy for retarded low-altitude bombing and the Broadhurst Trophy for conventional bombing, with Flight Lieutenant Kevyn Broadhurst achieving the maximum points total of 400. No. 20 Squadron operated the Harrier GR.3 at Brüggen before beginning conversion to the Jaguar on 1 March 1977. The first Jaguar had been delivered on 8 January. The squadron took part in the Jaguars' first *Maple Flag* exercise in 1980, when six Jaguars of 20 Squadron and six of 6 Squadron participated against RCAF CF-5s, CF-104s, CF-101s and C-103s, as well as USAF F-15s and F-5E Aggressors. During the first two weeks at RCAF Cold Lake 20 Squadron flew sixty-one sorties in atrocious weather, and victories were claimed consistently in poor conditions where others had failed.

Nos 14, 17, 20 and 31 Squadrons formed the largest operational wing in the RAF, with seventy single-seat Jaguars, which were 'declared' to the Supreme Allied Commander Europe (SACEUR) in the most demanding of all the flying roles – dual-role, strike/attack by day and night. In NATO terminology, 'attack' refers to operations with conventional weapons, whereas 'strike' refers to nuclear operations, the ultimate sanction. Additionally, from 1 October 1976, II Army Co-Operation (AC) Squadron's Jaguars under Wing Commander A. F. 'Sandy' Wilson at Laarbruch were tasked with tactical reconnaissance until re-equipment with the Tornado GR.1A on 31 December 1987. Unlike the Brüggen Wing, the squadron could be committed to any war in the central region. Its pilots were not qualified for in-flight refuelling, which was not considered a requirement in RAFG, and so for deployments the Jaguars either had to fly in stages or be flown by tanker-qualified pilots from UK-based squadrons. Mainly, the squadron was tasked with pre- and post-strike reconnaissance operation in support of the RAFG strike/attack Jaguar squadrons, and latterly the strike/attack Tornado units at Brüggen and Laarbruch. The secondary role of the squadron was attack using BL755 cluster-bomb units (CBU) and iron bombs.

The British-based Jaguar squadrons in 1 Group, RAF Strike Command, formed part of the Allied Commander Europe's 'ACE' Mobile Force in conjunction with the 3rd Division of the British Army. They had to be capable of rapid deployment overseas in times of crisis when additional aircraft and crews from the instructor staff of the Jaguar OCU would join them. No. 54 Squadron had re-formed at Lossiemouth on 29 March 1974 under the command of Wing Commander Terry Carleton to become the first operational Jaguar unit with aircraft from the JOCU and others minus the LRMTS nose or RWR fin. Though it was almost a month later, on 23 April, that 54 Phantom Squadron disbanded at Coningsby, the early days were spent putting pilots through a 26-hour type-familiarization course at the JCT. On 1 October 1974 Wing Commander Lavender handed over the 6 Squadron numberplate from the Phantoms to the Jaguar squadron, which had re-formed at Lossiemouth under the command of Wing Commander John Quarterman. On 8 August 1974 54 Squadron moved south to RAF Coltishall in Norfolk with seven aircraft, and a borrowed T.2 arrived on 23 December. No. 54 Squadron was declared combat ready on 1 January 1975. No. 6 Squadron followed in November, and 41(F) Squadron became the third Jaguar squadron in the 'Coltishall Wing', part of 1 Group, Strike Command, when it re-formed at Coltishall on 1 April 1977 with the primary responsibility for tactical reconnaissance. The 'Coltishall Wing' was assigned to the NATO-driven Regional Reinforcement and the Allied Commander Europe's Mobile Force, capable of rapid deployment overseas in times of crisis.

The Jaguar participated in the first NATO exercise between 10 and 14 September 1974 when 54 Squadron took part in *Bold Guard* operating from Karup Air Base in Denmark. Their first *Red Flag* followed in 1978. Two Jaguars of 54 Squadron crossed the Atlantic on Friday 14 July 1978, to re-create to the day a similar event that had happened thirty years earlier. On that occasion, six Vampire fighters from the same squadron made the first transatlantic crossing by jet-powered aircraft. Two Victor tankers of 57 Squadron from RAF Marham also flew the 2,260 miles to Goose Bay, refuelling the Jaguars, piloted by Wing Commander R.J. 'Kip' Kemball and Flight Lieutenant John Butler, six times each during the 5 hour 43 minute flight. Meanwhile, in February 1978 41 Squadron became part of SACEUR's Strategic Reserve (Air) and in 1983 was assigned to the Allied Command Europe Mobile Force (AMF), both involving regular deployments to northern Norway, operating from the often snow-covered runway at Bardufoss. To support the recce role the squadron had a Reconnaissance Intelligence Centre (RIC), which was responsible for the processing and interpretation of photographs taken by the aircraft. During the NATO Exercise *Arctic Express* in 1978, 41(F) Squadron joined detachments of fighter aircraft from a variety of NATO countries. Six Jaguar GR1s and a T.2 of 41(F) Squadron were based at Andoya on one of Norway's offshore islands, and they were employed in a variety of tactical reconnaissance, armed reconnaissance and simulated attack sorties. The squadron mounted up to fifteen sorties per day and achieved rapid response times from origination of task to time over target. In 1980 six aircraft of 6 Squadron (and six of 20 Squadron) took part in Exercise *Maple Flag* at RCAF Cold Lake with RCAF CF-5s, CF-104s, CF-101s and C-103s, as well as USAF F-15s and F-5E Aggressors. During the second phase 6 Squadron flew an impressive seventy-five sorties.

NATO assessed all its stations and units by TACEVAL (tactical evaluation), and each major headquarters, such as 2ATAF, had its own TACEVAL team under the command of a wing commander and with officers of all nations and specializations in the HQ.[3] Usually about every eighteen months, this team descended on a base without warning for what was normally a four-day exercise in a simulated war scenario to test war procedures. The surprise element is all-important, as NATO air forces in Europe are expected to maintain a very high standard of readiness. TACEVALs can come at any time of the day or night to the strident strains of a bull-horn, a wailing siren and a tannoy blaring 'Alert, Alert, Alert'. When it happens, RAF men and women have to move fast. Nine times out of ten the alert would be a wing-induced exercise, but the tenth would be the start of a Tactical Evaluation of the unit. During the Cold War there was always the thought that the 'eleventh' time could herald war. Traditionally RAFG stations did very well, often getting assessments of 1 (Excellent) in the various aspects.[4]

During the station work-up for TACEVAL, MINEVALS were held every six weeks or so. These were organized by the station, sometimes with participation of staff from HQ RAFG, and usually lasted only one or two days, with a three-day MAXEVAL just prior to the expected descent of the TACEVAL team. In addition to TACEVALS and MINEVALS there were frequent call-outs, usually in the small hours, to check that the station could be ready to react to an alert or repel surprise attacks by Soviet forces. The assessments in these preparatory exercises were often tougher than for the TACEVAL itself. The exercise continued twenty-four hours a day, so shifts were worked, with the early team normally starting at 4 a.m. and being on duty until 6 p.m., while the late team started at 11 a.m. and worked until midnight. The pilots lived and did their mission planning in the protected briefing facility (PBF), only coming out like bats to fly. They wore their charcoal-impregnated nuclear, biological and chemical (NBC) suits at all times, and so became pretty hot, sweaty and grubby as the black dust rubbed off into their clothes. Normally there was a simulated chemical attack on the airfield during the first day, so they had to live in gas masks thereafter, and life became even hotter and harder work for everyone. The ground crew lived in the HAS (hardened aircraft shelter), so food and drink were taken out to them. It was hard, grimy work for them, as the aircraft turn-rounds were hectic, getting them ready to fly again in the minimum possible time. This was followed by periods of quiet and boredom waiting for the aircraft to be scrambled and then again when they were airborne. The directing staff injected incidents such as simulating intruders, throwing thunder-flashes about and firing guns in an attack on the squadron site to complicate life and assess how the guards reacted. The RAF Regiment provided guards around the airfield, with the squadron engineers helping to guard the site;

GR.1s XZ378/CH and XZ374/CA of 20 Squadron flying over Neuschwanstein Castle overlooking the Rhine in December 1978. (MoD)

this meant more work and fatigue for them, and could be cold and miserable at times.

An intensive rate of flying was often called for, with up to three trips per day, to evaluate how the squadrons reacted under pressure, but sorties tended to be rather shorter than normal, averaging seventy or eighty minutes. Sometimes after flying one trip, the pilots were retasked while in the HAS, the second sortie being planned by pilots in the PBF, and the plan was brought out while the aircraft was being refuelled, serviced and bombed up. Formation briefings were then given over the inter-HAS telephone before engine start.

By the third day of the TACEVAL the wing's Jaguars would be flying hard in response to the flow of tasks flooding in from the NATO tasking centre. The missions might be attacks against airfields or interdiction targets such as bridges, convoys, storage areas or assembly areas. Alternatively the missions might be close air support to give immediate support to troops in the field, when pilots might be 'talked' onto their target by Army or RAFG forward air controllers. The pace was deliberately fast and rapid turnarounds on the aircraft essential to meet the requirement. Pilots would be taken by a TACEVAL team member to a quiet room and quizzed on procedures, knowledge of his own aircraft and weapons, the capability of the Soviet Defence Forces, how he would counter them, why he selected a particular route to his target and why he had chosen that heading for his attack. For the elusive top rating of 'One' to be achieved, everyone quizzed in this manner throughout the whole evaluation had to average over 85%. Pilots might find that they were flying the mission in a two-seat Jaguar with a TACEVAL team member in the back seat. Does he stay low and fast all the time, is his approach to the target tactically flown, does he keep a continuous look out for defensive aircraft, is his weapon attack flown accurately, is he on target on time, how does he control his formation? All the bomb plots throughout the evaluation were recorded and judged against the criteria. All the times-on-target were logged and judged.

'Red-Red-Red' signalled an air raid, and sirens sounded as a wave of aircraft from another base swept in to make their 'attack' on Brüggen. People dived for shelters and Rapier surface-to-air missile units would go through acquisition and launch sequences up to the point of button. After the 'attack' the Jaguars that had made it usually landed for cross-servicing (one of the problems of NATO 'standardization' with many kinds of different aircraft and weapons in service) to be practised and examined. After the attack the TACEVAL team would hand in slips of paper, or 'TACEVAL Injects', with a new set of problems resulting from the 'enemy bombing attack'. Typically they would be, 'Your No. 2 bulk fuel installation is on fire', There are unexploded bombs on the taxiway and runway at the following positions . . .', 'There is a fire in the bomb dump', 'You have fifty casualties in the MT section'. Firefighting forces are dispatched, damage support units react; medics prepared for a hectic period in improvised locations; taxiing aircraft are rerouted, returning aircraft diverted; tired armourers move more bombs to safety. All the while the TACEVAL team note and watch and time. 'Intruders' have been sighted on the station near one of the squadrons. Mobile defence forces are dispatched to deal with them, but can the Jaguars be taxied out of their hardened shelters while this activity is going on? The TACEVAL team introduce another inject: 'Launch missions 406, 407, 408 immediately', and missions are transferred to another squadron, which launches the Jaguars downwind. By Day Five of the TACEVAL, people are cold, hungry, tired and still operating hard. The engineers are improvising to maintain serviceability. The intelligence scenario shows that the point is being reached when NATO must contemplate nuclear operations. Security is increased, movement is restricted and nuclear fallout and chemical attack situations are injected into the scenario. Finally, at 1900 hrs on Day Five the formal scenario ends, and the next day is spent on qualification flying. At least 70% of the wing's pilots have had to fly and demonstrate that they could deliver weapons to the accuracy standard laid down by SACEUR. The resulting report is evaluated, and by the end of the week the TACEVAL team leader enters the Brüggen Station Commander's office and gives him the results. The evaluation team marks a wing in four areas: 1. Alert posture and reaction, or how prepared it is and how quickly it can get onto a full war footing, 2. Mission effectiveness, or how well the mission is executed, 3. Support functions, or how the engineering and ground operations complement the task, 4. Ability to survive, which includes a diversity of activities, including guarding and security, chemical warfare drill, firefighting, damage control and medical buddy-care, among others. By the end of the exercise everyone is extremely tired and glad to finish. If the results are good then it is time to party.

For others, their careers on the Jaguar are only just beginning.

GR.1 XX762 of 14 Squadron, RAF Germany in July 1979. XX762/28 crashed on the summit of Beinn-A-Chleibh, near Dalmally, Argyllshire, on 23 November 1979 in bad weather while acting as a chase aircraft. During the 'pull-up' the pilot ejected, possibly in the belief that the aircraft was about to strike the side of a hill. He was killed after suffering a severe blow to the head. (MoD)

CHAPTER TWO

Noble Endeavours

Looking back, the Jaguar was like most aircraft at the start of their careers – some way off being ready for what was demanded of them and us. The engines needed more thrust, the laser was not yet operational, there were no defensive aids, and the (not very accurate) navigation/weapon aiming system failed with monotonous regularity. But oh, Lord it was fun. The flying was challenging and the standards of one's peers were a constant incentive to do better. To do anything, actually, rather than to be awarded that great fat pink pig at the trip of the day debrief!

Air Chief Marshal Sir Jock Stirrup,
Chief of the Defence Staff, who in the late summer of
1976 finished the Jaguar long course on 226 OCU
prior to joining 41 Squadron

Kevin Graham Noble was born in Odstock Hospital near Salisbury on 15 June 1959. His father, Squadron Leader Bernard Noble, had been a Hunter pilot in the RAF and was a test pilot at Boscombe Down at the time. Young Kevin attended British Forces schools during the three years that his family was in Germany. By the summer of 1975 he had applied to the RAF for a University Cadetship and attended the Officer and Aircrew Selection Centre at Biggin Hill for three days of tests and evaluation. In 1978 he joined the Bristol University Air Squadron at Filton airfield, and during his final year at university he applied for a commission as a pilot in the RAF and was accepted for pilot training. He entered the service as an acting pilot officer at RAF Cranwell in August 1980, and passed out on 22 December that same year. At RAF Church Fenton, the home of 6 BFTS, he learned to fly on the Jet Provost Mk 3, usually referred to as the JP3. By modern standards it was a very simple aircraft with a pneumatic system operating the flaps and undercarriage, the later via a single cylinder and a system of bicycle-type chains. The Viper jet engine was originally designed in the early 1950s and was not very efficient by 1980s standards. On 27 March he made his eleventh trip, during which he satisfied his instructor that he was ready to go solo, and he accomplished this after a total of 8 hours 45 minutes of instruction. He was one of the lucky ones streamed for fast-jets, and he progressed onto the JP Mk 5A, a development of the JP3 with considerably more power, radio navigational aids and a pressurized cockpit. By February 1982 he was looking forward with great anticipation to the Advanced Flying Training School (AFTS) at Valley on the BAe Hawk. At the end of August he left for RAF Brawdy to join 1 Tactical Weapons Unit (TWU). His choices all the way through training had been Harrier, Jaguar and Tornado. He preferred the low-level ground attack role to air defence, and the

Jaguars on the line. (RAF)

Harrier was most pilots' dream aircraft. In the event the final choice was governed by supply and demand. As he had done better at the air defence skills he changed his choices to Phantom, Jaguar and Tornado. He would have been happy with any fast-jet apart from the Buccaneer, since he did not fancy spending most of his time over the sea, which he thought might be rather boring. At the end of TWU there was a single 'role dispersal board' for their course and for their compatriots from Valley on a parallel course at Chivenor. As it happened he was selected for Jaguars. He was overjoyed at hearing the news, and in retrospect was pleased not to be going to the Phantom. He had become engaged to Kate prior to starting at the TWU, and was married on 22 January 1983. Steve Hicks, his best man, was also posted to Jaguars. After his honeymoon Kevin then had to wait four months before reporting for the Jaguar OCU course at Lossiemouth in Scotland, so he made arrangements for a holding detachment at Boscombe Down.

He was attached to 'A' Squadron, which was responsible for testing fighter and trainer aircraft, and he found the aircrew to be very friendly and helpful. They were well aware of the relatively long period between his finishing TWU and starting at the Jaguar OCU in May, and did their best to get him enough flying to keep him in current practice. In the circumstances, he was fortunate to get twenty hours' flying in just over two months, most of it on the Hawk. He also managed to get trips in the Bulldog, Jet Provost and Hunter

Jaguar GR.1 cockpit (Author)

T.7. Undoubtedly the highlight of the detachment was a trip in a Lightning T.5. His main recollection is of the terrific power, which gave it rocket-like acceleration. Even in a loop he noticed that they were still accelerating as the aircraft climbed through the vertical. The fuel consumption with the afterburners in use was prodigious, and the flight lasted only thirty-five minutes. He later heard that Lightnings engaged on combat practice, which necessitated sustained use of afterburner, regularly logged sortie times of ten to fifteen minutes!

As he was going on to Jaguars, it was appropriate that his final trip at Boscombe Down was in a dual-control Jaguar T.2. He had already heard of the Jaguar's poor reputation regarding lack of power, coupled with its potentially dangerous handling characteristics at the limits of the flight envelope. The RAF had already lost a number of aircraft owing to the latter problem, but experience was to show that within its limitations and treated with respect, it was a good aircraft for the ground attack role. The T.2 in which he flew was in the clean configuration (without drop tanks or external stores), and at relatively low weight the take-off acceleration and ground roll did not seem too bad. The view from the rear cockpit was good and he was impressed by the then modern avionics. He particularly liked the head-up display (HUD) and the moving map, which were driven by an inertial navigation system (INS). The aircraft's present position was shown in the middle of the circular map display and the track-line vertically up from the centre circle showed the aircraft's track over the ground. Thus, to fly over a particular point, it was simply necessary to turn until the track-line was over that feature on the map and, hey-presto, it took you there. This first-generation INS was not perfect, and drifted a couple of miles from the actual position every hour, but it was much better than the one he had seen in the Harrier GR.3. It greatly simplified low-level navigation, especially when over featureless terrain or when the pilot was concentrating on other things. The INS had three gyroscopes mounted at 90° to each other, which measured the acceleration about their individual axes. A computer integrated these accelerations in each direction over time to calculate the aircraft's velocity, and then, provided the INS had been told precisely where it was at engine start, a second integration gave the aircraft's position. This was a very good system and he found it incredible that accelerations could be measured accurately enough to produce a meaningful result, let alone to within the fractions of a mile per hour that became possible with later systems.

Having been suitably impressed with the Jaguar, he was now keen to get to the OCU at Lossiemouth to learn more about this machine. However, before going to the OCU, he had to go to North Luffenham again – this time to get kitted out with Jaguar flying clothing and learn about the Jaguar oxygen system and ejection seat. On arrival he found that the rest of the Jaguar course were there, plus those who had been posted to the F.4 Phantom, and immediately a considerable banter started between the 'mud movers' (ground-attack pilots) and the fighter jockeys. After the customary beer and curry, they had a run in the decompression chamber the following day. But this time they were only decompressed to an equivalent altitude of 25,000 ft, because the Jaguar normally operated at low level and in any event only rarely exceeded that altitude if carrying any sort of load.

The Nobles drove up to Lossiemouth to join 226 OCU in mid-April 1983, and they soon settled in. Meanwhile, Steve Hicks and his wife Tessa had moved in about eight miles away. Eight students assembled for No. 60 course at the Jaguar OCU, which started in early May with the usual ground school. Three were experienced Jaguar pilots doing a short refresher course, while a fourth was an ex-Vulcan pilot who had successfully transferred to attack aircraft. He had been on Ascension Island during the Falklands War and was a member of the crew that had diverted to Rio de Janeiro during a raid on the Falklands, and he had some interesting stories to tell. Another pilot had been through training some time previously but had been delayed a number of times by problems with his sinuses and had finally undergone an operation. Unfortunately, about half-way through the course he collapsed in the cockpit while doing the pre-starting checks, and as a result lost his medical category for flying solo. However, all was not lost as he was later posted to Nimrods, where he did very well and was promoted ahead of many of his contemporaries. The remaining three, Kevin, Steve Hicks[5] and John Steven, had all started together on the same course at Church Fenton.

On the first morning in ground school, their new squadron commander welcomed them to the course. He was a great character and apparently had been a prizefighter before he joined the RAF. Kevin soon felt that he was going to enjoy this course: they were treated as responsible adults and the instructors made it clear that they were there to teach them as much as possible during their time at Lossiemouth. It was a marked contrast to the TWU.

The ground school phase was particularly interesting as it was no longer simply a matter of learning about the Jaguar but also its operational task. A relatively small aircraft, it could carry a large load of external stores, and in the clean configuration the performance was reasonably good, as it could attain supersonic speed in level flight at altitude. However, when loaded the performance and handling qualities deteriorated markedly. The British version had one of the most up-to-date navigation/attack systems of any aircraft in NATO at that time. It was centred on the NAVWASS (navigation and weapons-aiming sub-system), which used a Marconi inertial navigation system (INS) driving a moving map and a head-up display. The system relied on an 8 kB computer, which was quite powerful in the days when Sinclair Spectrums were the norm as home computers, but it was obviously working to capacity. For example, when weapon aiming was selected, the moving map froze, as the computer no longer had enough capacity to drive it, but following weapon release the map would suddenly leap forward to indicate the actual position. The lack of computer capacity was exacerbated by the workings of the INS, which also used computing power and meant that any momentary failure in the INS platform caused the system to 'dump' and revert to being an air data computer. In this mode the system worked on aircraft airspeed and compass heading, and required the pilot to insert the wind velocity so that it could compute aircraft track over the ground and still drive the moving map, albeit with a high rate of drift. Normally the pilot's first action if the system 'dumped' in the air was to ask his wingman for the wind speed and direction. But this could cause problems if he was given a wind vector that was grossly in error, and sometimes it was preferable just to switch it all off and revert to basics with map and stop-watch.

Coverage of the weapon system was another important aspect. Data inputs to the NAVWASS were made via the pilot's hand controller, which was just behind the throttles and operated with the left hand, the most important button being pressed by the left thumb. Having made the mode selection to start the digital display flashing, the thumb button had to be pressed once to display the number 1 and five times to display 5 for each digit. Thus to insert a position in latitude and longitude with a total of eleven digits was a laborious task. As a maximum of up to eight waypoints (turning points) might require insertion, plus the heights and times at these positions, this process took a considerable amount of time and button pressing, even for a practised operator. The hand controller was also used for slewing the weapons-aiming symbology in the HUD onto the target during attacks – a process known as 'ackling'.

The HUD was projected onto a glass screen in front of the pilot so that he still had a fairly unobstructed view ahead; this was a great leap forward, as he no longer needed to look down into the cockpit to check instrument indications. This display was driven by the INS, and showed the flight path in pitch and roll, as well as other parameters such as heading, airspeed and altitude. It was particularly useful for flying instrument approaches down a constant 3° glidepath with speed reducing and alpha (angle of attack) increasing for landing, or flying an accurate 5° dive for dive-bombing. Additionally, it had a mode called velocity vector (VV) in which the aircraft symbol actually pointed where the aircraft was going: placing the symbol just above a hilltop and following the indication

Back-seater's-eye view in a T.2. (Chris Bennett)

T.2 'X' of 41 Squadron taxiing in. (RAF)

T.2 'X' of 41 Squadron taxiing in. (RAF)

T.2 XX835/FY taxiing out at a snowy dispersal area. (RAF)

took the aircraft just over the hill.

Before a flight the pilot inserted details of the stores carried on each pylon into the weapon computer by rotating switches in the nosewheel bay. Considerable care was required, as incorrect selection could result in the release of the whole CBLS (carrier bomb light stores) instead of the individual 3 kg bombs carried on it. Although a few pilots were caught out, Kevin managed to avoid this particular mistake.

As with most computer-controlled equipment, the weapons-aiming system provided several different modes for attacking targets, probably more than most pilots would need to use, and it enabled weapons to be delivered with a very high degree of accuracy. A great deal of information regarding the aircraft's speed, height, attitude and many other parameters was constantly fed into the computer, which then calculated the best aiming solution. A radar altimeter (normally known as the rad alt) gave accurate height above ground for weapon aiming and general flying, while a laser rangefinder in the nose pointed straight ahead to measure the range to the target. However, the pilot still needed to make all the necessary switch selections correctly and fly the aircraft precisely, if the best results were to be obtained.

The fuel system contained several tanks and was quite complex, as these fed automatically in a set sequence to keep the aircraft's centre of gravity within limits. Unfortunately, the failure indications in the cockpit were just a couple of lights, and it was very easy to diagnose a fault incorrectly and get into serious problems. The advice was therefore to follow religiously the flight reference cards (FRC), usually referred to as flip cards, and land as soon as possible. The Jaguar carried 3,200 kg of fuel in the internal tanks, plus a further 1,900 kg in the two normal drop tanks. This was very good for such a small aircraft and typically was sufficient for an hour and a half to 1 hour 40 minutes on a low-level sortie. The aircraft had two Adour engines, with reheat, which were started by a small jet engine. These engines were quite efficient and used a total of 50 kg of fuel per minute at the normal low-level speed of 420 knots.

The Jaguar was legendary for its lack of thrust. The engines produced only 8,000 lb of thrust each in reheat and 5,000 lb dry (without reheat) on a heavy aircraft with a small wing. Although it weighed only eight tons empty and had a good thrust-to-weight ratio at minimum fuel, the normal take-off weight for training was 13.5 tons and the maximum weight was 15 tons. To ensure that maximum thrust was available for take-off, the cockpit pressurization was usually switched off to avoid bleeding power from the engines. In the event of one engine failing just after becoming airborne, the first action was to select maximum dry power, or even reheat on the other engine, to maintain flying speed; and under hot conditions at full load it might also be necessary to jettison external stores. Normally reheat was only selected at 100% r.p.m., but for the single-engine landing, maximum dry thrust was not quite enough on the approach. However, minimum reheat was too much, so the aircraft had a unique reheat system with part-throttle reheat (PTR), which enabled reheat to be lit from about 85% r.p.m. upwards.

With its small wing the Jaguar was fitted with full-span flaps and leading-edge slats to provide adequate lift at the lower speeds, and this necessitated the use of spoilers on the top surface of each wing for roll control instead of ailerons. To enhance roll control, differential movement of each side of the large tailplane was provided, using a variable gearing; maximum differential was available at low speeds, decreasing until there was no differential movement at speeds above 420 knots. To provide adequate longitudinal control at lower speeds the tailplane was very powerful, and this meant that it had to be handled with care at medium and high speeds if problems were to be avoided. As with many other aircraft with highly swept wings, the Jaguar did not have a conventional stall, although the wing continued to develop lift up to above 30° angle of attack. The aircraft lost directional stability well before this point. If the angle of attack was increased gradually there was some wing rocking, which could not be controlled, and this was followed by the nose slicing sideways, and shortly thereafter control was lost and the aircraft departed (from controlled flight). If the stick was snatched back by an inexperienced or ham-fisted pilot the whole process happened very quickly and the aircraft could enter a violent gyration from which it was difficult to regain control. Because of this the Jaguar had gained a reputation as a bit of a killer, with vicious handling characteristics and a high workload. A number had been lost following departures or from flying into the ground while operating at low level. However, treated with respect, it was a good aircraft, which fulfilled its operational role well. The problem was that it had hard edges to its flight envelope, and it was easy to snatch through the warning stages straight into full departure, from which the single-seat GR.1 took more than 15,000 ft of altitude to recover. In the low-level role, pilots simply did not have that luxury. The two-seat T.2 with its long and high cockpit canopy was even worse, and they were told that even under the most favourable conditions chances of recovery were slim.

To drive the message home, on the second day in the ground school they were shown film of single-seat Jaguar GR.1 spinning trials. This was very impressive and certainly grabbed the students' attention as the aircraft just rolled and tumbled end over end with fuel vapour pouring from the engine intakes when it was going backwards, as the engines had flamed out. Shots from inside the cockpit showed this to be a highly disorientating and uncomfortable experience, with the pilot's head flailing uncontrollably from side to side. They were then carefully briefed on the recovery action; it could not be practised, since it was too dangerous. The first action was always to unload the wing smoothly by easing the stick forward to the neutral position. Hopefully this steadied the gyrations. Then came the potentially difficult task of checking the speed under these arduous conditions. If speed was above about 170 knots and the alpha was oscillating between 50 and 250, the aircraft was in autorotation caused by coupling of the roll and yaw forces due to its long, heavy fuselage and short wing. Gently easing back on the stick increased the loading on the wing and slowed the autorotation, but pushing it forward in these circumstances merely increased the rate of rotation. If the speed was below 170 knots and alpha was 'off the clock', the aircraft was in a spin. The drill then was to let go of the stick and watch and wait. If the aircraft was out of control below 10,000 ft the answer was simple: eject.

Even if the pilot recovered from the spin or other departure, his troubles were not over, as both engines would probably have flamed out and the Jaguar would glide like a brick until they were started again. A general rule taught from the beginning of the course was generally to move the stick in only one plane at once – use aileron or tailplane but not both together. Bunting and rolling simultaneously was highly dangerous as it could cause the aircraft to flick into autorotation, which was fatal at low level. Although many fast-jets with long heavy fuselages and short wings exhibited these characteristics to varying degrees, the Jaguar was an extreme case. Modern fly-by-wire systems limit the amount of control the pilot can apply in given conditions, and so prevent the aircraft from getting into this situation. The only aid in the Jaguar was an audio warning that could be set to trigger at 12, 14 or 17 alpha – the setting depended on the aircraft configuration. The 17 alpha setting could be used for the clean aircraft and most training configurations. But heavy centre-line stores such as the reconnaissance pod reduced the directional stability, and 12 alpha was the limit at which a warbling tone warned the pilot of impending doom if he did not back off.

Another interesting feature of the Jaguar concerned the rudder and tailplane controls, the control rods for which ran down the spine on top of the fuselage. Under high g, the wings deflected up, but the fuselage bent down at the nose and tail, especially when the aircraft was heavily loaded. This caused the spine to lengthen, while the control rods remained unchanged; the result being that both rudder and tailplane were automatically applied above 4 g. This unhealthy situation, in which the rudder yawed the aircraft at high speed and g, was not discovered until the aircraft was under test. The remedy was to incorporate a 'spine-bending compensator' to activate the aircraft's autostabilization under high g conditions. The yaw damper then applied the necessary rudder deflection to prevent yaw, while the pitch autostabilizer did the same for the tailplane. The latter also cancelled the nose-down pitch caused by opening the airbrakes.

Inevitably, because of the greater complexity of the aircraft, the flight reference cards (FRC) were very thick and the checks more complicated than they had been on the Hawk, especially those covering emergencies. The ground school included several sessions in the flight simulator to teach the students the Normal and Emergency drills, and they spent a considerable amount of time in the evenings ensuring that they were fully conversant with them. Although they carried the FRC with them in their flying-suit-leg pocket, and initially used them for the Normal drills, those Emergency drills, which were printed in bold letters, had to be committed to memory. These covered the more serious emergencies for which drills had to be carried out immediately. Once this had been done and the situation was under control, the pilot could then get out the FRC and check that he had carried out all the actions correctly.

After two busy weeks in the ground school, they were all very keen to get down to the Flights and into the Jaguar. Kevin had his first conversion trip on 3 June 1983, and initially it took some time just to do the checks, but with practice he was soon able to streamline the procedure. These initial flights lasted only forty-five minutes to one hour, and included circuits and low-level flying to give them confidence and teach them to handle the aircraft safely. In fact the Jaguar proved quite easy to fly, and the moving map was a revelation, as it greatly eased the problem of navigation. Additionally, the HUD made accurate flying much easier. An abiding impression from his first trip was the poor view ahead, with so much ironmongery in the shape of the HUD supports and heavy windscreen frames, together with the thick, armoured windscreen, which dimmed vision noticeably. All this was in great contrast to the Hawk with its curved, frameless windscreen. However, he got used to it, and in poor light conditions he learned to look out of the thinner quarter-panels for a better view.

Although stalling was not permitted, the instructors demonstrated handling at high alpha (angle of attack), and showed that once the aircraft was below the minimum drag speed, more power was required to maintain level flight as speed was decreased. In this respect, probably the most effective demonstration was of flight on one engine, with the

Attending to the BAe recce pod beneath a Jaguar. (RAF Coltishall)

Jaguars of 31 Squadron at Red Flag *in 1981. Markings consist of a five-point golden yellow star surrounded by a green laurel wreath, flanked by green and yellow chequers and applied to the engine intakes. (Denis Calvert)*

other throttled to idle. In level flight the aircraft could maintain 330 knots at lower altitudes with one engine at maximum dry power, and would maintain height at lower speeds at reduced power. However, once below minimum drag speed, more and more power was required as speed reduced and the alpha increased, until finally at the lowest speed the Jaguar had a high rate of descent with one engine in maximum reheat. The only way out of this situation on one engine was to get the nose down to increase speed, but obviously, if the aircraft were on the landing approach, the only way out would be a 'Martin-Baker let-down' (ejection). In this context, the large and sturdy undercarriage produced a considerable amount of drag when down, so on one engine it was only lowered during the approach for landing, and even then part-throttle reheat was needed to prevent an excessive rate of descent from building up.

Starting on 3 June, only three dual trips in the T.2 were required before Kevin was sent off on his first solo for fifty minutes in a GR.1 on 7 June – a flight that he enjoyed immensely. After take-off he did a short low-level navigation exercise (Navex) before returning to Lossiemouth for circuits and landings, and he felt a great sense of achievement at having reached this stage. As before, low-level flying in Scotland was second to none, especially as he only had to go fifteen miles from Lossiemouth before letting down into a low-flying area.

Immediately after the first solo, he had a couple of instrument flying trips with an instructor in the T.2 before moving on to formation sorties, which built on his initial experience at Brawdy and introduced him to some new formations. Initially they flew in battle formation with pairs about two miles apart in line abreast, and also in arrow formation with the wingmen 150 yards back and 30° swept from their section leaders. When flying on the inside of a turn at low level in arrow, it was often difficult to see the leader over the nose, and they were taught to apply a small amount of bottom rudder to yaw the aircraft slightly away from the leader (plus enough opposite spoiler to prevent the aircraft from rolling) so that he remained in view. The first three formation trips were in pairs, and these were followed by two trips with four aircraft, using the formations they had been taught at Brawdy, plus a new one known as 'Card'. For the latter each pair flew in line abreast with two miles between aircraft, the second pair being about twenty or thirty seconds (2–3½ miles) behind the leaders, thus forming the four corners of a card. At this distance it was often quite difficult for the second pair to keep the lead pair in view, so precise timing was required; but the advantage was that the second pair were well positioned to attack any aircraft that tried to pull in behind the lead pair. The weather was marginal for the first four-aircraft formation, which was flown dual, so they spent most of the time tucked in arrow formation, flying down the valleys with cloud on the hilltops either side and going through showers. With their lack of experience it was hard work, but it was very enjoyable and gratifying to complete the trip satisfactorily.

For these trips they practised close-formation take-offs and landings in pairs. The use of reheat made the pairs take-off more difficult than on the Hawk; the reheat was lit before the brakes were released, but once airborne cancellation of reheat had to be co-ordinated if close formation was to be maintained. Take-off was also complicated by the fact that the pressurization had to be switched on once the aircraft was airborne. Unfortunately the switch was on the right wall of the cockpit: this meant that the pilot had to change hands on the stick without taking his eyes off the leader at this critical time, locate the switch by feel with his right hand and turn it on. Naturally, they first practised finding the switch by feel on the ground. Some years later, another Jaguar pilot recounted how, on an early OCU formation sortie, he looked down to find the switch and when he looked up he had slid in behind the leader and to his horror was looking right into the reheat plumes. Both his own engines then surged in protest at being fed so much hot turbulent air, but he managed to recover the situation after a few heart-stopping moments.

In close formation the leader normally gave specific hand signals to indicate selection of services such as undercarriage, flaps and airbrakes, although sometimes he did it by radio call. Initially the students found it quite difficult to stay in formation while taking their hands off the throttles to operate the undercarriage and flap controls. And in cloud it was easy to lose sight of the leader if one drifted more than a few feet away. However, it became second nature after a while.

Formation was followed by more low-level navigation trips, the main object being to get used to operating the navigation system. The rad alt (radar altimeter) was a great boon and an excellent safety feature: for the first time they had an accurate measurement of the actual height above ground, rather than an estimate. It also incorporated a low-height warning tone that could be set to sound at a selected height and left the pilot in no doubt of the need to pull up. These trips were initially flown with an instructor in the T.2 before flying solo in a GR.1 with an instructor flying chase in another aircraft to monitor progress, and finally they were completely on their own. Their routes covered most of Scotland, and the weather was glorious throughout that June. The scenery was spectacular and there were many remote areas with no roads or habitation, and accessible only on foot. The west coast is particularly beautiful, with barren rocky shores, purple mountains inland and a brilliant blue ocean. It was exhilarating flying down valleys and over ridges, instead of slavishly following the black line planned on the map, and it was easy to navigate around minor obstacles to keep exposure to simulated ground or air defences to a minimum. Going over small hills, the technique used for the Jaguar was to bunt (push over the top), whereas many other aircraft chose to roll over the vertical and let the nose drop. But this caused a conspicuous wing 'flash' from the rolling wing and made the aircraft easier to spot. The drawback to bunting was that negative g raised the dust and any small loose objects from the cockpit floor, and water, too, if it had been raining when the pilot got in. Kevin was soaked more than once by water flying up into the canopy then being dumped back down as the positive g came on. Over bigger, sharper ridges the technique was to roll over to 130–180° and pull down over the ridge. This maintained positive g when upside down and kept the aircraft closer to the ground on the far side of the ridge. It was great fun with rocks flashing by only a couple of hundred feet from your head when inverted.

At the end of June the course progressed to weaponry on the Tain range, which was only five minutes' flying from Lossiemouth, and they were now training to use the aircraft for its true purpose.[6] Unfortunately, on Kevin's first trip with an instructor in the T.2, the navigation system dumped, so they had to use the reversionary bombing mode with a fixed sight as they had done in the Hawk. Level bombing was carried out at 480 knots and 200 ft release height, and they also did 5° dive-bombing, using 3 kg practice bombs simulating the 1,000 lb retarded bomb. (Retarded bombs had a parachute tail, which deployed after release, greatly reducing bouncing or skipping after impact and ensuring that the aircraft was well clear before the bomb exploded.) The second trip was aborted because of bad weather, and they had to use the reversionary mode again on the third trip because the weapons-aiming system was showing excessive errors. Finally, everything worked on the fourth trip, and Kevin was able to use the continuously computed impact point (CCIP) mode; this was a great revelation after reversionary bombing, as it was much more accurate and forgiving of imprecise flying. Accurate weapon delivery was what the Jaguar was all about, as it had, and with its updated system still has, one of the best attack systems in operation.

On this trip Kevin also had his introduction to Jaguar strafing, and again the computing sight took care of the problems of crosswind and measurement of range from the target. The Jaguar had two 30 mm Aden guns mounted internally.[7] These were of the same type as that used on the Hawk (and the Hunter), but gun-firing ranges were much greater as the Jaguar was considerably less manoeuvrable and needed more height for the pull-out. Strafing was carried out in a 10° dive at 450 knots, but the firing bracket was now at a range of 2,600–2,000 ft, as compared with 1,800–1,500 ft for the Hawk. He found that the computing sight made a big difference to his efforts, and he achieved quite respectable scores; however, some of the other students preferred to stick to the fixed (reversionary) sight for strafing.

The course then moved on to a mixture of dual and solo weapons sorties, the solo flights being in the GR.1. In his first month he amassed more than thirty hours in the Jaguar, which was very good for continuity, and he really enjoyed the flying. July continued with more range trips – mainly solo – learning to use the different modes available in the weapons-aiming system. On his thirteenth weapons trip he moved on to toss bombing, which was an entirely new event for him. Using a 28 lb practice bomb to

With its small wing the Jaguar was fitted with full-span flaps and leading-edge slats to provide adequate lift at the lower speeds, and this necessitated the use of spoilers on the top surface of each wing for roll control instead of ailerons. On 19 April 1983 during air combat training (ACT) the pilot of GR.1 XX742/EF of 6 Squadron, seen here at RAF Wattisham on 8 August 1981, was unable to recover the aircraft from a roll to starboard, possibly due to disconnection of the roll control system. He ejected and XX742/EF crashed into the North Sea, forty miles off Bacton, Norfolk. The aircraft was not recovered. (Tom Trower)

simulate a slick (free-fall) 1,000 lb bomb, he approached the target at 500 knots at low level. At a range of about three miles he then engaged maximum reheat and pulled up at 3 g, following indications in the HUD. Passing about 20° of climb, the pilot pressed the pickle button and the bomb was then released automatically by the computer at about 30° of climb and two miles from the target. The bomb was literally tossed towards the target, but the accuracy was not very good, as it was almost totally reliant on how well the NAVWASS was behaving, and impacts were generally up to 1,000 ft or more from the target. This procedure was little used for ordinary bombing, but it could be employed for the delivery of nuclear weapons or laser-guided bombs (LGB), and it was used for the latter purpose by Harriers in the Falklands campaign using a ground-based laser designator. Modern navigational systems are now much more accurate for toss bombing.

Loft bombing was similar to toss, except that the bomb was released in a steady 30° climb at a nominal 1 g, and they practised reversionary loft bombing to simulate navigation system failure. Reversionary loft bombing on the Tain range was quite hard work but great fun, and as with all reversionary bombing, careful planning and accurate flying of parameters was crucial. They rolled out on the bombing run at precisely 500 knots and clicked the stopwatch when exactly abeam the Tarbat Ness Lighthouse, which was on a peninsula south of the run-in to the target. Some students even put a chinagraph mark on the canopy to help judge the exact abeam position. Switches were made live on the run-in, and an 'in hot' call was made. After a set time, adjusted for wind, the pilot pulled up smartly at exactly 3 g as measured on the g meter. At 30° of climb, the aircraft was checked to stabilize at 30°, and about two seconds later, at another predetermined time adjusted for wind, the pickle button was pressed and the bomb released. Strangely enough, the course generally achieved better results with reversionary Loft bombing than with Toss bombing using the navigation system. No reason for this anomaly was apparent, but Kevin maintains that it was due to the skill of the students.

For Loft and Toss bombing, safe recovery from the 30° climb back to low level after bomb release was a potentially disorientating and hazardous manoeuvre, as typically the aircraft reached 3,000 ft or more, and a normal recovery would increase exposure to enemy action in an operational situation. The danger was greatest if there was a poor horizon, it was night or the aircraft was in cloud, and the students were therefore taught the recovery manoeuvre extremely carefully and thoroughly. A set sequence of events was always followed: cancel reheat, transfer the instrument scan from the HUD to the head-down attitude indicator (AI) and roll to 135° of bank (half-way on your back) and pull 3 g, effectively stopping the climb and turning away from the target. When the nose came down to the horizon, as indicated on the AI, the aircraft was then rolled to 90° of bank and back to 60° of bank when the nose was 5° below the horizon. At this stage the aircraft was in about a 10° dive and a 2 g turn, and the wings were rolled level, continuing the descent. Approaching low level, the descent was stopped and the turn continued to roll out on the escape heading, which was normally within an arc of 60° on either side of the reciprocal to the attack heading. As all this happened at high speed and rates of climb and descent during a period of just over twenty seconds, it was hardly surprising that over the years a considerable number of pilots crashed during the recovery manoeuvre, mainly at night or in bad weather. The reason for changing to the head-down AI during the recovery was that this instrument was much easier to follow at high pitch and roll rates, whereas the HUD quickly became a mass of green lines flashing across the display. In these circumstances it was very easy to become disorientated, or just simply to miss the horizon

GR.1 XX119/01 of 226 OCU, whose aircraft were distinguished by a tartan stripe on the tailfin, which was introduced by Wing Commander John Lumsden (OC, April 1980 to December 1982), whose family tartan it was, although it was subsequently replaced by the more appropriate Lossiemouth tartan. Markings were a shaft of arrows and a beacon torch crossed and intertwined with a belt, usually painted on the tailfin, and for a brief period the unit carried a leaping Jaguar on the nose. XX119/01 was used later for ground instruction by 16 (R) Squadron at Lossiemouth as 8898M. (Gary Parsons)

bars and end up in a steep spiral dive close to the ground.

A graphic illustration of just how quickly things could go irretrievably wrong during the recovery from a bombing run had occurred on 7 March. No. 17 Squadron had brought its Jaguars over from Germany to carry out training in preparation for its participation in Exercise *Red Flag*, which was to be held over the Nevada Desert of the USA. On one trip, a formation carrying two inert (training) 1,000 lb bombs under the fuselage on the centre-line and 28 lb practice bombs under the wings went straight to the Tain range for a toss first-run attack (FRA). One pilot did a 'spotting recovery' in which he modified the manoeuvre so that he could see his bomb hitting near the target. Basically this was not particularly dangerous, but he ended up rather nose low, and rolled and pulled hard to recover. With the aircraft still almost full of fuel and with the extra weight of the 1,000 lb bombs, it rapidly departed from controlled flight and the pilot ejected without delay. Unfortunately, the aircraft was going backwards as the pilot ejected and the canopy, which would normally have been taken away by the airflow, slammed shut. The pilot was then ejected through the canopy, receiving substantial injuries in the process. He was only in the parachute a few seconds before he landed and the aircraft crashed nearby. Fortunately, he soon recovered and went back to flying.[8]

The weapons phase was completed after fifteen sorties, following which the students did a couple of instrument flying trips, culminating in the White Card instrument rating test. Kevin was thankful that his went well, and he gained a white rating. Having a rating made life easier as it meant that they could still fly when the weather deteriorated, while those who were unrated were more limited. They also did their night-flying in late July, although it was barely dark at midnight and they had to take off very late and fly into the small hours of the morning. Both of his trips were on the same night. The weather was beautifully clear, and on the first (dual) trip, as soon as they had climbed a few thousand feet, the glow from the sun was visible on the western horizon. The instructor then decided to see how high they could climb before going back to Lossiemouth for circuits. In maximum reheat they accelerated to Mach 0.95 near the tropopause, which was below 35,000 ft that night, before gently pulling up and into a ballistic trajectory that peaked at 42,000 ft with a speed of 150 knots indicated. Although they were flying a Jaguar T.2 carrying tanks and CBLS (Carrier Bomb Light Stores), it was apparent that it was no high-altitude machine. On the way back to Lossiemouth, while at around 30,000 ft, they could clearly see the lights of Edinburgh more than 100 miles away. After a few circuits, including a simulated single-engine approach, they landed after a total of fifty minutes. Following a quick debriefing, Kevin then took off solo in a GR.1 for another fifty-five minutes; he went up to the Shetlands and back at 20,000 ft, returning for some circuits before landing.

For the simulated attack profile (SAP) phase they flew low-level trips in pairs. Typically these included simulated attacks on two off-range targets, using the various attack modes and concluding with first-run attacks (FRA) on the Tain or Rosehearty ranges, or both. Rosehearty was a sea range thirty miles east of Lossiemouth. Initially Kevin flew in the No. 2 position as a wingman, but later he led pairs. The main difference from TWU was that the students now considered which weapons they would use for real operations, and planned realistic attacks. For most of the off-range targets they used either level or 5° shallow-dive attacks, simulating delivery of either 1,000 lb retarded bombs or the Hunting BL755 cluster bombs, which contained 147 bomblets for use against tanks, vehicles, aircraft on the ground or personnel.[9] When a 1,000 lb bomb explodes it throws shrapnel and debris over considerable distances, so that if a second aircraft were to fly through the explosion area, it would almost certainly be brought down. Hence, following pilots had to allow about thirty seconds for these fragments to fall back to earth. Second and subsequent aircraft therefore had to split from the leader as late as possible to maintain visual cross-cover and fly a dog-leg route to lose time. This had to be accurately planned, as it was desirable to get all aircraft over the target as quickly as possible, and each pilot was normally allowed only plus or minus five seconds on his planned time on target (TOT). Once past the target, the leader flew a planned dog-leg to let his wingmen catch up. With CBUs, the bomblets were small and fragments were generally not a problem; the wingmen could then fly as close behind the leader as they wished. The fragmentation effect of retarded bombs could be used to good effect against pursuing fighters, as dropping a bomb in front of them as they were approaching missile-firing range at least frightened the pilots, if nothing worse.

For the SAP it was normally planned to fly the route at 420 knots to conserve fuel and allow scope for speeding-up if time was lost, increasing to 480 knots for the run-up to the target, thus minimizing time in the target area, where defences were expected to be greatest. The standard practice was to load details of the latitudes, longitudes and heights above sea level, plus times of arrival at initial points (IPs) and targets into the navigation system. Small Casio calculators were used to convert grid positions on the 1:50,000-scale UK maps into accurate latitudes and longitudes; similar details for range targets were also included. Entering all this information into the navigation system involved much thumb work on the hand controller while trying to do the pre-starting checks in as short a time as possible. As the times for the weapons range targets were pre-booked, it was essential to take off on time to meet the TOT. Sometimes, when slightly late, the pilots had to enter the last details into the navigation system after take-off, before the workload built up in those areas where they were likely to be bounced by other aircraft. In these circumstances it was very easy to make a mistake in entering so many digits, and this could mean that the navigation system computed that the target was tens or even hundreds of miles from where it actually was.

To guard against incorrect information input, the pilots map-slewed (reset the moving map to each waypoint, using the hand controller) to ensure that each latitude and longitude was approximately correct. While flying the route they then compared progress on the moving map against a hand-held map on which they had planned the mission. All this had to be done while maintaining formation, keeping a lookout for bounce aircraft, checking on the time at which particular features were due to appear, maintaining a watch on aircraft position and fuel state and making general checks of the other important cockpit instruments. Although speeding up to 480 knots for a short period could remedy the loss of a few seconds, if a serious time loss of thirty seconds or a minute occurred, it could take six or seven minutes at 480 knots to get back on time. This was too long and used far too much precious fuel, which might be required for evasion later. To minimize these problems they turned at the planned time regardless of whether they had actually reached a turning point or not. If early they flew past the turning point and then gently converged onto the planned track on the next leg. By these means they kept to time without big speed changes, and the moving map made it relatively easy to get back to the planned track on time.

Night shift of OCU.1s and 1.2s of 16 (R) Squadron, the Jaguar OCU on the line. Nearest aircraft is GR.1 'A' with a black tail and the famous 'Saint' emblem in yellow, signifying the squadron's nickname 'The Saints'; because the unit had been formed at St Omer, France, on 12 February 1915 during the First World War. From 1 November 1991 16 Squadron was associated with the OCU, and the 'Saint' badge worn by Tornado GR.1s at Laarbruch until 11 September 1991 was applied to the fin of the Jaguars in addition to their 226 OCU quiver and torch air intake marking and fin band. On 24 June 1994 226 OCU became 16 (Reserve) Squadron. (RAF)

Since the navigation system drifted slightly with time, it was necessary to keep an eye on how accurately the moving map matched the real world outside, and any significant drift (greater than about a mile) was corrected by inserting a 'random' fix into the system. A prominent map feature shown on the track ahead was selected, and the 'fix' button was pressed as it was over-flown before slewing the moving map so that the feature was in the centre circle on the map display. The 'enter' button was then pressed and the map immediately leapt forward to the current (updated) position, making due allowance for the distance travelled in the time it took to make the 'fix'. If sufficient time was available during planning, the exact locations of prominent features were plotted and stored in the navigation system to provide planned fixes. When on the route, flying exactly over the feature and pressing the 'planned fix' button informed the system precisely where it was, and the moving map was reset.

To be certain of locating the target, it was vital to select a prominent feature as the initial point (IP) so that the accuracy of the navigation system could be checked and updated by pressing the 'planned fix' button as it was overflown. When on the last leg towards the designated IP, steering information appeared in the HUD and on the edge of the moving map display. Also, since the time at the IP had been inserted into the system, it calculated and displayed the ground speed needed to arrive on time. Finally, when within one minute of the target, a cross appeared in the HUD, pointing to the calculated target position, and a time circle appeared, which was increasingly obscured as the target was approached. The major shortcoming was that the system was not really accurate enough to give final guidance to very small targets, and so the pilots were forced to revert to map reading on a 1:50,000-scale map, as they had done in the Hawk. However, at least the HUD cross-pointed to the area of the target, and the demanded ground speed display greatly assisted in achieving the planned TOT. Once visual on the target, the pilot manoeuvred the aircraft for weapon aiming, and simulated the appropriate weapon selections, as well as obtaining film for the subsequent debrief. On operations he would also have to watch out for, and attempt to evade, any enemy threat. Once past the target the aircraft was flown straight ahead, making use of any gullies or other features in the terrain before turning onto the next leg.

On the final SAP trip, Kevin went to Spadeadam, the electronic warfare (EW) range north of Carlisle and close to the Scottish border, where ground radars simulated anti-aircraft radars and provided the correct indications on the radar warning receiver (RWR) fitted to the aircraft. Although the Jaguar had only a fairly basic system, it indicated the quadrant in which the threat lay, together with the frequency band and radar waveform characteristics. The students had to learn to recognize the individual threats by their various characteristics, and react accordingly. Initially this took considerable time and effort, as the indications were not easy to interpret. However, it was vital to determine precisely what the threat was and react accordingly if they were to survive in the face of modern air defence systems. Additionally, they had to be able to recognize the indications from the radars of friendly aircraft that might be operating in the area. This was their first encounter with EW, and the sortie on the Spadeadam range was simply to give them a foretaste of the training that they would receive on the squadrons. The range also had a number of simulated targets, including a dummy airfield with old aircraft hulks on it, and wooden tanks and missiles in various locations. These were very good for realistic SAPs, which they would later practice on their operational squadrons, since they could attack a realistic target while getting all the correct RWR indications in the cockpit.

Next, they moved on to Tactical Manoeuvring, which started with 1-v-1 air combat to get used to flying the aircraft to its limits. Much more care was required than on the Hawk, as pulling too hard could rapidly cause the aircraft to depart and probably end up with the pilot ejecting. For this reason, all air combat was carried out with instructors in the T.2. In the clean configuration, without tanks or CBLS, the Jaguar T.2 had a much improved performance as compared with the normal fit when carrying tanks and weapons. Even so, unlike the Hawk, the Jaguar did not turn well, and because of the relatively low power and small wing, it lost speed quickly when pulling g. For best performance, the majority of air combat was flown in full reheat, and fuel consumption was very high. At maximum dry power the fuel consumption at low level was about 80 kg/min, but with full reheat this soared to 250 kg/min – three times the fuel consumption for a 60% increase in thrust. Hence combat trips were short, lasting only twenty-five minutes on average, including ten to fifteen minutes spent in transit; but although the actual air combat lasted only about ten minutes, the activity was extremely intense and very enjoyable. As at the TWU, they quickly progressed from 1-v-1 to 2-v-1, and then on to low-level evasion. Although they used the same principles as at Brawdy, they now had a faster but much less agile aircraft, in which it was necessary to keep speed up to maintain manoeuvrability. First action was normally to go to maximum reheat (the R/T call was now 'Gate' instead of 'Buster'), and the bounce aircraft was now a Jaguar flown by an instructor. The moving map made getting back on track and time much easier, and it was also very useful for avoiding prohibited areas such as weapons ranges or Balmoral. Apparently overflying Balmoral is a career-limiting exercise if the Queen happens to be in residence. The initial evasion sorties were flown around several laps of a square route, starting off with simple situations where the position and direction of attack by the bounce aircraft were known, and gradually working up to surprise bounces. On later sorties these interceptions were made while flying on navigation routes, which included attacks on off-range targets.

On 19 September 1983 Kevin planned to fly to RAF Brüggen, just over the German border from Roermond in Holland and about thirty miles west of Düsseldorf, as four Jaguar squadrons were based there. During start-up the ground crew pointed to the far side of the airfield, where a thick black pall of smoke was rising, and a couple of minutes later the news came over the radio that a Jaguar had crashed near the short runway.[10] It turned out to be Ian McLean, a friend from the course below. He had hit a flock of birds, which had gone down the air intakes and caused both engines to fail at a late stage on the final approach to land. Without power the Jaguar fell like a stone, but the pilot ejected immediately; he was uninjured and was back flying within a couple of weeks. After some delay, the formation took off for a couple of days at Brüggen. From Brüggen they flew a low-level navigation exercise at 500 ft around southern Germany – this was interesting, as Kevin had never previously flown in this area. It was at the height of the Cold War and he was very impressed by the high morale of this front-line Jaguar wing.

The course had two weeks' leave at the beginning of October. On return he had a quick dual-currency ride to get back into practice. This was followed by a trip as a passenger in the T.2 with his flight commander as one of a pair on a staff continuation training sortie. They planned an evasion sortie off Flamborough Head against F.4 Phantoms from Leuchars and Lightnings from Binbrook. The former failed to appear, but they had a very exciting scrap with the Lightnings. With reheat going and heading south, they shot through the Lightnings, as the latter wheeled around them with afterburners blazing and vapour streaming off the wings as they turned hard. The Jaguars were travelling very fast, with the speed above 600 knots at times, as they turned and weaved to prevent the Lightnings getting into a firing position. After disengaging to the south, they turned and flew through the Lightnings again, heading north and keeping a sharp lookout. Kevin looked back and saw a distant dark shape closing very rapidly and very low. It was a Lightning. He reported this to the flight commander, and immediately they were off into hard evasive action again. This really was very exhilarating. By the time that they disengaged to the north, fuel was getting short, so they pulled up to about 25,000 ft for the return to base.

During mid-October Kevin flew to Aalborg in northern Denmark in a T.2 with an instructor in formation with another instructor and Ian McLean, who had recovered from his ejection and was already back on flying. The object was to take part in Exercise *Blue Moon* – a Danish air defence exercise. That night they stayed at a hotel in Aalborg, and the following morning they flew a route round Denmark at the minimum permitted height of 1,000 ft, practising evasion against Danish F-16 fighters before pulling up to medium level for the return to Lossiemouth. His final trip on the course was to lead a 2-v-1 evasion sortie with a first-run attack on the Tain range. He had passed the course with good results and had enjoyed himself in the process: in all he had flown seventy-six hours on the Jaguar, bringing his grand total of flying hours up to 521.

After the departure of the pilot who had suffered a medical problem, the remaining seven members of No. 60 Course graduated satisfactorily. Kevin was very gratified to win the prize for the overall best bombing scores. When the postings were announced, he was pleased to find that he was to join 17 Fighter Squadron at RAF Brüggen, while the others went to Jaguar squadrons at Coltishall, near Norwich, and Laarbruch, which is about thirty miles north of Brüggen. As these postings were not effective until December 1983, the OCU kept them in flying practice throughout the rest of October and November. They did a mixture of trips, including range sorties and bounced simulated attack profiles. These Kevin enjoyed immensely, especially the last trip, in which he flew in a pair. Each carried four inert 1,000 lb bombs, to gain experience of handling the aircraft at high weight. He found that it was even more important than normal to keep the speed high, especially as the loss of speed in turns was much greater. He also found it very satisfying and exhilarating to fly the aircraft bombed up in the configuration likely to be used if he had to go to war.

On 6 December 1983 Kevin and Kate Noble departed for RAF Germany on the ferry from Dover.

No. 14 Squadron in front of GR.1 'AM' at Brüggen in 1985. Normally, the Jaguars were housed in hardened aircraft shelters. 14 October 1985 was the end of an era with 14 (Jaguar) Squadron closing down and 14 (Tornado) Squadron being inaugurated; the four-squadron Brüggen Jaguar wing was no more, with the Brüggen Tornado wing taking its place. Kevin Noble is far left. (via Kevin Noble)

CHAPTER THREE

'Keepers of the Peace'[11]

I was on a 2-ship OLF (Operational Low Flying) mission routing north through the rugged terrain of NW Scotland, keeping a constant lookout for any opposition while hugging the terrain at 100 ft. To enhance the realism, we regularly routed through Spadeadam electronic warfare range NE of Carlisle, where 'threat simulators' would beam up a varying menu of emissions to emulate the real surface-to-air missiles (SAMs) or anti-aircraft artillery (AAA) systems that we could expect to meet from the Warsaw Pact. These emissions would trigger the radar warning receiver display in the cockpit and we would then execute the appropriate tactics including use of chaff, manoeuvre and terrain masking. As a real bonus, we also had a 4-ship detachment of Canadian CF-18s from Baden Solingen in SW Germany to provide a fighter threat. These were reckoned to be about as potent as anything in the West and certainly more so than anything in the Warsaw Pact. However, the WP had just recently acquired a new generation of highly agile fighters with a look-down, shoot-down capability, including primarily the MiG-29 Fulcrum and Su-27 Flanker, so the F-18 training was highly relevant.

Suddenly, the RWR display lit up, accompanied by a series of bleeps and squeaks. Against many threats, the RWR could be tricky to interpret but in this case it was obvious. A CF-18 was acquiring me on his radar in my front left quarter. Time to manoeuvre: full burner, hard turn starboard and chaff to try and get him on my beam so I would disappear in ground clutter on his radar. Roll out, dive behind the nearest hills and look out to port to try spot him. Speed increasing through 600 knots, back to dry power. Now balancing lookout between keeping low behind as much terrain as I could find (while avoiding meeting it) and looking high and left for the 'threat'. The RWR tells me I've broken lock on his radar but then I see them. Unfortunately, they've also seen me. Burners in again and hard to turn towards the lead fighter to go for the min-sep pass. Hopefully get inside his min missile range before he can lock me up and shoot with a Sparrow radar-guided missile. Then burners out as I roll out pointing towards him to try to deny the heat-seeking AIM-9L sidewinder shot. As I pass underneath him, it's full burner again and run. Dip my left wing down to keep and eye on him behind me – keeping low is now longer the priority. He's turning hard with vapour trails streaming back from the wings. As I begin to lose sight of him behind, its time to duck and try to lose him behind the terrain. A small ridge ahead – pull up over it, roll half on my back with the heather skimming by just 100 ft above my canopy and pull over the ridge, turning right before rolling out and looking back for him – he's still with me and closing. A call of 'Fox 2'. He's taken a (simulated) Sidewinder shot. I press flare button (no flares fitted for safety reasons) and jink low while trying to keep an eye on him in my mirrors – last-ditch stuff. He pulls up to look for more quarry and that bit's over. Relax a bit and now assess how to get back on track to the next target. At the debrief later with the CF-18s, it's confirmed that a high Pk (probability of kill) shot was taken on me – for real. My flares may have decoyed it but overall I was probably 'dead'. However, in reality I had survived to train another day and the memories remain of a totally exhilarating trip. Later in the evening, we all retired to the bar for a few beers and order a take-out of Lossiemouth's famous 'Brontosaurus (ribs) and chips' and banter with the Canadians and the rest of the squadron. Tomorrow it's more of the same – what a life.

Flight Lieutenant Kevin Noble of II (AC) Squadron on an Operational Low Flying detachment at Lossiemouth in March 1987, training to fly formation attack missions (two- and four-ship) at operationally realistic altitudes down to 100 ft, in preparation for participation one month later in Exercise Maple Flag from Cold Lake in Canada.

Kevin Noble was most impressed by a large sign at the Brüggen station entrance, which stated, 'The Purpose of this Station in Peace is to Train for War', and he realized that this was indeed the operational front line. He reported to 17 to discover that a considerable amount of ground study was required to start with. There were documents covering the orders and procedures for RAF Germany and HQ 2ATAF, who coordinated and controlled operations in major exercises and war. Additionally, there were the standard operating procedures (SOP) and the war procedures, which were both comprehensive and complex and were contained in a pile of A4-size books about 4 ft high. There was an awful lot to learn. Much of it was pretty dry stuff, which took several readings to absorb and understand, but it was vitally important and it required continual study throughout his time at Brüggen to become and stay fully conversant with all aspects.

No. 17 Squadron was equipped with the Jaguar GR.1 and had a T.2 for training. His first familiarization flight was in the T.2 with the Squadron Qualified Flying Instructor (QFI), who was responsible for checking the standards of all pilots on the squadron. They did a low-level navigation exercise around the 2ATAF area of Northern Germany, followed by circuits at base. He soon found that although the half-million-scale maps were the same, the 1:50,000 maps had very different cartography and symbols from the UK Ordnance Survey maps, but he soon got used to the changes. Brüggen was a 'hardened airfield', and all operational aircraft were accommodated in hardened aircraft shelters (HAS), which like the squadron operations room in the protected briefing facility (PBF) were constructed of reinforced concrete. The pilots lived and did all their operational planning and other work in PBF, while the 'soft' administrative accommodation and crew-room were adjacent. Operation from an HAS was very different from that from the flight line; the aircraft were a tight fit in the shelter, and only one or two Jaguars could be accommodated in each HAS. The engines were started with the HAS front and rear doors open, and care had to be taken to avoid scraping the wing-tips when taxiing out. When two aircraft were parked in the HAS, the front one was at a slight angle, with the rear aircraft to its left, and only one engine was started before taxiing out to start the second. One good aspect was that in wet weather the engine could be started and the canopy closed before moving out into the rain. When returning, the aircraft was turned round and the engines stopped on the pan, and it was then winched backwards into the HAS, with the ground crew steering via a long arm attached to the nosewheel.

Northern Germany was notorious for haze and poor visibility caused by the many industrial towns. The legal limit for low flying was a minimum of 5 km visibility – less than 30 seconds' flight time at 420 knots – and conditions were frequently near this limit. This, combined with a tendency for sudden deterioration to very poor conditions, was a factor that required some getting used to; fortunately the terrain on the North German Plain was very flat. The minimum limit for low-level flying was generally 500 ft throughout Germany, but there were eight areas where flight was permitted down to 250 ft in the north, and these were extensively used to get the best training value. Terrain in the 4ATAF area of southern Germany was much more rolling and interesting, but it was cluttered with control zones around airfields and other restricted areas, and the minimum height was 500 ft overall. At that time RAF Germany had three other operational airfields in addition to Brüggen. Wildenrath was eight miles to the south, with two squadrons of Phantoms operating in the air defence role. Laarbruch, thirty miles to the north, had two squadrons (XV and 16) of strike/attack S.Mk 2B Buccaneers and one squadron (II Army Co-Operation (AC) Squadron) of Jaguars operating in the reconnaissance role, while Gütersloh in the centre of northern Germany had two squadrons of Harriers, plus two squadrons of helicopters.[12]

Kevin's second trip was solo familiarization in a GR.1, and this was followed by a check down to 250 ft and a visit to the Nordhorn range in the T.2. Nordhorn was on the German–Dutch border about ninety miles north of Brüggen, and was operated by the RAF for laydown and dive-bombing, plus strafing. Toss and loft bombing were not permitted because of the proximity of towns. Three more navigation exercises and a bounced simulated attack profile in the back seat of the T.2 gave a foretaste of things to come and took him up to Christmas. Many trips included tactical air navigation (TACAN) recoveries to Brüggen, and involved flying a procedural pattern to specified points and heights, either all the way down to 400 ft on the final approach, or to intercept the instrument landing system (ILS) for a precision approach down to 200 ft. These TACAN approaches were much used by the other air forces in NATO as they minimized the use of air traffic control and it was easy to feed streams of aircraft to the airfields by giving them all exact recovery times to be at the initial approach position, which was the start point of the procedure.

Just before Kevin arrived in Germany, the Jaguars had undergone a modification programme to install electronic countermeasures (ECM) and chaff. The ECM equipment was contained in a large pod on the left outboard pylon and was balanced by a 'Phimat' chaff pod on the right outboard pylon. The ECM pod 'listened' electronically to radar signals, and if it perceived any that were classified to be a threat, it transmitted signals in an attempt to deceive the enemy radar and ultimately cause it to break lock. On a button in the cockpit being pressed, the chaff pod dispensed bundles of aluminized fibres, which

Aircraft of RAF Germany's five Jaguar squadrons. Nearest the camera is Jaguar GR.1 XZ109/O of II (AC) Squadron carrying a recce pod. Behind is XX960/AK of 14 Squadron, which on 18 July 1989 struck a TV mast and crashed at Iserlohn, West Germany while attempting to rejoin his formation. The pilot safely ejected. Next is XX768/BA of 17 Squadron, which on 29 September 1982 suffered an engine fire on approach to Brüggen, owing to fatigue failure of a low-pressure compressor, which ruptured several fuel system components. The pilot ejected before XX768 crashed at Heinsberg-Rauderath. Next is XZ374/CA, the first of 20 Squadron's Jaguars to arrive, on 1 March 1977. Last is 'DP' of 31 Squadron. (MoD)

looked like fine silver hair, cut to specific lengths to disrupt individual radar frequencies. Hopefully, if it was dispensed at the appropriate moment the enemy radar locked on to the chaff cloud instead of the Jaguar, but it took some practice to do all the correct switching at the critical moment. It was possible to carry an AIM-9G Sidewinder missile in place of the ECM pod, but this was not an ideal situation. The pilots would have preferred to carry missiles, pods and chaff, but, depending on the threat scenario, it would have been possible to have a mix of suitable fits in a formation. (Since the Gulf War the fitment of overwing rails for a pair of Sidewinders has overcome this problem.) Additionally, flare packs have been fitted to the engine doors between the ventral fins; these could be fired to decoy approaching enemy heat-seeking missiles. All this extra equipment was vital to survival in a modern hostile environment, but the big disadvantage was that it used two weapons pylons, and so with the standard fuel load, including two drop-tanks, the Jaguar was limited to only two bombs instead of four. Also, bombs would be dropped half-way though the trip, thus getting rid of a considerable amount of weight and drag, whereas the ECM and chaff pods were carried all the time. To get best results from the system it was necessary to interpret the bleeps, squeaks and visual indications from the RWR correctly and to use appropriate tactics with the right ECM being switched on at the critical moment, and this required a lot of practice. In Germany at that time, aircraft were allowed to dispense chaff almost anywhere at low level for ECM practice, but this situation has now changed.

Between Christmas and the New Year the squadron trained in preparation for Exercise *Red Flag*, which was to be held in the Nevada Desert in January, although, being a new arrival, Kevin was not scheduled to take part.[13] Jaguars had already been flown out by pilots from the UK Jaguar squadrons as they were trained in air-to-air refuelling (AAR), while those on the RAF Germany (RAFG) squadrons were not, and the aircraft were left out there for use by successive three-weekly detachments from the UK and Germany squadrons. The 17 Squadron advance party left by Hercules early in the New Year and was followed three days later by the pilots and ground crew in a VC 10, which arrived at Nellis Air Force Base, just outside Las Vegas, only one day after the Hercules. The VC 10 refuelled at Gander in Newfoundland, which was covered in deep snow, and flew on to find Nellis basking in sunshine with the temperature in the low 70s.

The USAF had discovered in Vietnam that if crews could survive the first dozen missions, their chances of surviving the rest of an operational tour were greatly improved, and they therefore endeavoured to replicate wartime conditions in Exercise *Red Flag*. Comprehensive exercise briefings covering the rules of play and safety procedures, plus films of aircraft, which either had narrow escapes or had actually crashed on previous exercises, were held on the Sunday in preparation for flying the following day. Despite these warnings, mistakes were made, and a pilot on the next detachment from Brüggen was killed when he mishandled his Jaguar at low level and lost control.[14] As one of the briefing officers pointed out, this was not war, just an exercise, and the probability of being killed was greater if you hit the ground than if someone fired a missile at you in anger.

The Nevada range contained many simulated SAM and AAA threats, as well as defensive fighters that endeavoured to intercept the attacking aircraft. There were also comprehensive facilities to record virtually every aspect of exercise play for use at the debriefings held after each flight. Kevin attended many of these debriefings and was very interested in the tactics used, especially those against SAMs. The Jaguars flew very low

GR.1 XZ373/BG of 17 Squadron over the North German Plain in typical training fit, with two 1,200-litre fuel tanks and CBLS (Carrier Bomb Light Stores) containing practice bombs. This aircraft ended its career with 6 Squadron, and was lost on 21 June 1995 during a training sortie from Italy while being flown by a USAF exchange pilot with 6 Squadron. Because of a fuel imbalance in the underwing tanks, control was lost during Air Combat Training (ACT). The pilot could not regain control and he ejected at 5,000 ft over the Adriatic Sea. A RN Sea King from the NATO base at Split subsequently rescued him. (via Kevin Noble)

– mainly at about at 100 ft above the ground. This was classed as operational low flying (OLF), as it was extremely difficult for SAMs and AAA to get a good shot and it was a very successful tactic; they also used ECM, chaff and flares to good effect. Video cameras were slaved to SAM and AAA radars and showed lots of Jaguars and other aircraft evading at high speed and low altitude while using these countermeasures – very exciting. Overall, *Red Flag* was excellent experience for Kevin during his early days on the squadron, but all too soon he was on the VC 10 back to Brüggen after two weeks at Nellis.

In late January and early February 1984, flying concentrated on unbounced SAPs, plus introduction to the Dutch ranges of Vliehors, the main range for toss and loft bombing, and Noordvarder, on the northern coasts of the islands of Vlieland and Terschelling respectively. These ranges were extensively used by the NATO air forces, and over the years had built up a reputation of being potentially hazardous, as 'goldfish bowl' conditions, in which the sea merged into the sky with no visible horizon, were prevalent, and many aircraft had flown into the sea. Fortunately, no Jaguars had ever been involved in this type of accident. The minimum permitted height over Holland was generally 1,000 ft but there were two specific routes down to 250 ft, one of which was from the ranges to the Dutch border near Brüggen. Kevin also did his initial night sorties: first a dual flight in the T.2, after which he did practice diversions to, and circuits at, local bases to check that he was competent, before being introduced to the night 'low-level' routes. At that time the Jaguars had a nuclear strike role by day and night, while they operated only by day in clear weather for the conventional attack role. The aircraft had no special night aids such as search or terrain-following radar (TFR), so under war conditions they would have had to fly as low as they dared, hopefully by moonlight. For training, there were specific routes around Germany with safe minimum heights specified for each leg. In peacetime, route navigation at night was not too difficult because of the lights from the towns, but it would have been a different story under wartime blackout conditions. The route around northern Germany terminated at Nordhorn, and, as finding the target at night would have been difficult, it was lit to ensure that other places in the local area were not bombed by mistake. On one night sortie he was on a night practice diversion to Manston, in Kent, but while passing 15,000 ft over Holland, he lit the afterburners to speed up the climb. However, as he pushed the throttles through the afterburner gate there was a loud bang and a huge flash up the left side of the cockpit as the engine pup-surged. This was a common occurrence in the Jaguar on lighting the afterburners, but the first time he had experienced it at night; the flash was very impressive and gave him quite a shock.

In mid-February 1984 it was down to Bad Kohlgrup in Bavaria for a two-week winter survival course. Back at Brüggen Kevin continued working up to obtain operational status in the strike and attack roles. The nuclear strike work was the highest priority, and a considerable amount of study was required on all the procedures involved. Flying training consisted of simulated strike profiles (SSPs), as distinct from SAPs, which were flown as single aircraft by day and night using the preset routes. March continued with a mix of SSPs, bounced and unbounced two-, three- and four-ship (aircraft) SAPs, plus the odd dedicated range trip to the Dutch ranges and a night trip.

In mid-March 1984 Kevin Noble had his first experience of strafing, using HE ammunition at Nordhorn, firing longer bursts of 1–2 seconds (as opposed to half a second), and soon learned to walk shells up a convoy target. Instead of splashes of sand there were red-black puff-balls erupting to obliterate the target – a very satisfying pastime. It was at this time that he experienced another close shave. On one run in hazy conditions he missed the small triangular wood at the end of the downwind leg and turned late, but another JP behind him turned in at the correct point and did not see him and so ended up very close above and behind. Both pilots called 'in live' at about the same time, and Kevin received 'clear live' and proceeded to fire. The other JP also thought he was cleared live and was about to fire when Kevin's aircraft suddenly appeared in his sights. He later told him in the bar that he felt hot and cold as he came very close to shooting him down. As the other pilot pulled off the target, his NAVWASS dumped, causing the HUD reversionary bombing symbol (which was the same as the strafe symbol but was depressed by about 5° instead of only about half a degree) to appear in place of the strafe symbol. Unfortunately, because he was flustered by the previous incident, the pilot failed to notice this and used the reversionary bomb index to aim on the next pass. He fired a burst, and not surprisingly his shells went well over the target. At least Kevin had the good grace to admit that the poor chap's second error was largely his fault.

Kevin received his check for proficiency in the strike role in mid-April. The Squadron Commander flew chase on this trip, and he passed quite well. This was the first step on the road to being declared fully combat ready. It meant that he could now do quick reaction alert (QRA); this was a regular 24-hour duty in which the pilots were ready to launch at short notice in the event of a surprise attack. This was quite a responsibility for a young pilot to handle. On QRA, they were frequently tested for rapid reaction and were called to the cockpits by the sounding of a klaxon. Occasionally someone was caught in the shower, and it was then amusing to see him dashing across to the HAS in bare feet, dripping wet in just a flying suit and carrying his flying boots, in his haste to get to the aircraft and check in. Once pronounced 'combat ready for strike', he was able to concentrate on attack work; this he found more interesting because they operated in formation and were likely to be bounced. Bounced SAPs were similar to those flown at the OCU but with slightly different tactics, and the separation between aircraft in battle formation tended to be greater. If bounced, the aim was to run away and hopefully lose the attacker. In the last resort a bomb could be dropped to deter the pursuer, and if necessary all tanks and stores could be jettisoned to survive. It was better not to hit the target and survive than to be shot down. He once had an interesting experience when running away from bounce in full afterburner at 250 ft. Watching the attacker over his shoulder, he suddenly became aware that he could not see out, as the canopy appeared to have misted up. When he looked through the windscreen the visibility was still good, and then he noticed the speed: it was well over 600 knots and rising fast. Apart from the nose, the rest of the aircraft was covered in a cloud of condensation: he was at transonic speed, and the limit for evasion was normally 480 knots, so he quickly throttled back.

During May he started on 1-v-1 air combat training (ACT) and was cleared for solo flying on this exercise. One day while on a SAP the aircraft suddenly felt very odd and yawed hard to the left as he rolled out of a turn. On checking around he noticed that the left leading-edge slat was fully lowered to the take-off position, while the right was still retracted. In theory, this could not happen, so he pulled up gently and slowed down before making a low-speed handling check at a safe height. Fortunately the aircraft handled satisfactorily in the landing configuration, and he made an uneventful landing. It transpired that the aircraft had recently returned from a major servicing in the Maintenance Unit at Abingdon, since when it had only flown a few sorties. During

GR.1 XX750/22, seen here in 226 OCU colours at Mildenhall on 26 August 1978, joined 14 Squadron and crashed inverted on 7 February 1984 at Red Flag *after loss of control while taking avoiding action after being picked up by ground radar. The USAF exchange pilot was killed. (Tom Trower)*

servicing the slats had been disconnected, even though the servicing schedule did not call for this, and on reassembly the bolts had only been done up finger tight. Naturally, after a few operations one fell out.

Although not its main rule, the squadron frequently practised close air support (CAS) on the battlefield in direct support of the Army: this was the main rule of the Harrier force. Army forward air controllers (FAC), either on the ground or in Gazelle helicopters, designated the targets and directed the pilots onto them. These missions were normally flown as pairs for flexibility and to ease the coordination of formations. Planning was normally carried out at short notice, although the pilots already knew the approximate area of the targets and had pre-briefed initial positions (IPs). The first problem was that instead of neatly folded strip maps, they now often had large square 50,000-scale maps, which could be a nightmare in the cockpit. Flying towards the target area they contacted the FAC at a pre-briefed position and time on a specified radio frequency, and were directed to an IP. The FAC then detailed target location, distance and direction from the IP and various other information, including location of friendly Army units; this was most important to avoid attacking our own troops. Having noted this information on a kneepad, the pilot then inserted the target position into the NAVWASS and plotted it on the 50,000-scale map so that he could pick out features in the target area; this was not easy while flying the aircraft and formating on the leader. On leaving the IP the FAC then gave further directions until he could see the aircraft approaching the target area, followed by left or right directions, referring to significant visible features, to lead the pilots to the target. The FAC often referred to features such as a 'bushy-top tree' but from the air hundreds of bushy-top trees were visible. To make a successful attack, the pilot needed to see the target for a minimum of about ten seconds (2 km) before overflying it, and it had to be almost directly ahead. This gave just enough time for a quick adjustment of heading, getting the sight onto the target and releasing the bombs. Typically the bombs were released 600 metres from the target, so if it was significantly off to one side it had to be picked out even earlier to give time to turn and line up for the attack. Camouflaged tanks and vehicles were particularly difficult to pick out against tree lines, and this added to the problem; fortunately there were plenty of Army training areas in Germany with real tanks and armoured vehicles to provide good training. On operations the aircraft would make a single pass to deliver their weapons and leave the target area. Previous wars proved that returning for a second pass was a recipe for getting shot down. However, to provide further training for the pilots and FAC they normally spent about thirty minutes making several passes on various targets from different IPs, and this gave the pilots a high workload.

Because of the many problems involved, this type of attack was not always successful, but the success rate was greatly improved if the FAC was able to mark the target with a laser beam. The Jaguar, Harrier GR.3 and Tornado GR.1 each had a laser ranger and marked target seeker (LRMTS) in the nose, which locked onto reflected laser energy and indicated the target to the pilot by means of a target marker in the HUD. The pilot would then normally fire his own laser to measure the range to the target, a crucial parameter for accurate weapon aiming at low level. The aircraft was then steered to fly the HUD bomb-fall line over the laser target cross, and the pickle button would be pressed so that when the computer calculated that it had a good aiming solution it released the bombs – easy if it all worked. Using this method the pilot could make a successful attack without seeing the target, and at the very least it normally gave an early and accurate steering cue. As the laser ranger was dangerous to the human eye, it could only be used in war or on specific weapons ranges, and even then only within particular headings and distances from nominated targets; for training purposes the FAC had a special device to render their laser target marker safe for use on exercise.[15]

Early in June 1984 the squadron set off to Decimomannu (known as Dechi) in southern Sardinia for the annual armament practice camp (APC). As a still relatively junior pilot (JP), Kevin had to travel in the support Hercules, which was definitely third-class travel, as it was slow, noisy and had uncomfortable paratrooper seats. Decimomannu was then a large NATO base run by the Italian, British, German and American Air Forces for weapons and combat practice. It had an air-to-ground range at Frasca half-way up the west coast, plus an air-to-air range over the sea to the west, which was not used by the RAF, and an air combat range, fitted with air combat manoeuvring instrumentation (ACMI) over the sea to the north-west. On this detachment 17 Squadron only used the Frasca range for three weeks of concentrated bombing and strafing in generally excellent

GR.1s XZ378/CH and XZ374/CA of 20 Squadron with a CBLS (Carrier Bomb Light Stores) pod on the centre-line over Germany in December 1978. Markings consisted of the squadron emblem, in front of a rising sun and eagle, wing elevated, perched on a sword, flanked by blue, red, white and green bars applied to the engine intakes. (MoD)

Mediterranean weather. The flights were short, lasting thirty-five to forty minutes on average, to give twenty minutes on the range.

It was nice not to have to do a lengthy plan before each trip. There was a briefing before take-off and a full formation debrief of HUD films immediately after landing. They flew up to three trips per day and relaxed in the evenings either at a local restaurant or in the quadri-national mess. All weapon scores were displayed on a large board for everyone to see, as this encouraged maximum individual effort and a healthy rivalry. The qualified weapons instructors (QWI) set the attack profiles for each trip. They started with basic reversionary level and 5° dive-bombing using 3 kg simulated retarded bombs, then working up to more unusual profiles not normally practised. They soon moved onto 20° dive-bombing, initially using the full NAVWASS, and then in the reversionary mode. As the dive started at 6,000 ft, they needed good weather. To simulate the 1,000 lb free-fall bomb they used 28 lb practice bombs, the bomb being released at about 3,000 ft before they pulled out of the dive. A new event was the 20° dive-toss manoeuvre using the NAVWASS. This was started from 4,000 ft by overbanking when turning onto the attack run, and allowing the nose to drop into a 20° dive. The HUD target bars were then slewed onto the target to indicate the precise target position to the computer, and the pull-out was commenced at around 2,500 ft before the pickle button was pressed. Computer bomb release occurred automatically in a 3 g pull-out at around 10° dive angle, and the recovery to level flight was then continued, normally dipping a wing to spot the impact of the bomb. This procedure provided good scores, with the bombs going in like darts. Landing after one trip, Kevin was on the final approach at about 100 ft when his Jaguar hit the jet wash from an aircraft ahead and rapidly rolled to nearly 90° of bank. Application of full opposite rudder and spoiler brought the aircraft level just in time to flare for the landing, and it was only at the end of the landing run that it occurred to him what a close shave it had been.

On the last weekend of the detachment he went to Gibraltar in the T.2 with an experienced pilot, accompanied by a single-seat Jaguar. The single runway was only 6,000 ft long (relatively short for the Jaguar), with water at both ends, so there was little room for error, and they always used the braking parachute to stop rather than the aerodynamic braking normally employed on longer runways. The road from Spain ran across the middle of the runway, and was closed for take-offs and landings. At that time there was considerable tension with Spain, and three Jaguars were permanently based there to show the flag. Care had to be taken not to infringe Spanish airspace, so a curved approach was required when landing towards the east, and the aircraft had to be turned immediately it was airborne when taking off towards the west: rather interesting in a loaded Jaguar on a hot day. Even some Buccaneers appeared to stagger as they took off in the heat of the day. Gibraltar had a chain arrestor gear (CHAG), an unusual device consisting of tons of ships' anchor chain laid up each side of the runway with a cable connecting the chains at the far end. The lowered arrestor hook caught the cable and dragged out the chains, bringing the aircraft to a stop – crude but effective. At that time the Jaguar was not cleared to use CHAG, but the pilots decided they would do so if necessary, rather than go off the end into the sea. The squadron flew back to Decimomannu on the Monday, and for Kevin it was back to Brüggen by Hercules the following day.

After only one week back at Brüggen, they were off to Cyprus for a fortnight's air-to-

GR.1 XZ370/BN of 17 Squadron in war fit with two fuel tanks, two blue (inert) 1,000 lb bombs on centre-line, a Phimat chaff pod under the starboard wing and an ALQ-101-10 ECM pod under the port wing. (via Kevin Noble)

air gun firing, 17 being the first Jaguar squadron to do so. Once more, and accompanied by another JP, Kevin had to travel by Hercules, but this time they had to go to Lyneham to start the flight to Akrotiri. One of the Jaguars in solo transit had diverted into southern Italy as the pilot had experienced 'break-out'. This was an uncommon phenomenon, which only occurred at high altitude and in which the sufferer felt a sense of complete detachment. In this case the pilot said he felt as if he was sitting on the wing looking in at himself, and felt an irresistible urge to let down to get closer to the earth's surface. After a period off flying, he recovered and went on to continue flying as an instructor.

For air-to-air firing the banner was towed by a Canberra over the sea to the south of Akrotiri. Although the firing pattern was basically similar to that used on the Hawk, the similarity ended there. To obtain reasonable manoeuvrability, the firing pass was made at about 420 knots, but at this speed there was very little time to track, differential tailplane movement available to assist roll control was very limited and the spoilers became ineffective above about 12 alpha. The net result was that when rolling and pulling to break away from the flag the roll rate was very slow, and they were briefed to use rudder to help the roll This was an unusual procedure for the Jaguar, or any other aircraft for that matter, and was alien to the pilots, who were briefed to use rudder with caution. Apparently Kevin did not obtain very good scores, and it is doubtful whether many other pilots did, either. To avoid the heat of the afternoon the working day started and finished early, thus giving plenty of time to sunbathe or windsurf from the beaches around the edge of the airfield. At the end of the detachment Kevin flew back to Brüggen in a Jaguar as a member of a three-aircraft formation, refuelling at Brindisi in the heel of Italy and Istres le Tube in France. The first leg took two hours across the Mediterranean and was his first experience of procedural flying on airways: there was only limited radar cover, so all aircraft had to adhere to flight-planned routes and report at specified points. Safety separation from other traffic using the airway was achieved purely on height and timing; typical heights and speeds used by the Jaguars were 25,000 ft and Mach 0.82–0.85. As their moving maps only provided coverage for Northern Europe down to the Alps, they had to use more basic navigational procedures than normal until they reached northern Italy. Overall it had been an interesting few weeks, with many new places visited and overflown.

In mid-August 1984 Kevin dropped his first live 1,000 lb bombs, at Garvie Island near Cape Wrath on the north-west tip of Scotland – the only place in Europe where this was permitted. He flew as No. 2 of a pair, the load was two 1,000 lb retarded bombs, and the aircraft landed at Macrihanish on the Mull of Kintyre to refuel. Unfortunately, due to an administrative mix-up, there was no range safety officer (RSO) available at Garvie when they arrived, so they had to land and spend the night at Kinloss. Garvie Island is a large rock, about 100 ft high and 400 ft long, and they returned the next morning, having to drop their bombs singly because of noise restrictions. On the run-in for the first attack Kevin was about seven miles behind the leader, whose first bomb exploded in a big puff of smoke and dust. He then checked and double-checked his switches to avoid any mistakes and made a level attack; there was a big thump as the bomb released and he dipped the wing into a turn to see a huge black eruption of smoke shoot up from the base of the rock. On the second run he watched in the mirrors, seeing the retarded bomb spinning slowly down to explode. With his leader he then pulled up to medium level for the return to Brüggen, and an hour later they were back on the ground.

August was a busy month, and he often flew twice a day, amassing a total of 39 hours 25 minutes – one of his highest monthly totals. There was plenty of variety with bounced SAPs, ACT and night-flying on the specified routes. During a large NATO exercise at the end of September he took part in a ten-aircraft airfield attack on a Belgian air base. For effective formation control and safety, good R/T discipline was essential with so many aircraft on the same frequency in a small area of sky. Belgium had low-flying areas cleared down to 250 ft in the Ardennes, with 500 ft minimum elsewhere, and their Air Force was renowned for flying lower than the limits, especially over Germany. One of Kevin's friends engaged on low flying actually had a Belgian Mirage 5 fly underneath him. The German authorities soon became fed up with this, and installed radars, with videos that recorded height and ground speed, to identify the culprits; anyone caught was in deep trouble. The RAF pilots meanwhile did their best to play by the rules, mainly

Jaguars of 17 Squadron in Cyprus for a fortnight's air-to-air gun firing. In 1984 17 was the first Jaguar squadron to do so. Nearest aircraft is XZ384/BJ, which went to RAF Cosford for ground instruction as 8954M after the squadron disbanded in March 1985. No. 17 Squadron codes BA to BZ were applied to the aircraft from March 1976. Markings consist of the squadron badge of a mailed red gauntlet on the intake sides, flanked by white rectangles containing black zig-zags. (via Steve Hill)

because they wanted to preserve the low-flying system for training.

Shortly afterwards Kevin took part in his first Exercise *Mallet Blow*, which was then the biggest and best annual air exercise in the UK, and lasted a week. The UK air defence aircraft flew combat air patrols (CAP) over the North Sea and Northern England to intercept the attack aircraft, which routed through Spadeadam in the Scottish borders. There they had to evade simulated SAM and AAA defences – their efforts being scored for exercise purposes – before attacking targets at Otterburn, an Army range about thirty miles to the north-east, in hilly terrain with very few features to help with navigation. The tactical targets on the range, comprising old vehicle hulks in 'convoy', bridges, simulated SAM sites and a runway with an old aircraft unit were therefore difficult to find and acquire. Army and RAF Regiment Rapier SAMs were also deployed on the range to take advantage of the targets provided by the attacking aircraft. As Kevin was not yet combat ready, he flew in the back seat of a T.2 with an experienced pilot in an eight-aircraft formation operating from Waddington.

Enemy territory started in Northern England, and they met some Phantoms from Leuchars between the Lake District and the Pennines. The Jaguar GR.1s initially picked up the Phantoms' radars on their RWR. As the T.2 had no RWR they had to rely on R/T calls from the GR.1s, while they endeavoured to evade the Phantoms by threading their way between the various radar threats and flying down the valleys when approaching Spadeadam. The Spadeadam defences launched 'smoky SAMs' if they managed to get a radar lock onto the Jaguars. These were polystyrene rockets that left a smoke trail up to 300–400 ft, giving some impression of the real thing. These rockets were very light, and so even if they hit an aircraft they would do no damage. On leaving Spadeadam the formation leader called an R/T frequency change to obtain clearance from the RSO to enter the Otterburn range, and each pilot called 'in hot' as he acquired a target. Keeping low to evade the Rapiers, switches were set to live for dropping the 3 kg bombs simulating a stick of four 1,000 lb retarded bombs.

When the last man left the target, they changed to the normal squadron frequency as they headed out to sea, looking out for the fighters. Most fighter interceptions took place over the sea, and these were very high-pressure and exciting moments as the fighters wheeled around them in full afterburner, attempting to get into position for missile or gun attacks. Evading hard, the Jaguars worked their way southwards until they eventually reached 'safe' territory, where they pulled up for the return to base. This was very exhilarating flying and probably the best training available apart from the USAF Exercise *Red Flag*. Back on the ground there was a formation debrief, followed by a debrief with the Ground Liaison Officer (GLO), an Army major attached to the squadron who liaised with the Army and intelligence organizations. All debrief details were passed on to Exercise Control, and in return they received bomb scores from Otterburn and 'shots claimed' from the Spadeadam and Otterburn Rapiers. Another IF on the squadron got into a bit of bother at Otterburn, as, having been cleared to strafe a target near the exercise runway, he could not find it and so strafed the hulk of an Andover on the runway threshold, chopping off one wing. The RSO was not amused at the wrecking of one of his targets, as these were normally reserved for attacks with 3 kg bombs, which only punched small holes. The following day Kevin flew over to Aalborg in Denmark for Exercise *Blue Moon*, staying the night and returning after the exercise the next day.

In mid-October 1984 the squadron held a navigation and bombing competition.

Although RAFG held a similar competition between squadrons for the prestigious Salmond Trophy, for some reason the Jaguars did not compete at that time. The 17 Squadron competition was therefore called the 'Sardine Trophy'. Each pilot was given a list of targets, including FRA delivery of retarded bombs on the Nordhorn range, with only limited time for planning; the targets were small and difficult to find and the attack results were assessed from the HUD film. The off-range targets were manned by squadron intelligence personnel, who checked that competitors flew precisely over the target at the specified time, and the range score was added to the total. Kevin came fifth out of sixteen pilots, which he considered to be quite good for a JR. Meanwhile he continued to concentrate on the work-up to achieve his attack combat readiness status with bounced two- and four-aircraft SAPs, interspersed with 1-v-1 ACT, dedicated range trips to the Dutch ranges and hi-lo trips to UK for lunch stops if the weather was not good in Germany. He had his attack combat readiness check on 27 November, leading a pair of aircraft in a bounced SAP, and although he cannot remember the details, he passed and was now fully combat ready, almost a year after arriving on the squadron. This was fairly standard at the time, although training later became more streamlined in an attempt to get crews combat ready sooner. Kevin had made it and was now a fully fledged combat-ready front-line pilot. This allowed him to do two new exercises: fighter affiliation and unbriefed evasion. The former comprised evasion sorties against air defence fighters, normally Phantoms from Wildenrath, while the latter allowed limited evasion to be carried out on meeting any other aircraft in Germany. This provided good training and encouraged the maintenance of good lookout and quick reaction to new threats, as it was very embarrassing if other aircraft were able to creep up on your formation unsighted.

Fighter affiliation was significantly different from bounced SAP. Their main opposition in war would have been the Soviet and East German MiG-23, code-named *Flogger-B*, a swing-wing air defence fighter, which did not have a look-down shoot-down capability and thus had to get in behind its target to fire its heat-seeking missile, normally the AA8 *Aphid*. The *Flogger-B* also carried radar missiles, but these were only effective against medium- and high-level targets. Although it could out-turn a Jaguar, it was not a very manoeuvrable machine, but it did have a very powerful engine, which gave it fearsome acceleration and speed. The MiG-27 *Flogger-D* was a development of the MiG-23, which was equipped for ground attack work and in some ways was the Soviet equivalent of the Jaguar. Several years later Kevin had the opportunity for a good look around a MiG-27 at an airshow: as compared with the Jaguar it had a very basic navigation system and the view from the cockpit was poor.

The Phantoms from Wildenrath were fitted with pulse-Doppler radars and thus had a look-down shout-down capability; the change of frequency in the radar reflections from moving targets enabled these to be differentiated from stationary targets or returns from the ground. Using this principle, the Phantom's radar could be locked onto an aircraft target instead of sweeping the area from side to side as it normally did in the search mode. The American Sparrow, or its British development the Skyflash, missiles were then able to home on the reflected radar energy. A means to avoid being shot down by one of these missiles was to break the radar lock. This could be achieved with the aid of the RWR by putting your aircraft beam on to the attacker. It then had the same relative speed to the attacker as the ground returns and the radar broke lock. Escape by flying very low was not possible, as evidenced by a story from the Gulf War. An American F-15 pilot locked onto a very low-level target, which he thought was a helicopter, travelling at about 100 knots, and fired a Sparrow. He followed the missile to observe results and to his amazement it homed onto and destroyed a car speeding down the Baghdad highway. His ground crew marked the kill by painting a car symbol on the side of his aircraft. Normally Doppler radars were designed to ignore any target with less than 100 knots speed relative to the ground, so this car must have been travelling pretty fast.

The Jaguar RWR detected when any radar, including that on the Phantom, was tracking the aircraft while it was still beyond visual range (BVR), and it was then possible to turn to put the fighter on the beam to break the radar lock. Having broken lock, any radar-guided missile fired would normally be lost and the fighter would have to start a new attack. However, with a head-on closing speed of about 1,000 knots, time was very short, so that having broken lock the Jaguars tried to edge around the attackers and get back on track to the target. The fighter meanwhile often tried to convert the encounter to a beam or stern chase for an AIM-9 Sidewinder infra-red missile shot when in visual range. The countering tactic by the Jaguars was then to straighten out when beam on and try to acquire the attacker visually; if he was picked up, the Jaguars then turned hard towards him to pass with minimum separation and tried to run away. Every intercept was different, and it took practice to quickly build up a mental picture of where all the players were and predict where they were going, while trying to keep them in sight. It also took a considerable amount of coordination on the R/T to maintain formation integrity and visual cross-cover; it was therefore very satisfying when everything went right and the attacker was avoided, or even better, it was possible to get a simulated 'shot' at him. When ECM and chaff were fitted they were used in the training modes to try to defeat attackers. Even if they were not carried, the pilots still made all the necessary switch selections so that the drills became second nature, since, in action, fumbling a switch could cost your life.

As already mentioned, carrying ECM and chaff on the outboard pylons halved the standard load from four 1,000 lb bombs to two. One way to rectify this was to dispense with the tanks fitted on the inboard pylons and carry a single tank under the fuselage centre-line instead. Tandem beams, which carried two 1,000 lb bombs one behind the other, could then be fitted on the inboard pylons to restore the maximum load to four bombs. This caused a small reduction in range, but the all-up weight remained pretty much as before. In the air, the front bombs could be seen to waggle around quite noticeably as the beam had a long overhang from the front of the pylon. Kevin flew in this configuration in mid-December to drop four inert 1,000 lb retarded bombs on the Vliehors range. The aircraft was in full war fit and weighed almost fifteen tons, so it was necessary to do a high-alpha take-off to get maximum performance. This meant lifting the nose at a slightly lower speed than normal to a higher angle of attack, thus shortening the ground roll, with the critical point at decision speed (when the aircraft was rotated to become airborne) a couple of seconds before reaching the rotary hydraulic arrestor gear (RHAG) barrier. In an emergency this then gave just enough time to lower the hook, engage the barrier and stop. Once airborne, the aircraft mushed away, slowly accelerating, and the aim was to reach safe flying speed as soon as possible. If an engine failed just after take-off, the drill was to jettison bombs and the fuel tank immediately; otherwise the aircraft could not maintain height. All aspects of normal and emergency procedures for heavyweight take-off were covered by the formation leader in his sortie brief. But in the

GR.1s of 14 Squadron over the North German Plain in various war fits. The nearest aircraft with centre-line tank, four CBU on 'tandem beams' and two AIM-9G Sidewinders. Middle aircraft has two LGB, ECM, Phimat and centre-line tank. Far aircraft is in original war fit (prior to installation of the ECM pod) of four 1,000 lb bombs and two fuel tanks. Markings consist of a winged crusader's shield, surmounted by a yellow helmet and shoulder-piece from a suit of armour, flanked by blue diamonds, carried on the intakes. (via Kevin Noble)

event they all took off with no problems, and they were helped by the cold air of December, with the engines producing more thrust than they would have done in mid-summer.

At Vliehors they bombed the special target reserved for inert bombs. Running in a couple of miles behind the aircraft ahead, Kevin saw the parachute tails open on the retarded bombs and the splashes of sand as the half-ton bombs hit the ground. Later, viewing his HUD film, it was just possible to see the bombs re-emerging from the sand a couple of hundred feet further on (minus their tails) and tumbling on into the distance. He then double-checked his switches and was cleared in 'hot' to drop his bombs, stabilizing the speed at 480 knots and height at 150 ft above the sea on the run-in to the target on the sandy shore. The pickle button was pressed and the computer released the four bombs in a stick in a fraction of a second. There was a quick ripple of thumps as the ejector units fired the bombs away from the tandem beams, and suddenly the aircraft was two tons lighter and felt much more responsive. His bombs straddled the target, as did those of the rest of the formation, and altogether it was a satisfying feeling to have accomplished this task successfully.

That afternoon, he did his first trip wearing the Aircrew Respirator No. 5 (AR5), which was worn in conjunction with the charcoal suit and rubber gloves to provide personal protection from nuclear, biological and chemical (NBC) agents. The AR5 consisted of a rubber head-piece resembling a scuba balaclava, with a perspex face-piece and an oxygen mask containing a built-in microphone; the normal protective helmet was worn over the top. A large rubber bellows around the neck allowed head movement and was attached to a mantlet, which lay on the shoulders to overlap with the charcoal NBC suit. Rubber gloves (like washing-up gloves) were worn under normal flying gloves. It was a hot and sweaty business donning this equipment, so what it was like to wear in hot weather can be imagined. The equipment was donned in the PBF, which was NBC-proof. A portable fan unit, or 'whistling handbag', which contained a battery-powered fan and filter pack, was then connected to the AR5 inlet hose to protect the wearer and to demist the faceplate when leaving the protected environment to go out to the aircraft. In the cockpit the portable unit was disconnected and the AR5 hose connected to the aircraft system. Misting of the faceplate was quite a hazard, especially if it happened in the air. Airsickness could also present a problem, as it was necessary to minimize any exposure to a contaminated atmosphere, and there was a special drill in the FRC checklist to cover this eventuality. For these reasons, the AR5 was only flown in the dual-control T.2, with a safety pilot in the rear cockpit. In the early days the AR5 was supplied, and the faceplate demisted, from the aircraft oxygen system, although filters and a fan were later fitted to the ejector seat for demisting and to conserve the oxygen supply.

Prior to this first flight, he had already done a couple of practices, wearing the AR5 in the flight simulator. The trip was a bounced four-aircraft formation to the Nordhorn range. This was really a baptism by fire, as most people seemed to have a fairly gentle ride for their introduction to the AR5. Initially, things were not too bad once he had strapped in and settled down, but it became hard work to keep a good look-out rearwards; the rubber bellows around the neck was not very flexible and his neck muscles soon became tired. To really look back, he had to resort to grabbing the mask with his left (free) hand and pulling it around. Pulling g is quite physical at the best of times, and in this equipment he was very hot and sticky by the time they reached the Nordhorn range,

GR.1 XX966 of 17 Squadron in formation with a CF-104 of the Canadian Armed Forces. (via Steve Hill)

and he was getting quite a lot of misting around the top of the faceplate. They spent the normal twenty minutes on the range before a steady return to base, which enabled him to cool off a bit. After landing, Kevin felt like a wet rag, and when he took the AR5 off, a pint of sweat splashed out from the neck bellows, and his shirt and flying suit were soaked. In retrospect, it had definitely taken the edge off his physical and mental performance in the air, and he noticed this in others when he later flew as safety pilot. However, this was a unique system, which allowed RAF aircrew to continue to operate in NBC conditions when others could not, and although no one would wish to fly in it, the alternative was death or incapacitation, so there was really no choice.

A couple of ACT trips; 1-v-1 and 2-v-1, completed 1984, and they then stood down for the normal, very social Christmas. Then it was off for a fortnight's skiing at Oberstdorf in Bavaria. Meanwhile, the two Buccaneer squadrons at Laarbruch had already re-equipped with the Tornado GR.1, as had 20 and 31 Squadrons at Brüggen, and 17 (Jaguar) Squadron was getting ready to wind down, as new aircraft and crews arrived to build up the new 17 Squadron with the Tornado. (17 Squadron received its first Tornado GR.1 on 16 August 1984.) As the Tornado carried a pilot and a navigator, the new squadron was twice the size of the original; the big Jaguar wing was already fading and both the station and mess were changing with the rapid influx of new faces. However, the Jaguars continued normal flying throughout January and February, and Kevin took the instrument rating test (IRT) to gain his Green Card rating in February. This was a big step forward, as he no longer had to add 200 ft to the minimum approach height and so could fly to lower cloud and visibility minima. This was important to him personally as he had been left on the ground on several occasions when the weather was not fit for those holding White Cards but was acceptable for Green-rated pilots. During the last couple of weeks the squadron practised the handover parade for the new Tornado squadron. His last trip on 17 Squadron was on 28 February 1985, when he ferried a Jaguar back to Shawbury for long-term storage. Shawbury was then a training school for helicopter crews and air traffic controllers, so when he called them he was asked to do a precision approach (GCA) for controller training. A very interesting approach ensued, as the poor girl under training was used to handling the Jet Provosts that were established for controller training, and the Jaguar was considerably faster. Very quickly they were into a situation of large heading changes, with the Jaguar diverging farther through the approach centre-line with each one. Eventually the calm voice of an instructor took over, and with one heading change it was all sorted out. Kevin flew back to Brüggen in a Pembroke from the Communications Flight at Wildenrath, and he found it old and noisy. Unknown to the pilots, he plugged his helmet into an intercommunication socket and could hear their conversation. He overheard them grumbling every time one of the passengers went back to the toilet in the tail as it upset the trim of the aircraft and they had to keep adjusting it.

The handover parade from the Jaguars to the Tornadoes took place on 1 March 1985, and this was followed by a Station Dining-In Night in the mess, during which members of the Jaguar squadron were dined out. Along with another JP, Kevin was posted to 14 Squadron, which was on the opposite side of the runway at Brüggen, and he was able to transfer his combat readiness status without having to go through the work-up and being checked out again. However, they already knew that their time on 14 Squadron would be limited, as it was the last Jaguar squadron at Brüggen and was due to be re-equipped with Tornadoes at the end of the following October. During his time on 17 Squadron, Kevin had flown 280 hours in just over a year, bringing his total on the Jaguar to 418 hours and his grand total to 854 hours. Although he realized that he still had a lot to learn and felt that his ability would improve, he was now fully combat ready and confident that he could do a good job, and that his future as a front-line Jaguar pilot was assured.

As he was simply changing squadrons at Brüggen, he was spared the arrival procedure associated with posting to a new station, and he was able to start flying on 14 March 1985 without going through all the preliminaries normally required. A few days later he was off to Garvie Range in an aircraft carrying two drop-tanks and four 1,000 lb retarded bombs, flying as leader to his flight commander. The loaded Jaguars would have taken some time to climb to the cruising height of 20,000 ft. As this would have caused problems in transiting the busy Dutch airspace, one of the senior flight lieutenants suggested that the best way to go was low level across Holland at 1,000 ft before pulling up to medium level once some fuel had been burned off. The alternative was to climb to 20,000 ft before crossing the Dutch border, which lay only a couple of miles to the west. At engine start, the flight commander had problems with his aircraft, so Kevin took off alone. Flying at low level seemed a good idea at the time, but the weather deteriorated soon after he entered Holland, so he requested approval to climb from the Dutch Military ATC; unfortunately, to avoid entering controlled airspace, the clearance required him to reach 20,000 ft in a short distance. As this would have necessitated using the afterburners, with consequent high fuel consumption, he decided to remain at 1,000 ft, although this meant scudding in and out of cloud and maintaining height using the radar altimeter. Luckily, Holland is pretty flat, but even so it was not very comfortable, and later, with greater experience, he realized that it would have been better to accept the increased fuel consumption entailed by climbing in the first place. Eventually the weather improved as he crossed the Dutch coast and he began the long slog up to 20,000 ft *en route* to Macrihanish, where he landed to refuel. The flight commander landed about thirty minutes later, and after a further briefing they set off for Garvie Island. Having dropped his first bomb from a lay-down attack, Kevin then found that the remaining three would not release normally and he had to jettison them into the sea near Garvie: it later transpired that the main weapon system fuse had blown. They returned to Macrihanish to refuel and he then led the flight commander at low level across the Spadeadam range and eastwards through the low-flying system, pulling up to medium level after crossing the east coast on the way back to Brüggen. Overall he considered this to be a rather disappointing trip, but it provided some very useful experience.

A few days later he went to Vliehors with four inert 1,000 lb retarded bombs to drop a stick onto the special target. It was necessary to press the pickle button throughout release of the stick for all the bombs to be dropped; unfortunately, being used to dropping a single 3 kg bomb on most range attacks, he took his thumb off the button prematurely. The result was that the release was terminated with two bombs remaining, and as the bombs were ejected in sequence to minimize trim changes, he was left with one bomb on the centre-line and one on an outboard pylon. He soon discovered that the aircraft did not handle very well in this asymmetric condition. He gingerly made his way round the range circuit for a second run, and the remaining pair were dropped without incident. This showed why constant training was needed in all aspects of operations if mistakes were to be avoided. Later in March he did three 1-v-1 ACT trips in one day, and was gratified to confirm that he could hold his own against most other pilots on the squadron.

At the time 14 Squadron had the specialist role of dropping the laser-guided bomb, which was then the only precision guided munition (PGM) available to the RAF for air-to-ground use. The USAF had developed this system during the Vietnam War, where its initial use had been dramatically demonstrated by the destruction of a bridge using a single LGB after hundreds of conventional bombs had failed to score a hit. The RAF weapon was code-named Paveway II, and consisted of a standard UK 1,000 lb bomb and fuse, with a guidance system bolted to the nose and a new tail with flip-out fins to give improved stability and control. The laser seeker was mounted in the tip of the nose and detected laser energy from an external laser marker reflected from the target. These laser signals were passed to the guidance computer, which controlled four moveable canard fins to guide the bomb towards the laser spot on the target. The laser spot was provided either by a ground-based laser target marker or an airborne designator from a podded Pave Spike system on a Buccaneer. A toss manoeuvre from low level was used to deliver the bombs, and this could be a particularly complex operation. One squadron pilot counted twenty-six switch selections required for a particular mode of attack, although this did include use of the ECM equipment, and one incorrect selection could nullify the whole operation. Switch selections therefore required careful rehearsal on the ground to ensure that the switching sequence could be carried out almost automatically in the air, when there were many other things to think about.[17]

The Buccaneers also practised steep-dive delivery of the LGB from medium level, although the Jaguars did not use this method. Since the Gulf War, Jaguars have also had the capability to deliver LGBs in level flight or in a dive from medium level using their own target designator. The Pave Spike designating pod contained a TV camera mounted on a rotating ball in its nose and could view in any direction, right back to within 30° of the tail; operation of the pod was controlled by the navigator. Initially the pilot flew towards the target until the navigator picked it up on the Pave Spike TV screen, and by use of a small joystick zoomed in to track it with the aiming cross. The pilot was then able to turn away – hence the need for the TV to be able to look backwards. The aiming cross was partially stabilized, but it still required considerable skill for the navigator to track the target smoothly and precisely, and the whole operation became very tricky if poor visibility made the target difficult to acquire and track throughout the attack. Co-operative designation missions were practised with Buccaneers from Lossiemouth on a regular basis, as it took precise timing and co-ordination to have a good chance of success. The Jaguars could carry either one LGB on the fuselage centre-line with two drop-tanks on the wings, or two LGBs on the inboard wing pylons with a single tank on the centre-line.

At the end of April 1985 the Buccaneers visited Brüggen to practise with 14 Squadron. Normally they flew in formations of six aircraft – four Jaguars and two Buccaneers – with the Jaguars leading because they had the better navigation system. In spite of the limitations of the Jaguar INS, it was still superior to the Buccaneer, which at that time relied on map and stopwatch. During one evasion sortie, on the call of 'Buster' (maximum dry power) the Buccaneers quickly started to overhaul the Jaguars, and even when the latter went to full afterburner it took some time before they started to pull away. With its two big Spey engines and large fuel capacity, the Buccaneer was fast and had a long range, and in this role it could also carry four 1,000 lb retarded bombs in the bomb-bay, for dropping in front of pursuing fighters. It was interesting to operate with a different aircraft type on missions that required such close co-ordination. The Buccaneers with Westinghouse AN/AVQ-23E Pave Spike laser designator pod were eventually used in anger during the Gulf War, where they initially operated with Tornadoes aiming LGBs from medium level and eventually designating targets for bombs, which they dropped themselves.[18]

In mid-May the squadron flew down to Decimomannu for the annual APC, and this time they were to use the air combat manoeuvring instrumentation (ACMI) range for the first time, as the Jaguar had just received clearance to carry the ACMI pod. Kevin took a Jaguar, but over France one drop-tank stopped feeding at about half-empty, although this was not apparent initially since the drop-tank fuel indications in the cockpit only showed when the tanks were full, empty, or somewhere in between. As he did not have enough useable fuel to reach Decimomannu safely, he diverted to Nice along with a T.2 flown by one of the senior flight lieutenants. From Nice he phoned the ground crew who were already in Decimomannu, and after obtaining advice he was able to refuel the Jaguar and continue the journey. The first trips were on ACMI with 1-v-1, initially doing simple ranging exercises before graduating to ACT. This was great sport, and they used the full switching sequences for their weapons and equipment in the knowledge that any mistakes would be revealed in the subsequent replay. On the third trip they played 1-v-1-v-1, which involved three aircraft, all enemies. Although this was not a realistic situation, it was good training as it meant that in addition to attempting to get into a position for a shot at one of the opponents, a good look-out had to be maintained on the other one to prevent him creeping in unobserved and obtaining a shot on you. Similarly, it constrained your manoeuvres to some degree, as it was important in making a successful attack on one opponent not to place yourself in a vulnerable position to the other.

For the remaining three weeks they did a mix of ACMI and APC, and this constant variation made for an extremely interesting detachment. As he was now fully combat ready, Kevin was now permitted to take part in dissimilar air combat training (DACT), and for the first exercise took part in a 2-v-2 against a pair of German F-4 Phantoms. The Jaguars were fitted with the AIM-9L Sidewinder, which could home onto targets from any aspect, whereas the earlier models were effective only for stern attacks, where the missile seeker head could lock onto the heat of the engine exhaust. The German F-4 did not have the Doppler radar or Sparrow missiles of the RAF Phantoms, but it still had superior speed and turning ability to the Jaguar. However, their engines smoked considerably when in dry power, which made them easy to see from considerable distances against a sky background, while the Jaguars were small and more difficult to acquire visually. Overall, the Jaguars did very well and more than held their own. Later they did a 2-v-2-v-2: two Jaguars against two pairs of German F-4s, which provided a very good scrap and was a real 'multi-bogey environment'. It was quite different and more realistic than anything that he had previously experienced. He soon found that the only way to survive was to keep the speed up to Mach 0.9 or better, and fly through a fight, taking the opportunity to get a shot at any opponent who appeared within a narrow cone ahead. Any attempt to pursue an opponent by turning through a large angle almost invariably allowed another aircraft, which you had not seen, to obtain a quick kill on you.

For the third trip that day Kevin was a passenger in a Navy Hunter T.8M[19] on ACMI against a student in a Sea Harrier from the OCU at RNAS Yeovilton. The aim of this sortie was for the student to entice them into a slow-speed fight so that he could use vectoring in forward flight (VIFF) to tighten his turn to get a shot at the Hunter as it flew through his gunsight. In the air Kevin was surprised at how easily the Hunter out-turned the Sea Harrier, but even with his limited experience he was not impressed by the way the student handled his aircraft and never really achieved the aim of getting into a position for a shot at the Hunter. The student led on the return to Decimomannu and succeeded in getting lost despite the mountains down the west coast of Sardinia, which provided a prominent navigational feature. Embarrassingly, the instructor then had to lead back to Decimomannu. Kevin did not attend the debrief, as the instructor probably had some hard words to say. However, a couple of days later, one of the 14 Squadron flight commanders also had a trip in the Hunter T.8M, with the same student leading, but it was to be his last flight, as he was subsequently removed from the OCU course.

For the second weekend Kevin flew to Naples in a formation of three two-seat T.2s plus a GR.1, carrying a total of seven pilots. When contacting Naples on the R/T they were instructed to hold off over the bay, and about five minutes later an airliner called up and he also was told to hold off as the runway was blocked. Apparently an airliner had burst its tyres on landing and the runway would be obstructed for some time, so the formation leader quickly set up a diversion to Grazzanise, an Italian Air Force F-104 base about twenty miles north of Naples. This was a dilapidated place, which appeared to be disused, with rusty Nissen huts and grass growing up through joints in the concrete. However, the Italians were very friendly and helpful and soon had the Jaguars refuelled, so that they were able to take off on the ten-minute flight to Naples as soon as the runway was clear. On the downwind leg for landing they flew over Naples, and even from 1,000 ft it looked a bit rough. The formation flew back to Decimomannu on the Monday morning, and overall it had been a fascinating weekend.

Back at Decimomannu he flew in a Jaguar T.2 with an RN lieutenant-commander from the Sea Harrier detachment in the rear cockpit. The mission was to Frasca Range to drop eight bombs and fire sixty rounds in strafing attacks, and he really had his eye in, scoring a number of direct hits, or 'bull's eyes', as the Italian RSOs called them, and hitting the target with forty out of the sixty rounds on strafing. These were very good scores and his passenger was suitably impressed. The next day he had another trip

A 17 Squadron GR.1 dropping a stick of eight (inert) retarded 1,000 lb bombs over the Vliehors range in NW Holland. (via Kevin Noble)

in a Navy Hunter T.8M – this time in a 2-v-2 with two Hunter T.8Ms against two Sea Harriers. His final trip on ACMI with 2-v-2-v-2 was the best, with pairs of Jaguars, Hunter T.8Ms and Sea Harriers competing. Each type used its own attributes to best advantage; it was great sport and although it all ended fairly even, it again re-emphasized the need to keep the speed up and not to get involved in a turning fight. The tactics were to fly through against individuals or congregations of targets, taking any shots that reasonably presented themselves; this was difficult as firing opportunities only lasted a few seconds and it required considerable anticipation and good co-ordination with one's wingman to achieve success. The squadron returned to Brüggen in early June after a most rewarding and enjoyable three weeks of flying, with plenty of sun, sea, socializing and visiting new places thrown in.

June 1985 provided a good mix of laser-guided bomb simulated attack profiles, work with forward air controllers (FAC) and normal SAPs. With increasing ability and experience, Kevin was now frequently authorized to lead SAPs; this was part of the normal squadron policy for giving pilots the opportunity to develop new skills at leading and controlling formations when they were considered fit. Early in July he did his first operational low-flying (OLF) sortie over the North Sea in a Jaguar T.2 with the squadron commander. This was in preparation for a forthcoming detachment to Gibraltar, where they would be exercising with some RN frigates that were about to deploy to the Falklands. From the normal low flying at 420 knots and 250 ft they eased down to 100 ft in stages, before practising normal turns at 2 g and hard turns at 4–5 g. Flying at 100 ft felt much lower than the usual 250 ft, which he equated to driving down a motorway. He realized that they were travelling fast, but the ground just seemed to glide by. At 100 ft the sea zipped past and he was much more aware of the close proximity to the surface, especially in hard turns at high angles of bank, where it entered his peripheral vision and flashed by very close. Initially, it was only possible to look straight ahead; snatching quick glances out to the sides for look-out, but eventually, as confidence built up, he learned to look out all round and behind. The margin for error was significantly reduced at this height and speed, where small changes in the angle of bank in hard turns led to rapid gain or loss of height, the latter being extremely important when flying so close to the surface. However, he soon learned to control height accurately, and it gave a great sense of achievement to master this new aspect of operational flying.

Accompanying the squadron commander, one of the flight commanders and another junior pilot, Kevin caught the Boeing 737 Trooper to Luton in mid-July, from where they took another Trooper to Gibraltar for a two-week detachment. They were to fly the three Jaguars, which were permanently based on the Rock; as well as exercising with the Navy, they were to show the flag and establish the British presence following some problems in relations with the Spanish. The first day was spent in briefings on procedures and the effects of wind around the Rock, which gave problems in using the single runway. Conditions were worst when the wind was from the south-west, as it caused considerable turbulence on the approach and gave a tailwind component on both ends of the runway – most unusual. The Jaguars were always flown clean, that is without external tanks or stores, and flying started early and usually finished by lunch-time because of the heat: the afternoons were then available for sun-bathing and windsurfing. For the first couple of trips he did general handling and aerobatics while accustoming himself to the local area over the Mediterranean to the south and east of the Rock, followed by circuits to get used to the relatively short runway, which was only 6000 ft long. The next day came two OLF trips over the sea in preparation for working with Navy ships. The first was just to get back into practice, and then as a member of a pair, getting used to looking out to the sides to check behind the leader's tail and practising battle turns. That evening they were invited to the sergeants' mess and had a very pleasant time, but the gin and tonics were very strong and Kevin woke up feeling terrible the next day. He did not fly until the following afternoon, when he thought he had recovered, but the feeling of being rather remote and not up to speed with the aircraft provided a very salutary experience, which he took care not to repeat.

A few days later, they conducted OLF attacks against the RN frigates, HMS *Penelope* and HMS *Amazon*, in preparation for the ships' deployment to the Falklands. The ships' radars tracked them throughout the attacks and Kevin felt certain that they would have been shot down in a war situation, as there was nowhere to hide over the sea. A couple of days later one of the pilots, Bob Judson, went on *Amazon* to watch weapon firing against a target towed by a Canberra from Gibraltar. The 4.5-inch gun was very impressive, but the now obsolete wire-guided Shorts Sea Cat missiles were not so good, as two splashed down into the sea shortly after launch. One evening while in the officers' mess bar, he saw a Boeing 737 touch down about half-way down the runway, leaving only 3,000 ft in which to stop. Everyone rushed out onto the patio, expecting to see the aircraft go off the end into the water, but somehow the pilot managed to stop, although it must have been rather exciting for those inside – that is if they realized what was happening. At the weekend, they went to Spain and headed west along the coast away from the tourist traps; the scenery was marvellous, with beautiful villages and brilliant whitewashed cottages, plus empty beaches.

A new experience, which Kevin greatly enjoyed, was strafing against the splash target – a raft made of wood and fibreglass towed about 400 yards behind a naval launch travelling at 20 knots, which created a wall of water about ten feet high to aim at. It could also be used as a target for 3 kg practice bombs, but they did not have any of these. At shallow attack angles there was a considerable risk of ricochet from the water, so HE ammunition was used. Aimed at the splash, the shells naturally hit behind the target, but this was done to preserve the raft as the Navy tended to be rather upset if it was destroyed too quickly. From the air the explosion of the shells looked like the splashes made by throwing gravel onto water. Later trips of the detachment were taken up with ACT including 1-v-1-v-1 by all three Jaguars, which he considered to be the sport of kings. On the final flying day he did four trips, each of thirty to thirty-five minutes, with two sorties of 1-v-1 ACT before lunch, followed by two strafing trips against the splash target in the afternoon, using the full ammunition load of 120 rounds HE for each gun. At the end of the second sortie the Navy said they were happy if the target was hit. So on the next pass Kevin pulled a little lead on the splash and took great delight in seeing rounds hit all over the raft, which was totally destroyed. The launch crew later presented him with some of the bits. Overall it had been an excellent detachment, with varied and exciting flying, and he was sorry when they handed over to the detachment that had arrived from II (AC) Squadron.

Back at Brüggen it was straight into bounced SAPs before going off to a multinational NATO exercise at Fassberg – a *Luftwaffe* helicopter base near the border with East Germany. Before departure they were warned to beware of Soviet spoof radio beacons, which would attempt to lure them into East Germany and thus cause embarrassment to NATO. Sure enough, when he selected the airfield TACAN beacon as he approached Fassberg, it locked onto a beacon that was obviously situated well inside East Germany, but this caused him no problems as he had the moving map, which indicated precisely where he was. The exercise involved mainly FAC work on the Sennelager range, which was operated by the British Army and provided live targets of real armour on the move. He was also lucky to get a trip in a two-seat French Mirage IIIB on a pairs SAP mission to Sennelager. Unfortunately his pilot spoke very little English, and Kevin's pidgin French was limited. Nevertheless he enjoyed the trip, although because of the language problem he could not do any of the flying. The Mirage was like a fast Hunter, but the instrument fit was very basic and it had no navigation system to compare with the Jaguar. Also, with its delta wing, it buffeted and slowed markedly in turns. Altogether it was a thoroughly enjoyable week working with and getting to know pilots of other NATO air forces.

By this time Kevin was frequently leading SAPs, although it was rather frustrating that no effort was made to clear him as a pairs leader since the squadron was disbanding. On their final exercise as a squadron, the squadron commander decided to lead a formation of fourteen aircraft in an airfield attack on Brüggen. Unfortunately the weather was deteriorating as they taxied out, and at take-off it was looking distinctly poor, with low cloud and rain, but they got airborne anyway and were quickly in cloud. The net result was that they ended up in pairs scattered over the area, with clutch radar (which controlled aircraft from Brüggen, Wildenrath and Laarbruch) struggling desperately to get them under control and feed them back to Brüggen for pairs GCAs to overshoot before the final radar pattern to land. He spent the majority of the trip in cloud in close formation on his leader. Finally, as 14 was the last Jaguar squadron at Brüggen, he was on the penultimate Jaguar strike QRA standby, the squadron commander taking his place for the last duty.

At the end of October a large parade was held, closing down 14 (Jaguar) Squadron and inaugurating 14 (Tornado) Squadron. This was the end of an era. The four-squadron Brüggen Jaguar Wing was no more, and the Brüggen Tornado Wing took its place. This was made up to four squadrons shortly afterwards by the arrival of XI Squadron, with 20 Squadron, one of the original Brüggen squadrons, having been re-formed at Laarbruch. The Jaguar pilots' final presentation to the new 14 Squadron was a snake, which was the squadron emblem. It was a Burmese python, and only about eighteen inches long: some ten years later 'Sid' had apparently grown to fifteen feet and lived in a large tank in the crew-room. Kevin's final trip on the squadron was to ferry a T.2 to Shawbury, and he was gratified to receive a flying assessment of high average at end of his tour. His total flying on the Jaguar was now 545 hours, and with increasing experience and confidence he now knew that he could do a good job as an operational Jaguar pilot. Meanwhile the Air Secretary's Branch had given him a choice of postings, either to go onto the Tornado GR.1 or join II (AC) Squadron[20], which operated Jaguars in the reconnaissance role at Laarbruch. He opted for the latter, as did Bob Judson, and so in November 1985 the Nobles moved up to Laarbruch, which was only thirty miles to the north.

Before joining the squadron, Kevin and Bob Judson did a three-week Weapons Employment Course at Cranwell. The course, sometimes referred to as the 'Whitbread Enjoyment Course', included both air defence and ground attack crews (mud-movers), and they found it very interesting to learn the theory of air-to-air, surface-to-air and air-to-surface weapons, covering such aspects as guidance systems, weapon effects and weapon effort planning. It soon became apparent that the air defence weapons were much more advanced than the basic bombs and rockets used for ground attack, most of which had hardly changed since the Second World War. The course provided a wealth of background knowledge to help them as squadron pilots and gave them an understanding of other systems so that they could get the best results from their weapons while creating problems for the air defences opposing them. This further fuelled Kevin's interest in weapons and confirmed his desire to become the qualified weapons instructor (QWI) for the squadron.

Back at Laarbruch in late November, the first few days on the squadron were spent in reading through the piles of books covering rules and procedures. Thankfully most of them were the same as he had studied at Brüggen. A TACEVAL took place during the following week, and Kevin was put onto the night shift as a mission planner. Many of the reconnaissance tasks came in during the night, and it was his duty to do the planning ready for the pilots as they arrived to fly the dawn missions.

Just before his arrival, the II Squadron Jaguars had been fitted with a package of modifications to bring them from GR.1/T.2 standard to GR.1A/T.2A standard. The most important change was incorporation of the Ferranti FIN 1064 inertial navigation system, which was a great step forward in being much more capable, accurate and reliable than the old system. Switches and controls in the cockpit were also rearranged, making it ergonomically much superior to the previous version. Additionally, the new system had many more functions and was mechanized in a much more user-friendly way than the original. A rotary switch controlled the mode of display and numbers were entered into the system by a telephone-type keypad, which was easy to use in the air. Positions could now be entered either as latitude and longitude or directly as Universal Transverse

Mercator (UTM) or Ordnance Survey Great Britain (OSGB) grid references, and the computer then converted them to latitude and longitude. A total of thirty-two waypoints could now be entered as opposed to eight previously, and up to thirty-two offsets, either in range and bearing from a waypoint or a specified number of feet north or south and east or west of a given position. The system also had an offset TACAN facility by which the aircraft could be directed to any position some miles from the TACAN beacon.

It was much quicker and easier to input data into the FIN 1064, although it was rarely necessary to use all its capabilities. Groundspeed (G/S) and demanded G/S were displayed as before, but there was now the option of displaying the calculated time early or late at a waypoint; these facilities were very useful as they showed the precise change of speed required to attain the planned time of arrival. The reversionary navigation modes were also improved so that if the system started to run away, the input of a wind velocity obtained from another aircraft damped down the errors. However, the fully reversionary mode using a standby gyrocompass and the air data computer (ADC) with manually input winds was still not very good because of the limitations of the standby gyro. In spite of this, the system was much more accurate and reliable than previously, and much easier to use. The system software was initially upgraded about every six months, and each squadron had a FIN 1064 representative who attended regular meetings with the Ferranti software programmers, providing suggestions on how to improve its operation – a very effective method of improving what was already a very good system.

There is a tendency to believe that sophisticated new equipment has greatly simplified the pilot's task, and it has even been suggested that all he has to do is to press a few buttons and sit back and allow the electronics to do the work. Nothing could be more misguided, as, although introduction of the first-generation systems provided a marked improvement in operational capability, they also greatly increased the pilot's workload and were often unreliable. The capabilities of later equipment have increased dramatically, and it is much more reliable as well as being simpler to operate. Even so, to obtain optimum performance the pilot must have a comprehensive understanding of equipment capability and operation and be able to make the necessary switch selections while carrying out the many other tasks required by his operational role. Provided he is able to do this, it is now possible to locate and destroy targets in bad weather or at night, which would previously have been impossible to find, much less attack. And, far from reducing the need for aircrew to have abundant mental capacity and to be given comprehensive training, it has augmented these requirements.

Kevin had an initial flight check with the squadron's QFI, combined with an introduction to the FIN 1064, in a T.2A in mid-December 1985. A large removable pod, which was fitted to the centre-line pylon beneath the fuselage, provided the reconnaissance (recce) capability, and he was given a full briefing before his first flight in a GR.1A. This flight was devoted to checking how the pod affected aircraft handling and to practise using the cameras. Much of the space in the pod was taken up by a large air-conditioning pack, which was disconnected, as it was never used. There was one forward-facing camera plus a fan of four cameras that covered the ground laterally from horizon to horizon, and all were housed in a large rotating drum, only the bottom half of which was exposed below the pod. When the aircraft was on the ground, the cameras faced upwards, keeping their optical windows clean; in the air, the drum rotated when the pod was switched on and a test was then made to cheek that the film counter on the recce control panel moved. In the rear of the pod was an infra-red line scanner (IRLS), which contained a single IR detector with a multi-faceted gold mirror rotating at very high speed beneath it. The incoming infra-red light from the left horizon all the way underneath the aircraft to the right horizon was reflected onto the detector by a single mirror facet before the next one scanned across, covering a new strip of ground as the aircraft moved forward.

Electronic signals from the detector were amplified and passed to glow tubes, which recorded a dim or bright image on ordinary wet film, building up a picture of the area covered. Unlike normal cameras, which produced individual frames, the IRLS picture was built up from the myriad consecutive strips, and the film produced a continuous heat-map image, with hot spots showing up white and cooler areas dark. The scale and resolution of the IRLS picture was inferior to that produced by ordinary cameras but it was very useful for locating hot objects such as vehicles under camouflage nets, which were virtually transparent to IR. However, the equipment was temperamental and required very careful maintenance and setting up to ensure that it worked correctly. On the clear edges of all films, navigation system data was printed, detailing height, speed, location and time, to enable the photographic interpreter (PI) to locate the precise position photographed. This was vitally important when he was faced with hundreds of feet of film from up to six cameras, as, in an operational situation, time was limited if newly located targets were to be hit before they moved away.

The IRLS system carried sufficient film for about thirty minutes' running time, so it was switched on just before reaching the IP and turned off after passing the target, while the normal cameras, which ran at very high speed, were only switched on for a few seconds on either side of the target. To prevent blurring of the film picture because of aircraft speed, a process of image motion compensation automatically moved the film in the opposite direction to aircraft travel, so that the image passing through the lens thus appeared to be stationary on the film. This process was controlled by the navigation system and ensured that the correct velocity:height ratio was fed to the compensator at all aircraft speeds and heights. If the navigation system failed, the pilot could set the velocity:height ratio manually for the planned height and speed. The frame rate of the cameras was also controlled by the velocity:height ratio to provide an overlap of at least 60% between each frame, and this allowed stereoscopic viewing. A pair of lenses on legs were placed over the film to view adjacent frames, the three-dimensional stereoscopic effect being obtained by viewing one frame through one lens with one eye, and the second frame, which was taken from a slightly different position because of the forward speed of the aircraft, with the other.

The recce pod was of similar weight and drag to a 1,000 lb bomb, but as it was much larger it had an aerodynamically destabilizing effect. This was hardly noticeable in normal flight but became very significant at high angles of attack, and the aircraft was therefore limited to a maximum of 12 alpha except when the flaps were down for take-off and landing. Great care had to be taken not to exceed the limit, especially if speed was allowed to decay during hard manoeuvring. The standard war fit was the recce pod, with inboard tanks plus outboard ECM and chaff pods. For small targets the normal technique was to track slightly to one side in order to get the best view and camera cover. Running directly over the top caused the target to disappear under the nose much earlier and prevented the pilot from obtaining complete information for the in-flight report (IFREP), or for the visual report, which was especially important if the cameras failed. The IFREP

GR.1 XZ108/28 of II (AC) Squadron carrying a recce pod and two fuel tanks. On 9 January 1990 the port wing of XZI08/GD struck the tailfin of Tornado GR.1A ZA394/11 of II (AC) Squadron after they approached each other head-on at the Spadeadam weapons range in Northumberland, neither pilot being aware of the other's presence. The Tornado crew ejected after being unable to control the violently rolling aircraft, and it crashed near Hexham. The Jaguar pilot managed to correct his rolling aircraft and made an emergency landed at Leeming. On 3 September 1998 Flight Lieutenant Whittaker, the pilot of XZ108, lost control of the aircraft when acting a singleton during a 2-v-1 air combat sortie over the North Sea with two other Jaguars. He ejected and the aircraft crashed into the sea thirteen miles north-east of Cromer, Norfolk. It was the second time Whittaker had been forced to leave a Jaguar, having ejected from XZ362/GC in Alaska on 24 June 1996 during Exercise Cope Thunder*! (via Kevin Noble)*

was passed over the R/T to Army listening posts at a convenient time after leaving the target. For larger targets, or if the target was obscured in trees, it was necessary to fly directly over the top to get the best cover. Most recce trips were flown by single aircraft, since this normally provided adequate cover, although a pair of aircraft could be used for very large targets such as airfields. Because of the amount of film carried, one aircraft could normally cover several targets.

Attack squadrons did recognition training of the basic types of enemy armoured fighting vehicles (AFVs) and aircraft. On the reconnaissance squadrons this was carried out in much greater detail, covering literally hundreds of different types of AFVs, down to individual marks of tanks, plus radars and other electronic equipment. This was extremely important, as, if particular vehicle types could be recognized, it might allow identification of the enemy unit involved. All spare time when not planning, flying or doing other secondary duties was spent in the training cell of the Reconnaissance Intelligence Centre (RIC) where the PIs lived and worked, learning to recognize all the different types of both NATO and Soviet vehicles and equipment. There were thousands of slides to go through, and as some types were very similar it took months to acquire a good knowledge of all of them. It was also necessary to be able to identify many items of non-military equipment and installations, and to report using specific terms that were standardized throughout NATO. All targets were grouped into seventeen NATO standard categories: for instance bridges were Category 12, and there were many types of bridges. Other categories covered items varying from industrial facilities to missile systems. As there were limited numbers of recce aircraft in the NATO Central Region, in war the squadron could be tasked to provide reconnaissance, not just for 2ATAF (including the Belgians, Dutch and Germans), but also for US forces. In Germany there were plenty of military training targets, varying from barracks to Hawk and Nike Hercules SAM sites.

There were also many military training areas where tanks and other AFVs were frequently exercising. Using a master map, all pilots on the squadron produced their own maps covering military barracks and training areas so that they could select almost any type of desired target. After checking the weather forecast each morning, one of the senior pilots selected the 'trip of the day', normally providing five varied targets chosen from the large library maintained by the RIC. Additionally, there were many civilian targets, which were frequently used.

There were several different types of recce targets and searches. The most common were:

    a) Point targets, which were contained within a small area. These were normally tasked by category, with the position in latitude and longitude.

    b) A strip search along a straight line between two points, normally several kilometres apart.

    c) A line search along a line feature such as a road, railway or river between specified start and end points, and often via quoted intermediate points. These were commonly used in war to search major roads and locate the main lines of enemy advance and reinforcement.

    d) An area search, either within a specified radius of a given point, or in a box, which could cover an area of several square kilometres.

Training started with point targets, moving on to strip and area searches and finally line searches, the latter being preceded by a line search in the T.2A with an experienced pilot. In those days there was a considerable mystique about tactical reconnaissance, but after flying in the attack role, Kevin found that there were really only a couple of difficult aspects to master. The first was in actually seeing and remembering everything about a large target, which contained many different pieces of equipment. The second was in line searches, where following a winding road at 500 knots was very difficult. However, these problems were counterbalanced by the fact that there was little or no formation flying, and life was easier in many other ways.

Considerable practice was required to become proficient at line searches. Most of these were on roads; initial planning was similar to that for a point target and an IP lined up with the first stretch of road was selected. Maximum dry power was set before the IP, and the left hand was then used for thumbing down the map, power not being reduced unless it was absolutely necessary. In full war fit with ECM and chaff pods, this gave a speed of about 500 knots, but it was easy to lose nearly 100 knots by pulling hard in a 90° turn at high fuel load, and greater anticipation was required to reduce g and maintain speed. The turning radius at 480 knots when pulling 3–4 g was about two kilometres, so it was necessary to select a feature this distance before the turning point, and start the turn when passing over it. A classic error was to turn late and then pull hard, causing the aircraft to lose speed and end up having to reverse the turn because the road twisted the other way, the ensuing zig-zag leading to further loss of speed. In turns, the road disappeared under the nose, so it was necessary to roll out on the next heading and look for the road again. Any large feature such as a wood could be used as a reference to turn onto, and it was often necessary to fly from feature to feature without seeing much of the road, especially in summer when it was frequently obscured by foliage. All military equipment seen on the road had to be noted, together with its position, for the IFREP and the visual report (Vis-Rep) required after landing. It was extremely difficult to follow the map and simultaneously to follow the road and note any activity, especially if it was a complex line search, and pre-flight study was even more important than with a normal target.

Line searches frequently covered a considerable distance and required the use of several 50,000-scale maps, and it needed a certain amount of manual dexterity to thumb the map with one hand. Ideally the road was near the left side of the map so that it was possible to thumb the way along the edge. Correct folding of the maps was crucial, as it was easy to lose the way when turning the map over, and it was normal to fold maps in a zig-zag style so that they could be unfurled continuously without actually having to turn them over. Overall, line searches took some time to master, and Kevin initially found them hard work and frequently lost the line, so he started adding his own line searches to the standard sorties to obtain more practice. This eventually paid off and he became quite proficient.

Most of January and February 1986 were taken up with single-aircraft day recce (DR) sorties ranging all over Germany and Belgium, although some of these were chased to enable squadron staff to monitor his progress. There were more barracks and military equipment in the 4ATAF area of southern Germany, but unfortunately all the 250 ft low-flying areas were in the 2ATAF area of the north. Additionally, as a single aircraft it was easier to go to the less accessible parts of Germany and to see new areas he had not visited before. Late in January he did a dual line search in the T.2A and he was then able to do the full 'trip of the day'. Typically it took about one and a half hours to plan a five-target mission, walking out thirty minutes before the take-off time to allow target data to be inserted into the navigation system. The flight itself normally took an hour and 20 minutes, all at low level. With six maps (one route plus five target maps), careful cockpit management was essential to stow them in the right order and re-stow them after use. The IRLS was switched on during the approach to each IP and the cameras were used over the target itself, while the event button on the throttles was pressed on crossing the target. This marked the film at the target and eased the PI's task of locating the important areas in hundreds of feet of film. Comments on the cockpit voice recorder were used by the PI as he examined the film, and they also formed a very useful record if the cameras failed. Important points, including the time-on-target (TOT), were also noted on the knee-pad for use in the IFREP and for the visual report after landing. A special recce form for the PI, giving basic details of each target, was normally completed while taxiing after landing. Thus, the whole period from commencing planning was an extremely busy one for the pilot, and he was working at maximum pressure for most of the time. In these circumstances it was easy to forget things, such as leaving the IRLS switched on after leaving a target, and running out of film before the last target was covered. After shut-down in front of the HAS, the RIC personnel downloaded the film cassettes from the reconnaissance pod and had usually completed this task by the time the pilot reached the bottom of the ladder. The films were whisked away to the RIC for processing as the pilot returned to the flight-line control to sign the aircraft servicing documents before going back to the PBF to sign the flight authorization document. He then went straight to the RIC to write his visual reports before seeing the films. These preliminary aspects took about ten minutes, and by the time that he arrived in the RIC the processed films were arriving on the light tables for the PIs to examine. There were six films lying parallel on the table so that the PI could match them together to obtain complete data on each target. Writing the visual reports and then debriefing on each target normally took about an hour, and the whole cycle from the start of planning to the end of debriefing took about five hours.

After a holiday it was straight back into single-aircraft DR trips before moving on to a 1-v-1 ACT phase in early March. Part of the aim of the ACT was for pilots to become accustomed to handling the aircraft to its limits at a safe height, but it was not permitted with the recce pod fitted because of the increased danger of loss of control. Despite its reputation, the Jaguar could be flown largely by feel, since, provided the limits were approached cautiously, it gave adequate warning of impending doom. The problems occurred if the stick was snatched, pulling to high

Flight Lieutenant Kevin Noble in front of his Jaguar GR.1 of II (AC) Squadron near a HAS at RAF Laarbruch in late 1985. (via Kevin Noble)

alpha (angle of attack) and going straight into a full-blown departure, without giving the warning signs a chance to show. Wing rocking was common in ACT, and it was tempting to try to fight it, but this just made matters worse; the only solution was to reduce the alpha. As a junior pilot during a very early 1-v-1 combat at Brüggen, Kevin managed to get into a tail-slide through over-exuberance. In the first combat of that sortie he met his opponent head-on at Mach 0.9, before they both pulled into a looping manoeuvre, unloading the g when vertical to get as much height as possible, before pulling over the top. The aim was to gain maximum height so as to drop behind the opponent on the way down for a quick kill, or at least to gain an initial advantage. This he failed to do and quickly lost the fight. In the second combat, he was determined not to make the same mistake again. The opening gambit was a repeat of the first fight, and he unloaded g in the vertical to gain as much height as possible while watching his opponent doing the same about three miles away. When his opponent started to ease over the top, Kevin attempted to do the same, but there was little response from the controls and he looked through the HUD just in time to see the speed decaying through 50 knots (the lowest displayed) with the aircraft still in the vertical. Sensibly, he just held the stick neutral and waited, and he remembers seeing clouds above and in front of him starting to recede – he was going backwards. After a couple of seconds, the aircraft flopped over forwards in a hammer-head stall, so that he was now pointing vertically downwards, and it was then that he started to worry as a violent wing rock commenced, and for a moment he thought that it was about to depart. Luckily he held the controls central and after a few gyrations it died down and he was able to ease out of the ensuing dive without any further problem. Amazingly, the engines and afterburners remained lit, without complaint, throughout. This was not a combat-winning manoeuvre, but he certainly learned about handling at high alpha; he also counted himself lucky not to have ended up in greater difficulties.

During an ACT sortie on II Squadron, Kevin had another interesting moment in combat with a senior flight lieutenant. They were in a vertical rolling scissors, spiralling downwards in a high g barrel roll, each trying to get behind the other, and this entailed rolling and pulling simultaneously. Suddenly, he felt the aircraft start to go; the rate of roll increased without any control input and he instinctively unloaded the wing by centralizing the stick, but the roll rate then became very high indeed. He immediately checked the HUD alpha and speed as they were trained to do and noted that the speed was around 300 knots, so the aircraft was obviously in autorotation. Easing back on the stick stopped the roll immediately and he was able to recover without further incident.

At the end of March 1986 he had his limited-combat-ready recce check and was given a set time to plan a five-target mission, which was chased by a flight commander. Fortunately the sortie went well and he passed this important stage in becoming combat ready as a recce pilot. A station MINEVAL was held in early April and he did five sorties in two days; these involved rapid planning and typically only covered two targets each. During exercises there was insufficient time to go to the RIC for a post-flight debrief and to complete visual reports, and each target was therefore reported to a NATO fixer post by IFREP, which was repeated to the RIC. The PIs then relied on the voice recorder tape, the recce form, maps and films, as they had very tight reporting times to meet, especially with several recce sorties landing within a short period.

In early May the squadron deployed to Akrotiri for a two-week air-to-air gun firing practice camp. They refuelled at Nimes-Garons in France before flying on to Brindisi in Italy for a night stop, completing the final two-hour leg to Akrotiri the following morning. Although 100 Squadron Canberras were in residence, they were fully committed to flag towing for 92 Squadron Phantoms, so the Jaguars had to tow for themselves. For this the flag cable was attached to the braking parachute mechanism in the tail of the fuselage and was released in the same manner as the parachute. The flag was laid on one side of the runway ahead of the aircraft, with the cable looped back before being attached, so that as the aircraft accelerated the loop was taken up and when the cable became taut the flag was snatched to aircraft speed in very short order. This reduced the distance the flag was dragged along the runway and the consequent danger of it fouling something in the process. Kevin's first trip at Akrotiri was to tow the flag, but the crimp on the cable-towing eye failed and the flag was left on the runway. The squadron had a number of similar failures before a revised cable crimping procedure cured the problem.

His second sortie was a dual check in the T.2 with the flight commander QWI, who unfortunately failed to connect the gun safety-disconnect before engine start, so the single gun did not fire. However, Kevin was allowed to go solo for dummy (dry) attacks on the next two trips before doing two live (hot) sorties, but he missed the flag altogether before getting nine hits out of sixty rounds on the third and final sortie. This compared favourably with the results achieved by the rest of the squadron. Between firing sorties Kevin did a number of flag tows, each lasting about an hour and three-quarters, with the aircraft carrying full underwing tanks. On take-off the technique was to accelerate as normal until a gentle tug was felt as the flag was snatched, then to rotate for a high alpha take-off and steep climb-out, to get the flag airborne as quickly as possible. On the range a racetrack pattern was flown with flap down at a speed of 200 knots – the same as we had used for the Meteor. Normally either two or three pairs of Jaguars fired on the flag during each towing sortie, after which the aircraft returned to Akrotiri and the flag was dropped alongside the runway. One pilot did not quite get the take-off right and the flag hit the runway arrestor gear, losing half its length and causing the sortie to be aborted. Normally, Kevin did one or two trips per day, and this included some 1-v-1 ACT. Afternoons were spent on the beach, windsurfing and water-skiing. During the middle weekend he toured Cyprus with three other pilots in a hired mini-moke. Overall, it was an enjoyable detachment in spite of the small amount of gun firing, and he flew back to Laarbruch in a VC 10, which was much more civilized than in a Hercules.

After three weeks back at Laarbruch, he was off again in mid-June – this time on his first NATO squadron exchange. Paired NATO squadrons visited each other for a couple of weeks to learn about the other's aircraft, capabilities and method of operation. Refuelling at Bordeaux, they flew to Monte-Real, about mid-way down the Atlantic coast of Portugal, to visit *304 Esquadra de Ataque* of the Portugese Air Force, which was equipped with the Vought A-7P Corsair II single-engined attack aircraft.[21] Kevin flew in the T.2A and was thus able to do his procedural instrument rating test (PIRT) on the second leg. The Portuguese officers' mess was being renovated, so they were accommodated in a hotel in the local village but took lunch in the main base canteen – the food was not very good but at least they could eat out in the local restaurants in the evening. There were the usual briefings on Portuguese rules before flying, and on the first full day there was a low-level trip around Portugal by a pair of Jaguars led by a Portuguese A-7 Corsair. The latter was a very good aircraft, which carried a lot of fuel and thus had a good range and large bomb load; it also had an excellent navigation/attack system with a moving map and terrain-following radar, which operated in the manual mode only.

On average they flew once a day and were led by Corsairs on a couple of occasions. They flew at 250 ft over the rolling and scrub-covered terrain, although the Portuguese seemed fairly relaxed about the rules and appeared to fly as low as they wished. Kevin was impressed by their level of skill and professionalism, as well as by their determination. On the last trip he got a ride in a two-seat Corsair as part of a four-aircraft SAP of two Jaguars and two Corsairs. They spent almost an hour at low level and at 480 knots for much of the time, before the Jaguars returned to base while the Corsairs pulled up for some formation aerobatics, which they apparently did quite frequently. Service rules prohibited the Jaguars from carrying out these manoeuvres. The Corsairs finally landed after about an hour and ten minutes, in spite of the fact that they were not carrying drop-tanks; with the latter they could do around two hours – a very impressive performance. The members of *304 Esquadra de Ataque* were good hosts and entertained their guests extremely well with barbecues and parties on most nights. Their stay lasted only for a week, including a weekend during which they visited Lisbon; it was a beautiful town and the people were very friendly. Unfortunately, *304 Esquadra de Ataque* was unable to pay a return visit to Laarbruch because of Portuguese budgetary restrictions.

Back at Laarbruch Kevin did a few more day recce trips before his operational readiness check with the squadron commander flying chase; this included landing away

SR-71A 'Blackbird' 64-17962 of Det 4 of the 9th Strategic Reconnaissance Wing cruising at 420 knots at 2,000 ft en route to RAF Mildenhall on 2 May 1985. On either side are Jaguars T.2 XX841/S flown by Squadron Leader John Butler and GR.1 XZ119 flown by Squadron Leader (later Group Captain) Steve Griggs AFC, both of 41 Squadron. This unique formation was photographed by Squadron Leader Mike Rondot, Flight Commander, 6 Squadron, flying GR.1 XZ359, using an F95 camera in the Jaguar Recce pod. (XZ359 crashed on 13 April 1989 north of Berwick-on-Tweed. Squadron Leader Paul 'PV' Lloyd of 54 Squadron was killed.) On 25 May 1982 Steve Griggs had been forced to eject from a Jaguar thirty-five miles north-east of Brüggen, when it was 'shot down' by a Sidewinder missile accidentally fired by a 92 Squadron FGR.2 Phantom. SR-71A 64-17962 is now on display at the IWM Duxford where it is one of the star exhibits in the American Air Musuem. (Mike Rondot)

at Gutersloh for refuelling and replanning the second part of the sortie. Although he passed, the trip did not go as well as he had hoped since he departed from the line search route on each occasion; it was very disappointing, as he knew he could do better. He also felt that this probably left a permanent impression with the squadron commander and flight commanders, and his progress thereafter was not as he would have hoped. This was a blow to his confidence, which took some while to overcome.

In mid-July they went to Decimomannu for the annual three weeks of armament practice camp and air combat training on the ACMI range, and he had the usual good time, with excellent flying. Two of the pilots managed to get flights in the two-seat American F-15 Eagle, an awesome aircraft with terrific power combined with an outstanding turning performance. Kevin tried to get a trip but failed this time. When the F-15s departed to return to Bitburg in Germany, they took off singly and disappeared down the runway in the heat haze from their afterburners, before reappearing going vertically upwards, even though they were each loaded with three external tanks. The Jaguars returned to Laarbruch early in August. The flight took an hour and 45 minutes and was routed over France to avoid Switzerland, which did not permit military overflights.

Following the return it was back to DR, which was getting rather monotonous by this stage, although they also did the occasional SAP. Late in August Kevin went to Strasbourg to spend the night at the French reconnaissance base near the beautiful old town, and the next day he flew a low-level recce trip around eastern France at 500 ft before returning to Laarbruch. France, he discovered, was a huge place, with open rolling agricultural countryside in the central and eastern regions. Later he did a couple of lunch-time land-aways at NATO bases to allow their ground crews to practise turn-rounds (refuelling and rearming) on the Jaguar. This was standard NATO practice and a regular occurrence for all bases and squadrons to ensure that everyone maintained the ability to provide good cross-servicing.

Members of the Standardization Flight from the Central Flying School (commonly known as the 'Trappers') arrived early in October for the annual visit that was paid to all squadrons. Together with QFIs and QWIs from the 'Standards' Flight of the Jaguar OCU, they talked to members of the squadron and flew with a number of them to check that all aspects of the flying organization met the required standards. Kevin's trip with one of the CF staff passed off satisfactorily.

On 8 October a Tornado from one of the squadrons at Laarbruch diverted into Leuchars following a bird strike and needed a borescope inspection of the engine to check for damage. The borescope was a long probe that could be inserted through special orifices in the engine to allow visual inspection of the compressors and turbines. At that time Leuchars was still a Phantom base, so the necessary engine specialist and equipment had to be flown in. Since it was much simpler to do this with the Jaguar T.2A than in the rear cockpit of the Tornado, the squadron agreed to undertake the task, with Kevin as the pilot. The engine specialist from the Tornado squadron had to be kitted out and given a briefing on emergency procedures before they set off for Leuchars. It then took some while for him to carry out the inspection, which showed that there was no damage and that the Tornado was serviceable to fly. By this time it was dark, but as they would be able to get back to Laarbruch inside the normal fourteen hours crew duty time, they took off and transited down the North Sea at medium altitude and a speed of Mach 0.95. *En route* they were intercepted by a Phantom, which obviously had to be supersonic to catch them, and Kevin saw the flames from the afterburners for some miles as it curved in behind them. The Phantom next reappeared alongside before lighting the afterburners again and pulling up and over them in a large barrel roll. It was a most impressive sight, with huge blue conical burner plumes from the twin Spey engines, as the Phantom rapidly accelerated away into the distance.

During October Kevin was gratified to be told that he had been selected to become the Squadron Instrument Rating Examiner, whose job was to train squadron pilots in instrument flying and also to be the examiner on the annual instrument rating tests, which all pilots had to pass. The first step was to be qualified to act as captain of the aircraft from the rear cockpit, so he did three trips in the back seat of the T.2A, including a check by the Squadron QFI to ensure that he was competent. This he passed, and thus achieved another useful qualification. Flying from the back seat was relatively straightforward, as the T.2A had been designed as a trainer: most front cockpit instruments and controls were duplicated and it had a HUD. The back seat was raised above the level of the front seat, so that the forward view was relatively unobstructed, the only problem being that the top of the front seat blocked the view forwards and downwards in low-level flying and the final stages of the landing approach. This situation on landing was worse if there was no crosswind, when it was necessary constantly to scan as far forward as possible from each side of the cockpit canopy. With a crosswind, the normal crabbing approach gave the pilot in the rear seat a good view down the runway.

At the end of October it was down to Villafranca, an Italian base near Verona in the Po Valley, with another Jaguar to take part in a recce exercise. Initially they flew low level to Bremgarten in southern Germany, where they stopped for the night. It was often very hazy in the Po Valley, and this time was no exception, but luckily Villafranca had a good GCA and ILS. As was common with many NATO bases, Villafranca was a joint civil/military airfield, with two F-104 reconnaissance squadrons on the north side and a civil terminal on the south side. Following a briefing on low-level flying in the area from one of the F-104 squadron pilots, they planned a trip around the Southern Alps and the Dolomites for the afternoon. This was to be one of most spectacular low-level flights that Kevin ever made, passing 500 ft above the mountains, which soared up to above 12,000 ft and then dropping steeply down into valleys several thousand feet below. They flew in arrow formation, and on passing over a peak they rolled inverted and pulled down into the valley, keeping the speed high at all times. They had to be very cautious of bad weather, as the climb angle required from the bottom of a valley could easily exceed that available in a Jaguar, even using afterburner. It was also necessary to keep a sharp lookout for cables strung across valleys. These were very difficult to see, so they looked for the pylons, and it was therefore safer to fly well up the side of the valley rather than in the bottom. They also avoided habitation if possible. Using the cameras they took several shots of each other against impressive mountain backdrops and obtained some very good pictures. As there was no suitable accommodation at Villafranca, they stayed at a hotel in Verona, where they spent a pleasant evening, walking miles before having a good meal out. The next morning they flew at low level through the Italian Alps, up the Aosta Valley and passing close to the peak of Mont Blanc at 15,800 ft on the Italian side, before turning south and pulling up to join the airways. This led them back into France and then on to Bremgarten for refuelling and another low-level recce trip back to Laarbruch. It had been a most memorable detachment, for both the scenery and the flying.

Early in November Kevin flew up to Lossiemouth in a T.2A for a one-week course, satisfactory completion of which would qualify him as an instrument rating examiner (IRE) on the Jaguar. He was taught basic instructional technique and fault analysis, plus the detail of instrument flying and procedures. Altogether, six trips were flown, initially concentrating on flying using the HUD as well as the normal head-down instrument display. They practised diversions to civil airfields via the airways, plus the standard arrival and departure procedures at military airfields, as well as TACAN let-downs, ILS and GCA approaches. The instrument rating test (IRT) required two flights: the first was the normal test, while the second was the procedural flying test. The first test comprised an instrument take-off, climb and transit for a practice diversion to another airfield, including a radar-controlled precision approach using the HUD, followed by an overshoot and low-level steep turns using first the HUD, then the head-down instruments. The latter was made much more difficult because of the limitations of the attitude indicator, which had a tendency to drift during manoeuvres. This emphasized the need to maintain a rapid scan of the other instruments, including the vertical speed indicator, compass, altimeter and air speed indicator, which is what the previous generation of pilots had to do before the HUD was invented. It was much easier using the HUD since all the information appeared on a single display and the indications were totally dead beat as they were provided from INS data. Low-level abort procedures and recovery from unusual positions were also carried out. For the latter, the pilot under test in the front cockpit closed his eyes

GR.1 XZ361/25 of II (AC) Squadron over the Dolomites in northern Italy on a recce detachment to Villafranca (Verona). The recce pod of another Jaguar took this photo. (via Kevin Noble)

and lowered his head, while the instructor carried out various manoeuvres before leaving the aircraft in an unusual position and saying, 'You have control'. The pilot then opened his eyes and quickly assessed the situation before recovering the aircraft to straight and level flight with minimum loss of height. The flight was concluded with ILS, TACAN and GCA instrument approaches at base, in which both the HUD and head-down instruments were used. The second flight was the procedural IRT, and covered all aspects of procedural flying on civil airways and the standard arrival and departure procedures used at civil airfields; this was to allow them to fly on airways across Continental Europe and the Mediterranean. Kevin's PIRT test included all these elements, plus some fault analysis in which the instructor, flying in the front seat, made deliberate mistakes and Kevin had to spot them and diagnose what the instructor was doing wrong. The squadron pilots normally flew the IRT and PIRT tests at alternating six-month intervals. The whole week went very well, and he passed with flying colours – to quote his instructor, 'flown to Master-Green standards'. By this stage his instrument flying was good; it was smooth and accurate and he felt confident he could do well as an examiner.

His first trip back at Laarbruch was an IRT. Normally on an IRT the subject was slightly apprehensive, but this time it was Kevin who was apprehensive, as he did not want the subject to fail. Fortunately all went well and he passed. The next two trips in the back seat were as safety pilot for a subject who was wearing a new version of the AR5 NBC helmet, the faceplate of which could be ripped off if it steamed up or the pilot was sick. Each pilot had to fly a low-level trip wearing the AR5 and then pull up and rip the faceplate off, using a special handle attached to a 'cheese wire', and everything worked as planned. Throughout November Kevin continued doing day recce sorties, and he became impatient to get on with some evasion and bounced SAPs for his attack readiness work-up. Even allowing for detachments and the instrument course, he had now been at Laarbruch for a year, and the fact that he was not attack ready pointed to poor squadron organization. The second IRT was on the squadron commander, who was very good and passed without problem. The next was on a flight commander, who did not do so well. On an ILS approach at a German base, he flew down to the decision height with an incorrect altimeter setting, which meant that he was actually down to about 50 ft (instead of 200 ft) at the overshoot. This was potentially a very dangerous mistake, of which the flight commander was unaware until after landing, and that made it all the more difficult to tell him he had failed, the only time Kevin had to do this. The flight commander passed the retest the following day. Late in November Kevin did a check for captaincy from the back at night, and this then allowed him to test other pilots for currency and to do procedural IRTs at night. It was often convenient to do this, but they could not carry out a full IRT since they could not do recovery from unusual positions and the low-level part of the test.

During later IRTs, he derived considerable satisfaction from being able to help other pilots sort out various minor problems. As I had discovered many years previously, it was very interesting to fly with other squadron pilots and see how good they were. The best were not only smooth and accurate, but always well ahead of the situation and could anticipate events, making it all seem easy. Kevin also carried out a few IRTs where pilots made the work unnecessarily hard through lack of foresight; such as planning an approach for a particular runway without first checking on the R/T that this was in fact the runway in use. This, for him, confirmed the old saying that 'an exceptional pilot uses his exceptional foresight to anticipate and rectify situations that would otherwise demand the use of his exceptional skill'.

Squadron life continued through December 1986 and into January 1987 with a mixture of reconnaissance sorties, IRTs and the odd bounced SAP. Kevin finally had his attack check in early February 1987, leading a bounced SAP pair, and at last he was declared combat ready for attack operations fourteen months after he had arrived at Laarbruch. Bob Judson was also declared combat ready at about the same time, and they were both now cleared to do fighter affiliation and unbriefed evasion again. The remainder of February contained a good mix of SAPs, affiliation and IRTs, and this variety definitely added to the spice of life and kept his interest, motivation and skill levels high. Continual recce exercises became monotonous and did not stretch the skill and imagination of the pilots, and the formation flying skills of the squadron also suffered.

The squadron was nominated to take part in Exercise *Maple Flag* in Canada during April 1987, on a joint detachment with 54 Squadron from Coltishall, and as only half the squadron could go, Kevin was extremely glad to be chosen. Before the exercise the whole squadron had to complete an OLF work-up in March, and pilots were teamed up into constituted pairs, which meant that they flew together on every mission during the work-up and on *Maple Flag*. Kevin was fortunate in being paired with a very good pilot of similar experience and with whom he got on well. Constituted pairs enabled pilots to get to know each other so that they were able to anticipate what the other would do in most situations and thus work well together. This reduced the need for use of the R/T and made for a more effective and smoother operating tactical pair. In mid-March they deployed to Lossiemouth for the OLF training and were joined by four Canadian CF-18s from Solingen in southern Germany, whose pilots included an RAF exchange officer whom Kevin had known on 14 Squadron. Although Kevin had previously done OLF, it had only been over the sea, and this was very different. There were three OLF areas in the UK: those to the north-west of the Great Glen and in southern Scotland they used from Lossiemouth; the third was in mid-Wales. His first overland OLF dual flight was amazing flying and he could hardly believe they were allowed to do it. He vividly recollects going down a valley at 100 ft towards a spur at the far end, when a lorry appeared on the road level with, and heading straight for, him. The lorry driver must have had quite a shock. At these heights, they were fully aware of the need to avoid habitation, and made special efforts to do so.

The OLF syllabus was very strictly supervised and controlled, as power cables, small masts and trees posed a much greater threat than when at 250 ft. Training built up from single aircraft to OLF in pairs, then pairs with a bounce aircraft, four aircraft formations and finally four aircraft with a bounce. They frequently used the Spadeadam Electronic Warfare Range, and the last three trips were with CF-18 affiliation. This was low-level operational flying of the highest quality, and they were able to use the aircraft tactically over the hilly terrain. The principles for CF-18 affiliation were the same as described for the F-4 Phantom, the CF-18 carrying Sparrows and Sidewinder missiles, albeit later models. However, the CF-18 was a much more modern aircraft with better radar than the Phantom, and as it was highly manoeuvrable it proved an extremely difficult adversary. Being co-located at Lossiemouth, the two units could brief and debrief together, including looking at the CFIS radar and HUD videotapes to see which tactics worked and which did not. Kevin was chased around the hills by a CF-18 while flying at 100 ft and glancing behind to keep an eye on his pursuer, pulling hard over ridges while overbanking to about

130° to stay low and try to avoid giving his adversary a shot – all very exhilarating. The Canadians were very sociable, and they had an excellent time with them and with other friends from the Jaguar OCU and the Buccaneer squadrons at Lossiemouth. They finally returned to Laarbruch after a fortnight of the best tactical flying training he had ever done.

After two weeks back at base, those members of the squadron selected for *Maple Flag* flew out to Cold Lake, which was about 100 miles north of Edmonton in mid-western Canada. To pick up the VC 10 they were transported to Coltishall, the home of 54 Squadron, in an RAF bus. They then flew to Goose Bay for refuelling before continuing to Cold Lake. Each leg took approximately the same flying time, indicating the vast size of Canada. They had three days to acclimatize before the exercise started, so some of them went to Jasper National Park and Lake Louise in the foothills of the Rockies to the south of Edmonton. There was still plenty of snow, so they decided to go skiing, using hired kit. The pistes were as wide as motorways, and with hardly anyone else around they had a very good time. On their return to Cold Lake, a day was taken up with pre-exercise briefings before starting flying in pairs, progressing to four-aircraft formations on the second day; as with all these exercises, the start was relatively low key, and activity built up steadily. Unlike *Red Flag*, the exercise area was large and free of restrictions, with just one electronic warfare site in the middle and plenty of wooden targets to bomb. Because of the fire risk, only inert weapons were allowed, so they were not able to use smoke/flash practice bombs. Most of the terrain was gently undulating, with pine forests and lakes, and a particular hazard was from dead trees standing well above the tops of the surrounding forest. As the radar altimeter measured height above the ground, one could be caught out by a dead treetop suddenly appearing very close in front, as they were extremely difficult to see against the forest background. Opposing (Red) aircraft were CF-18s based at Cold Lake and the USAF 'Aggressor Squadron', which flew Northrop F-5Es and used Soviet tactics.[22] Friendly (Blue) aircraft were USAF E-3 AWACS, F-15 fighters and ground attack aircraft, including US F-16s, Canadian CF-5s and USAF reconnaissance RF-4Es from the Reno Air National Guard. The latter were a very good bunch of people, many of whom were airline pilots during the week: One flew DC-9s for a living, plus RF-4Es in the Air National Guard and a Bearcat in the Reno Air Races. Some USAF FB 111s also participated, as they were just starting to do conventional attack work, having been purely nuclear strike up to that time. There were even appearances by individual B-52s flying twelve-hour missions, which included forty minutes at low level in the exercise area.

Many of the lakes looked the same, and because of the lack of good navigational features, the Jaguars relied on the navigation system to a greater extent than usual; in any event they were very busy looking out to avoid SAM/AAA threats and defensive fighters. As the area was uninhabited they were able to use the laser ranger to obtain accurate fixes on salient navigational features, as these were more accurate than the normal 'on-top' fixes. Similarly, the laser ranger was used for fixing on the IP and the attack on the target. The second day started with a meteorological briefing and an intelligence briefing on a simulated war scenario to make it as realistic as possible. A package leader, who was in charge of all attack aircraft, outlined the overall plan for hitting the nominated targets. Crews of the national formations then returned to their crew rooms to plan the mission, liaising with the package leader if required and walked out to the aircraft in plenty of time to allow for minor snags to be fixed before take-off. This was sequenced to get all aircraft airborne in a short time (R/T silence was maintained during the second week of the exercise), before setting off to the range area. Trips normally lasted about an hour, of which forty minutes was spent in the range area on OLF. The Jaguars flew with a centre-line tank, tandem beams on the inboard pylons and ECM/chaff pods on the outboard pylons. After the mission, there would be a quick 'hot debrief' followed by mass debriefing of all players, including representatives from the electronic warfare site. All kills claimed by the AAA and SAMs were detailed, together with ground target claims, which were validated by HUD films from the individual aircraft. Good and bad points in the operation were covered in the debriefing, and major lessons were emphasized by the package leader and the *Maple Flag* staff, as these debriefings were a very important part of the exercise. Normally each individual started with a joke as he got up to do his part of the debrief, and this helped to create a relaxed atmosphere among all the crews; it was professional and yet lighthearted. The later trips were all flown in formations of six, and each Jaguar pilot had eight inert retarded bombs to drop – a stick of four on one mission, plus two sticks of two on later missions.

Kevin's trip with four bombs was to attack a simulated airfield set in the forest. After releasing his bombs, he looked across and saw his wingman's bombs coming off and retarder tails opening. He then noticed an Aggressor F-5E pulling up into the vertical; apparently the F-5E pilot had been just about to take a missile shot when he saw the bombs release and the tails opening, and wisely decided to clear the area. All the Jaguar pilots claimed hits, but after the debriefing, the squadron's Dutch exchange pilot, who had been flying as wingman to the senior flight commander leading the formation, said that the leader had missed the target and dumped his bombs into a lake three miles beyond. Naturally, the flight commander lost a great deal of credibility over this incident, and he was not aware that everyone knew of his error until an article appeared in the Laarbruch Station magazine a couple of months later. This incident confirmed Kevin's belief that honesty was always the best policy in that sort of situation.

One mission was led by an American package leader, whose plan was to concentrate all aircraft as they reached the simulated forward line of own troops (FLOT), to overwhelm the defence as they entered enemy territory. To do this each aircraft type was allocated a separate height block, starting with the Jaguars at the bottom and working all the way up to the F-15s at 40,000 ft. As each type flew at different speeds, they converged at the FLOT and then started to spread out again, so they then had to fly different routes to co-ordinate their time-on-target (TOT). Whether this complicated plan worked satisfactorily is not known, but on the premise that the best plan is a simple one, there must be some doubts. Typically the Jaguars flew at 450 knots when *en route*, and 480–540 knots in defended areas, accelerating to over 600 knots when evading defences. The Jaguar became rather twitchy in pitch above about 550 knots, and concentration was then needed to avoid over-controlling when flying at 100 ft. One of the II Squadron pilots had an interesting experience: while flying at 480 knots at 100 ft, an FB-111 flew about 200 ft above him, doing in excess of 700 knots, so he was well supersonic and gave the Jaguar pilot a fair boom as he passed.

During one of the mass debriefings, the usual film from the electronic warfare site of simulated SAM and AAA kills was shown, which picked up an FB-111 approaching at very high speed and low level. The Canadian Marines on site were equipped with shoulder-launched SAMs, but as the FB-111 was supersonic no-one heard it coming; the video cameras recorded an enormous boom and immediately fell off their stands to film the ground. The boom also knocked out the main radar on the site for a day, and the Marines threw their SAMs to the ground to cover their ears, so it seemed a very effective way of taking out a SAM site. By the end of the exercise, all the paint had been burned off the leading edges of the FB-111s by the high-speed flying. In another debriefing a video of a B-52, apparently pouring out smoke from its eight engines, was shown, but the B-52 liaison pilot clarified the situation by saying, 'That's not smoke; that's chaff.' The B-52 appeared huge on video, prompting a wag to dub it 'aluminium overcast'. Normally, gun or missile shots and claims are called Fox 1 to 3, but on this exercise they heard the claims of 'Fox 4' for the first time; this was for the B-52 tail-guns used against defensive fighters. In general, not much was seen of the defensive (Red) fighters, as they tended to stay at medium level fighting the Blue escorts, while the Jaguars remained at low level; this seemed to happen on most exercises.

The middle weekend was spent in Edmonton, which was an excellent town for relaxation as it had a huge indoor water-sports park with massive slides, and also an adventure park with roller-coaster rides, all of which suited Kevin very well. During the second week he had only three more trips, all in formations of six aircraft. Normally they avoided flying over lakes as the aircraft were much easier to see from above, but on the last trip they were routed over a large lake, which it was impossible to circumvent. He and his wingman let down below the level of the trees to about 20–30 ft above the water, and as he looked across Kevin was amazed to see a white rooster tail wake on the water from his wingman's jet wash. This was not tactically sound, and was the equivalent of leaving a contrail at high level; it was easy to see, and pointed straight at the aircraft. Kevin had a spare day before leaving and managed to get a trip in a CAF Lockheed T-33, the trainer version of the P-80 Shooting Star, as a member of a pair on a training mission. It initially carried a lot of fuel in the wing-tip tanks, so the roll inertia was high until the tanks were empty. The engine was a licence-built Rolls-Royce Nene with a centrifugal compressor, which had a slow wind-up from low r.p.m. The pilot let him do most of the flying, and he remembers the aircraft as being quite sensitive in pitch. *Maple Flag* had gone well for him and he was confident that it went some way to resurrecting his reputation with the squadron commander and flight commanders.

Back at Laarbruch a new squadron commander arrived, and as the runway was being resurfaced the aircraft were moved down to, and operated from, Brüggen. This was a nuisance, as the squadron crews then had to commute thirty miles each way every day. The squadron's 75th Anniversary was on 13 May 1987, and Kevin was given the task of organizing the celebrations. However, because of the recent disruption caused by Exercise *Maple Flag*, the ceremony was deferred until July, and it was to prove a major undertaking. Commemorative first-day stamp covers were obtained, and these were flown by Jaguar to Farnborough, where they were franked before being flown back to Laarbruch. Four Jaguar GR.1As flew in box formation over south-east England and were accompanied by a T.2A to obtain photographs. It had been hoped to include some formation shots of a Jaguar with a Spitfire from the Battle of Britain Memorial Flight, but unfortunately the Spitfire had been damaged in a ground incident some weeks earlier.

Shortly after his arrival the new squadron commander briefed Kevin on comments made by the previous CO regarding his progress, and he was extremely annoyed that the former CO had not spoken to him personally about his perceived shortcomings. The new CO assured him that as far as he was concerned, all that was in the past and he could now make a fresh start. Things looked up from that time. In June he had a pairs leader check, leading the CO on a pairs SAP; all went well and he had climbed the next rung on the ladder. On attack squadrons it normally took about two years to become a pairs leader, but on II Squadron it took up to three years since so much time was spent on recce and there was little opportunity for pairs or formation practice. Because of the two changes of squadron it had taken Kevin three years, and it took Bob Judson about the same. The excessive time taken to reach attack combat readiness and pairs leadership was a source of considerable frustration among the junior pilots on II Squadron. The time for approval to lead formations of four aircraft was even greater, since the squadron rarely flew formations of this size. Kevin still considers that the squadron did too much recce at the expense of attack and formation training, so that flying became monotonous and did not stretch the pilots. Since becoming an IRE he had been allowed to authorize his own flights, but soon after gaining pairs leader status he was allowed to authorize flights by other pilots.

The approval to authorize flights by other pilots now made him eligible to control and supervise the flying programme; this was a major increase in responsibility, which entailed doing regular half-day stints as authorizing officer at the operations desk. For morning duty he had to go in early to check the weather state and forecast, choose the best areas for low flying and check that suitable weather and crash-diversion airfields were available. A weather-diversion airfield was required when the base weather was poor or liable to deteriorate and was usually some distance away, while a crash diversion was the nearest suitable airfield in case the runway at base became blocked. While on the desk, the weather had to be monitored constantly, especially if conditions were poor or deteriorating; this was most important if pilots who only held a White Card instrument rating were airborne or programmed to fly. Kevin also had to liaise with the engineers regarding aircraft serviceability and availability, and amend the flying programme as appropriate. The mission planning of junior pilots also had to be checked, and he was required to sit in on the briefings for formation flights if no one in the formation was approved to authorize flights. The authorizing officer's final action before each individual or group of pilots left the PBE was the authorizing officer's out-brief, a final check to ensure that each sortie was correctly planned and that all relevant factors had been taken into account. For inexperienced pilots especially, he had to attempt to foresee any particular difficulties they might encounter and check that they had considered these problems and knew what they had to do in any given situation. When all this had been done, the authorizing officer entered precisely what the pilot or formation was permitted to do on the authorization sheet, and initialled it before each pilot entered his initials as understanding his duties.

Normal squadron training continued while preparations for the 75th Anniversary celebrations were made. Permission was obtained from HQ RAF Germany to repaint the fin of one aircraft with the squadron crest on a black background, and also to fly a formation in the shape of a figure '2'. Ideally they wished to fly a roman II, but in the event it was simpler and safer to fly an arabic 2. The figure had to be readable from the ground (it appeared as a mirror image when viewed from above), and comprised three aircraft leading in vic formation, with another three in echelon to form the diagonal and

Box 4 of II (AC) GR.1s passing Farnborough on 13 May 1987 to commemorate the birth of the squadron there seventy-five years previously. Kevin Noble is flying XZ364, nearest to the camera. Four years later XZ364 was used in the Gulf War, when it flew forty-seven missions in Operation Granby *and was painted as* Sadman. *(via Kevin Noble)*

three in line abreast for the base – nine aircraft in all. A 'whipper-in' flew with them on all flights to pass advice and criticisms on the formation, although he peeled off as they approached the airfield on the big day. The formation was led by the CO, with Kevin as his No. 3 on his left, in vic, and wider spacing than normal was flown to improve the appearance of the figure. As it was a large and unwieldy formation, all manoeuvres were very gentle, rolling slowly into and out of turns. Practices were flown on 6 and 8 July, with the ceremony being held on 10 July, when they overflew Brüggen and the Joint HQ at Rheindahlen before doing the flypast at Laarbruch to open the celebrations. As the Laarbruch runway was still closed, the formation then landed at Brüggen, where the pilots were picked up by a Puma helicopter for a rapid return to Laarbruch.

In mid-July Kevin led a pair of Jaguars to take part in the static display for the International Air Tattoo at Fairford. Unfortunately the weather was terrible for the whole weekend, as it poured with rain, turning the grass areas into liquid mud, and overall it was not much fun. Thankfully, by August the work on the runway at Laarbruch had been completed and it was no longer necessary to commute to Brüggen. That month he completed his one thousand flying hours on the Jaguar. In mid-August he took the airman who had painted the squadron crest on a Jaguar fin for a trip in a T.2A to reward him for his efforts. The trip was a pairs low-level recce mission led by a GR.1A. Despite efforts to keep him relaxed, it was apparent that the passenger was very nervous even when strapping in, and by engine start he was almost hyperventilating. Kevin kept the flight smooth and gentle, and he thinks that his passenger enjoyed it, although it was difficult to get much response from him. To provide a memento he had briefed the pilot of the GR.1A to ease up at a suitable point, so that he could formate on one of the recce-pod camera ports to get some pictures for the passenger to take home. This they did, but on pulling away, the GR.1A pilot said his passenger did not look too well, and on checking in his mirrors, all Kevin could see was the top of his helmet. He was being violently ill, so they went straight back to base. The subsequent pictures showed just the cockpit area of the T.2A, with Kevin looking up at the camera but all one could see of the passenger was the top of his helmet and his white gloves holding a sick-bag, so it was not quite the memento intended.

Early in September the Nobles went off on another holiday to northern Italy. He then had only two trips at Laarbruch before setting off for the annual three-week APC/ACMI detachment to Decimomannu. After a week he was tasked with taking a Jaguar back to Abingdon for a major overhaul and to bring back another aircraft that had just been overhauled. Since the aircraft had to be delivered without pylons and drop tanks, he studied the operating data manual carefully and came to the conclusion that he could just make the distance direct to Abingdon on internal fuel. To save fuel he only lit the afterburners prior to rotating at take-off, and cancelled them as soon as he reached safety speed when airborne. Although he knew that pilots had taken off without using afterburner, this entailed some risk if an engine failed at the moment of rotation, as there would then be barely sufficient power on one engine, so he lit them as an insurance policy. All went well during the climb and he soon levelled at 35,000 ft, which was about 10,000 ft higher than when carrying tanks. Having started with 3,200 kg of fuel, he had only about 2,000 kg remaining when crossing the southern coast of France. However, cruising at 35,000 ft he was now in a very fuel-efficient regime, and as more fuel was burned he was able to climb to 39,000 ft, where he was using only about 20 kg per minute and cruising at Mach 0.92. The plan was that if he was short of fuel he would land at Manston, but in the event he was able to make Abingdon without any problem after one hour and 50 minutes. Some years previously, a Jaguar pilot had flown an aircraft without tanks from Portugal to Lossiemouth without refuelling; this was quite incredible, although apparently he had very little fuel on landing. This showed what a difference it made to a small, clean aircraft when it was not encumbered with external stores. For the return trip, again without tanks, he had to land at Laarbruch, and there was no problem as both legs of the journey were relatively short. Although he was well used to Decimomannu by now, it was no less enjoyable, and it was always good to get way from the planning of normal operations and concentrate on weapon delivery and ACT. Another weekend trip to Gibraltar also proved to be very pleasant.

Two weeks after returning from Decimomannu, the squadron hosted an Italian Air Force F-104G reconnaissance squadron from Villafranca on exchange for a week, and Kevin's first trip with them was to lead a pair of F-104Gs on a reconnaissance sortie. Apparently they relied entirely on map, compass and stopwatch for navigation, and were rather bemused by the navigation system and the projected map display (PMD), as well as by the Jaguar pilots' planning methods. The Italians always turned on overflying a turning point, correcting the track error on the next leg. Jaguar pilots selected a point on the PMD, not necessarily a feature, but perhaps a letter on the map, to start the turn, so that the aircraft was on the new heading when it passed over the turning point.

The next major event for Kevin was another reconnaissance exercise at Villafranca. This time he led another junior pilot, flying at low level to Bremgarten for lunch and refuelling before crossing south-eastern France at medium level to land at Villafranca. Again they stayed at a hotel in Verona, and after a briefing to bring them up to date on low-level procedures in Italy, they planned trips to and from Brindisi in the heel of Italy. The weather was beautiful and they had a very enjoyable flight down the eastern side of Italy to Brindisi – another joint civil/military base – with Aeritalia (Fiat) G.91s, which were small, single-engined attack aircraft. After refuelling the Jaguars they had lunch with a G.91 squadron, before setting off for Villafranca, flying up the western side of Italy. Southern Italy was very rocky and barren with scrub vegetation; there were quite large hills up the spine of the country and many small villages with red terracotta-tiled roofs. Next day, the weather forecast for Bremgarten was very poor, but they were accepted for refuelling at Ramstein, a large USAF base south-west of Frankfurt. They again flew the scenic route at low level through the Alps and up the Aosta Valley, climbing up to medium level across France to Ramstein. After a typical American lunch of burgers they had a meteorological briefing and phoned Laarbruch before setting off at low level. Kevin let the other pilot lead, and they had just got airborne when he noticed that a link-bay door on the other aircraft was open. This was a small rectangular door under each gun bay, hinged fore and aft, and it was normal practice to stow the Form 700 servicing document there when landing away. The JP had put his F700 in the bay and had failed to close the door properly; fortunately the airflow kept the door pressed firmly against the recce pod, so at least it did not beat itself and the airframe to pieces. Although the F700 was now probably scattered somewhere on the runway at Ramstein, it could pose a significant threat to the F-16s with their big chin intakes. Kevin therefore instructed the JP to slow down and pull up for return to Laarbruch, while he informed Ramstein of the situation before setting course for home himself. The F700 was never found, but in the follow-up he was given a minor wigging by the CO, as he should have instructed the JP to land back at Ramstein in order to close the door. In retrospect he agreed that this would have been the best solution.

Late in November he was leading a pair of Jaguars on a recce trip when they came across a pair of Lightnings in the low-flying area to the north-east of Laarbruch. The Lightnings were based at Wildenrath and on their final detachment to Germany, and Kevin with his wingman had an excellent dogfight with them. It was one of the best unbriefed affiliation exercises that he had ever had, and they thoroughly enjoyed themselves. December consisted mainly of single-aircraft day reconnaissance exercises, but ended with four IRTs in succession, and these he enjoyed. Owing to the limited amount of formation work, they normally did not get much opportunity to see how the other pilots flew, and in any event it was always different to fly in the same aircraft with another pilot. In addition to accurate flying, anticipation and smoothness were required for instrument flying, especially when leading a wingman through bad weather. At the end of one IRT he felt that his new flight commander, who had already passed the test, was about to do a rather heavy landing, and so, as captain, he took control in the final stages. During the debriefing the flight commander assured him that the situation had been perfectly under control, and Kevin must have borne this in mind some months later on a procedural IRT with the same flight commander. Again, he thought that the landing was likely to be rather heavy, but this time he did not take control. They hit the runway with a tremendous thump, but fortunately the aircraft was undamaged – a testimony to the strength of the Jaguar's undercarriage, which was designed for rough field operations. This remains the heaviest landing he has ever experienced.

The normal flying programme continued throughout December and January 1986, the most interesting trip being a high-level flight up to Scotland, dropping down to low level for the overland section to Lossiemouth and using a low/high profile for the return. This was in order to obtain some target photographs in preparation for an impending OLF detachment to Lossiemouth. Both were very enjoyable trips in beautifully crisp, clear weather over the mountain scenery of northern Scotland in mid-winter. The squadron deployed to Lossiemouth at the end of January, in company with four Canadian CF-18s from Solingen, for two weeks of OLF. Again they went through the standard work-up from single aircraft to pairs, then bounced/affiliation, but this time they also did OLF

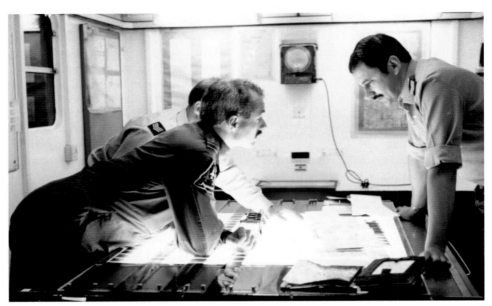

Debrief of recce imagery in the RIC (reconnaissance intelligence centre) after a sortie. All spare time, when not planning, flying or doing other secondary duties, was spent in the training cell of the reconnaissance intelligence centre (RIC) where the PIs lived and worked, learning to recognize all the different types of both NATO and Soviet vehicles and equipment. (via Kevin Noble)

recce trips. It was very hard work doing line searches at 100 ft above the ground, but it also provided excellent close-up camera shots of targets, especially as the squadron GLO and RIC teams went out with Land Rovers on the tasked line searches to find them specific targets to look for. As before, the best part of the detachment was the CF-18 affiliation, and Kevin even managed to get a shot on a lone CF-18 by sneaking up behind him unseen at low level. This was another good detachment, with outstanding tactical flying in some of the world's best low-flying country.

At the end of March Kevin led a pair of aircraft on a short reconnaissance exercise for his first visit to Norway. The Norwegian Air Force had very few recce aircraft, so the Jaguars were tasked to photograph various targets for them. They flew at high level to Rygge in Southern Norway for lunch, and then planned a low-level trip to the F-16A base at Ørland, twenty miles north-west of Trondheim. Each low-level route plan had to be checked by Norwegian pilots, as there was danger from the cables strung across valleys and fjords; it was impossible to expect to see these cables in time, and some were not even marked on the maps. It was also necessary to avoid the hundreds of mink farms at that time of year, as it was the whelping season and the mothers attacked their young if disturbed by loud noise, leading to costly compensation claims on the government. Fortunately, farms tended to be around the coast, and all were marked on the map.

He had expected to have to fly from packed snow runways, but in the event they were all clear. The snowfall in Norway was normally so heavy that it was impossible to keep the runways clear, so they rolled and compacted it, crushing grit into the surface to provide reasonable friction for braking. North of Rygge the terrain quickly became more mountainous, covered by a mixture of pine forest and bare rock, with snow everywhere except on the low-lying regions near the coast. Since it was necessary to avoid the Swedish border by several miles, and Norway was very narrow from east to west when going north, this left only the narrow coastal strip available to fly over. Further north, when flying over the high plateaux at low level, crossing the cliffs almost gave a sense of vertigo as the rock faces dropped away vertically by a thousand feet or more to the fjords. The Norwegian weather could change dramatically from blue skies to heavy snow showers in minutes, so it was very important to check the weather forecast, as the nearest suitable weather-diversion airfield could be hundreds of miles from the intended destination. Luckily, the weather was good throughout the three days they were there.

They arrived at Ørland after heading north for an hour and a quarter. It was a very enjoyable trip and they were still only one-third of the way to the North Cape. Having supervised the refuelling of the Jaguars and completed the after-flight cheek, they went down into the small fishing town to find a hotel. The normal breakfast was raw fish, which they did not find very appealing, so they stuck to the standard continental fare of meats, rolls and jam. Later they flew a mission up to Bødo, which was still only about two-thirds of the way to the North Cape, covering a number of targets *en route*, and did the same on the return. In the mountains they flew up a glacier at an altitude of several thousand feet; it was both beautiful and breathtaking. Much of Norway was sparsely populated, and Kevin felt that low flying was a tremendous privilege, as it was the only way to see so much spectacular country at close quarters in a short time. In any event, most of it was inaccessible by other means. After a second night at Ørland, they set off south the following morning, retracing the route home via a lunch stop at Rygge. His main impressions were that everyone they met was very friendly and hospitable, and the scenery was marvellous; this detachment had provided three very enjoyable days in another extremely interesting country.

A three-day exercise was held at Laarbruch early in April, and he flew three trips on each of the first two days, plus four on the third, a total of almost fifteen hours' flying. It was very tiring, with early starts and long days of frenetic planning, followed by the relief of escaping to fly. At least he was then free of the exercise injects, which caused much additional work and the simulated air raids that necessitated wearing gas masks for hours on end. The maximum crew duty time was fourteen hours, with ten hours off before starting again, and they worked to these limits every day. By the end of the third day he was definitely feeling rather jaded, as were the rest of the pilots and the ground crew, and as always it was a great relief when Endex (the end of the exercise) was declared. After debriefing it was the tradition to go to the bar for a few drinks to relax, and it was a good way to wind down in the company of the officers of the station.

Late in April 1986 the squadron went to Decimomannu again, this time for a fortnight's ACMI only. Some of the latter trips included 2-v-2 Jaguars against Jaguars, and it could be quite confusing trying to keep track of who was who, but it was excellent for practising formation control and co-ordination. Kevin also took part in a 2-v-1 Jaguars against a CF-18; even with two of them it was very difficult to beat the CF-18, although he was not using his Sparrow radar-guided missiles. Throttle management now became extremely important in dogfighting where IR missiles were involved. The plan was to join the engagement at high speed with engines throttled right back to minimize the IR signature, but aircraft energy then quickly bled off, especially in any turning manoeuvres, and it was straight back to full afterburner when inside minimum missile range for the close fighting. The best fighters, such as the F-15, F-16 and F-18, all had plenty of thrust and generally had to slow down to obtain the best turning performance at the 'corner velocity', which for these types was about 350 knots. 'Corner velocity' was the minimum speed at which the aircraft could attain the airframe g limit: at lower speeds the maximum g could not be attained. At higher speed more g could be pulled at the expense of overstressing the airframe, and in either case the turn rate was less than the maximum. At low altitudes these fighters had sufficient power to sustain 'corner velocity' at maximum g, whereas the Jaguar and Tornado, and the older fighters such as the Phantom, could not. Thus, in the Jaguar 'corner velocity' was rather academic, and the aim was to try to conserve energy and only use maximum alpha and g on those occasions when it was most advantageous. Since they operated over a sea range at Decimomannu, they were permitted to carry and use flares to counter enemy IR missiles, and this provided good practice at using the correct procedures and switches. Kevin led a four-aircraft formation for the return to Laarbruch, a sign that he was now accepted as one of the more experienced pilots.

This time he was only home for a week before going off again, leading a detachment of two aircraft for a week at Villafranca to take part in a NATO exercise with reconnaissance aircraft from other nations. He had already flown down for a pre-exercise conference about a month previously, and stayed the night, but unfortunately he had forgotten to take civilian trousers with him. On arriving at the hotel he put on a civilian sweater over the top of his flying suit and sauntered down the back streets to find some trousers, encountering the odd strange look on the way. Thankfully, he soon found a suitable shop. The squadron Dutch exchange officer led the pair on the medium-level trip down to Villafranca, but while over France he suddenly stopped answering French ATC, so Kevin took the lead. It transpired that the other aircraft's REF transmit button and its spring had popped out of its housing when released at the end of a transmission. Luckily, the ground crew, who were already at Villafranca, managed to find all the pieces and reassemble the switch.

It was very interesting to work with the other recce squadrons and see how they operated. The weather was very variable and occasionally poor, but using their projected map displays the Jaguars were usually able to navigate around the bad weather at low level and fly down the valleys to stay below cloud. They reached their targets on all but one occasion, and this led to an interesting involvement with Italian ATC, which then tried to route them at medium level to a suitable point to let down to the low-level route again. This just reinforced the view held by many of us over the years, that the British ATC is without doubt the best and most flexible in Europe, if not the world. However, it was useful experience, since one of the aims of the exercise was to become familiar with the ATC and working in the airspace of different nations. Again, it was a very fruitful week, both operationally and socially. At the end of the exercise the Italian ground crew towed all the aircraft onto a large pan for a photograph. Unfortunately, the towing arm became disconnected from a French Mirage 5, and as the brake accumulator was unpressurized the brakes were inoperative, and the aircraft gently rolled off the taxiway and onto the grass, where it very quickly sank up to its axles. It took several hours to defuel it and get it back on the taxiway.

On return to Laarbruch they were straight into a MAXEVAL the following week.

Thankfully, it all went well, and everyone was confident that they were ready for TACEVAL in July. In early June, Kevin led three aircraft to Akrotiri for a long weekend in the sun, refuelling at Villafranca and Brindisi. This was his swan-song ranger flight in the Jaguar, as the squadron was planned to re-equip with the Tornado in September 1987, and a number of pilots were already scheduled for posting. Kevin, with one of the flight commanders and two other pilots, was posted to the Tornado Conversion Course, for return to the re-equipped II (AC) Squadron. Initially he was slightly unhappy at not getting another Jaguar tour, but soon realized that this was a great opportunity to fly another type operationally and see different aspects of the job. On his last trip to Vliehors in a Jaguar, he achieved about fourteen hits on each strafing pass, and he knew his aim was good because he could see the impacts in the sand behind the panel. Even so, he suspected that the system was over-scoring somewhat, and it finally reached 108, when he estimated that he still had sufficient ammunition left out of 120 rounds for one more pass. He knew that the score would be nullified if it exceeded 120, so he fired well to the right of the target on his final pass and settled for 108 out of 120.

The TACEVAL in early June went very well, and he did thirteen trips in three days. Two of these trips were with members of the TACEVAL distaff (directing staff) in the T.2A – one with a wing commander who said he had been at Brüggen in the Jaguar days. Kevin naturally assumed that he was a pilot, and was rather surprised at how 'rusty' he was when he let him take the controls. He later discovered that the wing commander had been a navigator on a Phantom squadron at Brüggen during the handover to the Jaguars. That particular trip went very well, and the wing commander was suitably impressed until they were winched backwards into the HAS. The ground-crew man who was guiding the Jaguar by means of a steering arm on the nosewheel got well off the painted line, and a wing-tip hit the HAS wall. Luckily the damage was minor and the aircraft was flying again later that day. At the end of the TACEVAL they had the traditional party in the mess, and after that Kevin had only three more trips in the Jaguar as an active member of the squadron. The last one was leading four aircraft that were attacked by a bounce aircraft, and this was followed by F-16 affiliation. Following the normal tradition for 'last trips', the rest of the squadron turned out to meet him as he shut down after landing.

In all, he had flown 1,270 hours on the Jaguar – quite a respectable total, although this was not quite the end, as during his initial Tornado conversion at Cottesmore, the squadron sent a T.2A over to pick him up on four occasions, so he finally reached 1,275 hours. On one of these trips, a new issue of software had been installed into the navigation system, and he was gratified to see that some ideas he had suggested had been incorporated. Overall he had enjoyed his time on Jaguars and had recovered from the bad patch early in his tour on II (AC) Squadron. His last two annual flying assessments were 'high average', the scale running from 'below average' to 'average', 'high average', 'above average' and 'exceptional', which was rarely given. In many ways, he wished that he had stayed on an attack squadron, since he found working in formation with regular combat training more rewarding, as it added to the general interest and unpredictability of the task. Reconnaissance, on the other hand, although interesting as another facet of combat aviation, was more limited in scope, and he felt that too much time was spent on it at the expense of maintaining other skills. By the end of his tour on II (AC) Squadron, he knew Germany pretty well, as he had flown over most of it many times, and he now looked forward to something new, in the shape of the Tornado.[23]

GR.1 XZ109/O of II (AC) Squadron piloted by Flight Lieutenant Bill Langworthy on his 1,000th-hour flight mission over hardened air shelters at Brüggen. The introduction of the multi-role Panavia Tornado during the mid- to late 1980s saw RAF Germany-based Jaguars being replaced by the newer aircraft. Though the threat from the former Soviet Union had diminished, the Jaguar force in Britain remained, and the three Coltishall-based units were strengthened and their out-of-area commitments increased. (BAC)

CHAPTER FOUR

Worldwide Versions And Variants

JAGUAR A

A1 flew for the first time on 20 April 1972, and a total of 160 A models were delivered to the *Armée de l'Air* by 14 December 1981. The aircraft had a less sophisticated avionics equipment fit than its RAF GR.1 counterpart because of its intended role as a battlefield support/stand-off aircraft role. Beginning in February 1977 with airframe A81, Jaguar As received a Thomson/CSF CILAS TAV-38 laser rangefinder in an undernose blister fairing, and the window for the Omera 40 panoramic camera was moved to the rear of the fairing. (Eventually this was fitted or retrofitted to all A models.) The laser rangefinder, which had been developed for the Jaguar M, was also retrofitted to a small number of earlier aircraft. It had an air-to-ground range in clear conditions of 6.3 miles (10 km) and was accurate to 16 ft (4.8 m). A131 to A160 were modified to carry the Thomson-CSF/Martin-Marietta ATLIS I and later ATLIS II targeting pod, designed for use in conjunction with the Aérospatiale AS.30L laser-guided missile or for the stand-off/self-designation of laser-guided bombs. (ATLIS allows the aircraft to launch the missile and break away, while the laser pod continues to designate the locked-in target for the missile.) From aircraft A81 the Jaguar As were fitted with a TAV-38 rangefinder under the nose.

JAGUAR E

E1 first flew on 14 December 1981, and a total of forty two-seat Jaguar Es were delivered for basic conversion and combat training. Fitted with only the most basic of flight systems based on a master gyro and TACAN (SEIM 250-1 twin-gyro inertial platform and an ELIDA air data computer), it also had no in-flight refuelling capability. The Jaguar E was armed with two DEFA cannon with 130 rounds of ammunition, whereas the RAF two-seater had none. The E differed principally from the A model in having a lengthened fuselage of 57 ft 8 in (17.57 m) including the pitot tube and a tandem bubble canopy, the second seat replacing one of the internal fuel cells and being raised 15 inches (38 cm) higher than the front position. From airframe E27 onwards a fixed probe was fitted on the production line in place of the nose pitot/probe.

JAGUAR (S) GR.1 (GROUND ATTACK/RECONNAISSANCE MARK 1)

The first of 200 production Jaguar S (XX108) models for the RAF flew on 11 October 1972, and the last aircraft was delivered in 1983. From the outset the GR.1 was much

more sophisticated and technically advanced than the Jaguar A, the central hub being the Marconi NAVWASS (NAVigation and Weapons Aiming Sub-System). At the time of its introduction this was one of the most comprehensive and accurate computerized digital inertial navigation and attack systems in the world. It was capable of guiding the aircraft to a target for a single-pass attack without having to use a radar system that could be detected by the enemy. It consisted of the Marconi-Elliott Avionics Systems E3R three-gyro inertial platform; a projected map display; a navigation control-unit weapons-aiming mode selector; a hand controller and air data computer; the Sperry Gyroscope Divisions gyromagnetic compass and a Smiths Industries diffractive-optics head-up display (HUD), which used a low-light-level TV camera. Also installed was the Marconi-Elliott MCS 92CM computer, which had an 8,912-word store machine to receive inputs from fourteen different sources through the interface unit. The pilot would enter waypoint and target co-ordinates into his MCS 92CM before the mission got under way. During flight, heading, velocity and acceleration information provided by NAVWASS was passed to the pilot via the platform electronic unit and the interface unit via the 92CM computer. Also fitted were a horizontal situation indicator; ARJ 23232 radar altimeter; ARI 23205/4 TACAN and a fin-mounted Ferranti ARI-18223 radar homing and warning receiver (RHWR). Early in the production run a Ferranti ARI 23231/3 laser ranger and marked target seeker (LRMTS) was added, which resulted in the familiar 'chiselled-nose' appearance of the RAF single-seat Jaguars.

JAGUAR GR.1A

Beginning in 1978, the original Adour Mk 102 engines were replaced by Mk 104 (RT172-26) engines very similar to the Mk 804 used to power export versions of the Jaguar, which

added between 10% and 15% increase in thrust. The engine replacement programme began with the re-engining of all Jaguars in RAF Germany, and Adour 104s were eventually retrofitted to all aircraft. Beginning in 1983, the original Elliott MCS 920M system was replaced on eighty-nine Jaguars by the smaller, lighter, more reliable and more accurate Ferranti FIN 1064 INAS (inertial navigation system) NAVWASS II. No. 54 Squadron was the first to receive the NAVWASS II, which can give twenty types of information on the NCU and PMP showing the aircraft's present position, track and direction to selected waypoints. These are presented to the pilot on his HUD, which, in addition to the 'regular' flight information, also shows angle of attack, vertical speed, time to go and weapons-aiming information. Among other new innovations for the aircraft was the Ferranti TABS (total avionics briefing system), which was a ground computer linked to a digitizing map table. By placing the cursor over a point on his map, the pilot could plot his route, and the computer in turn displayed the completed route, annotating any threats and giving error and time-on-target cues. A hard-copy printout showing grid references and up to thirty-one targets or turning points were then downloaded into a Ferranti PODS (portable data store) a 32k erasable memory module, or 'brick', that could be inserted into the aircraft computer via an interface. Jaguars were also provided with an increased weapons fit. This consisted of a Westinghouse ALQ-101 jammer pod and a Phimat chaff dispenser mounted on their outer wing pylons, and two Tracor AN/ALE-40 flare dispensers scabbed onto the underside engine access panels, while provision was made to carry the AIM-9G Sidewinder AAM.

JAGUAR T2/T.2A

Unlike the Jaguar E two-seater operated by the French Air Force, the Jaguar T.2 was designed from the outset to have a full operational capability. Originally, thirty-five T.2 operational conversion trainers were ordered for the RAF, though this was later supplemented by three additional T.2s – one for trials work with the Institute of Aviation Medicine and two for the Empire Test Pilots School at Boscombe Down. The first T.2 (production B) first flew on 22 March 1973, with the last being delivered in 1983. It differed from the GR.1A in having an elongated nose section to accommodate separate and divided cockpits for instructor and student in tandem beneath a large bubble canopy. The aft section was raised by 15 in. (38 cm) to permit better visibility for the instructor. The avionics were identical to the single-seat version, though there was no internal RWR to permit a smoother transition from training to front-line aircraft. Like the GR.1, the original Elliott MCS 92CM system was replaced by the Ferranti FIN 1064 INAS, and the original 102 Adour engines were replaced by 104s, all aircraft being redesignated T.2A. Every T.2 aircraft was fitted with a retractable IFR probe and a single 30 mm Aden cannon.

JAGUAR INTERNATIONAL

Overseas sales of the Jaguar never reached the epic proportions set by American aircraft such as the F-86, Sabre, F-104 Starfighter and the General Dynamics F-16, but BAC still managed to pull several export orders out of a very small hat. Dassault was not really interested in selling Jaguars to potential overseas markets, especially since it could offer more lucrative deals on its range of Mirage fighters, when all, and not just half, the revenue went into its pocket directly. The export version of the Jaguar remained a

The considerable array of weapon options available on the Jaguar. (BAe)

collaborative effort, but it was BAC which conducted much of the trials work and weapons clearances, using British prototypes at Warton. And the Jaguar International was based closely on the GR.1A, whose proved avionics and weaponry offered better export potential than the much simpler French version.

BAC targeted in excess of thirty countries as potential customers for the Jaguar. West Germany eventually acquired the Panavia Tornado, while Japan decided to produce the indigenous Mitsubishi F-1 instead. In Switzerland the Jaguar International was one of nine types under consideration before it lost out to the Mirage, while Brazil's and Argentina's interest in a naval version ended when the Jaguar M was cancelled. In the mid-1980s Chile considered buying eighteen ex-RAF Jaguars to be armed with Exocet anti-shipping missiles, but funding problems resulted in no orders being placed. In 1974 a BAC sales team visited Kuwait, but Dassault, having received a tentative order for

sixteen Mirage F.1s and fifty Jaguars, finally obtained agreement for the Mirage F.1s only. At one point Turkey considered acquiring twenty-four Jaguars, and Egypt around 200 Jaguars, but nothing came of the Turkish enquiry. Having acquired thirty Alpha Jet MS1 trainers from 1982 onwards, Egypt eventually obtained fifteen Dassault-Dornier MS2s, the close-support version of the Alpha Jet. When in 1976 Abu Dhabi expressed an interest in buying the Jaguar as an alternative

Omani Jaguars streaking low over the desert terrain. (BAe)

to a second squadron of Mirage IIIs, the Mirage was eventually selected. Later that same year Pakistan considered buying 100 Jaguars if the USA would not supply them with A-7 Corsairs, but once again a contract for Mirage 5s went to Dassault. When a European consortium of Belgium, the Netherlands, Norway and Denmark was seeking a successor to those countries' F-104 Starfighters, BAC again offered the Jaguar, which with overwing Magic or Sidewinder AAMs was better equipped for the air defence role than its rivals. It was also considered superior to the Mirage and F-16 in the ground-attack role. BAC proposed that Dassault offer the Mirage F.1 to re-equip the European consortium's interceptor units, while the Jaguar would be offered to re-equip the ground-attack units. The potential deal failed, mainly because M. Dassault, backed to the hilt by the French government, wanted the entire order, and the F.1 was offered as a replacement for both the air defence and the ground-attack aircraft, while the British government remained strangely unequivocal. In the end, 521 examples of the General Dynamics F-16A/B were produced under licence in Belgium and Holland for the air forces of the four European countries.

B(0).2 203 of 20 Squadron of the SOAF (Royal Air Force of Oman) taking off from Thumrait. (Rolls-Royce)

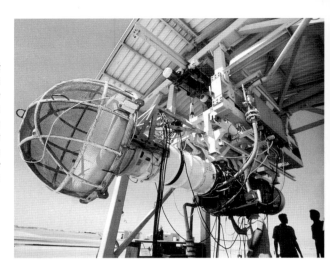

Thirty-five of the Omani Jaguar's Mk 811 Adours are being put through a mid-life upgrade, which effectively breathes new life into the engine for an additional 1,200 hours. Once the engines have been upgraded at the East Kilbride facility in the UK they are then shipped to Oman and run in an open-air test facility. (Rolls-Royce)

Royal Air Force of Oman engineers with an Adour Mk 811 engine at Thumrait. Rolls-Royce is currently engaged in a programme of activity designed to extend operations of the Jaguar in Oman until at least 2010. (Rolls-Royce)

Flight Lieutenant Andy Cubin, who completed an exchange postin̄ with the Omani Air Force and later returned to Oman as a Jaguar QF hugs the ground in Oman before exiting between the hangars! C completion of a three-season stint in 1993–6 as display pilot flyin̄ XX116, 'Cubes' was selected to join the Red Arrows aerobatic disple team. (Author's collectio̊

Jaguar Versions Worldwide

Jaguar A	Appui (support) French single-seat attack aircraft. Two prototypes (A03, A04) and 160 Production aircraft (Al to A160)
Jaguar B	British two-seat conversion trainer prototype (B08/XW566)
Jaguar E	École (school) French two-seat conversion trainer, two prototypes (E01, E02) and forty production aircraft (El to E40)
Jaguar M	Marine, navalized carrier-based aircraft prototype, one built (MO5IF-ZWRJ) replaced by Super Étendard
Jaguar S	Strike, British single-seat strike aircraft prototypes 506/XW560 and 5071XW563
Jaguar GR.l	Production version of the Jaguar S for the RAF, 165 aircraft built. Adour Mk 102, later to Mk 104
Jaguar GR.1A	Seventy-five GR.ls upgraded with FIN 1064
Jaguar GR.1B	Unofficial designation for TIALD-equipped GR.1As
Jaguar T.2	Production version of the Jaguar B for the RAF, thirty-eight built. Adour Mk 102 to Mk 104
Jaguar T.2A	Fourteen T.2s upgraded with FIN 1064
Jaguar T.2B	Unofficial designation for the two TIALD-equipped T.2s
Jaguar 96	Pre-military aircraft release designation of GR.3 and T.4
Jaguar 97	Pre-military aircraft release designation of GR.3A
Jaguar GR.3	Ex-Jaguar 96 single-seaters, from mid-1999
Jaguar GR.3A	Ex-Jaguar 97, from January 2000
Jaguar T.4	Ex-Jaguar 96 two-seaters, from mid-1996
Jaguar T.4A	Ex-Jaguar 97 two-seaters, from mid-2000
Jaguar ACT XX765	Active control technology, fly-by-wire (FBW) flying demonstrator
Jaguar International EB	Two-seat Ecuadorian version of the B. 2 built
Jaguar International ES	Single-seat Ecuadorian version of the S.10 built
Jaguar International OB	Omani version of the B.4 built
Jaguar International OS	Omani version of the S.20 built
Jaguar International SN	Nigerian version of the S.13 built
Jaguar International BN	Nigerian version of the B.5 built
Jaguar International IM	Anti-shipping version of the Jaguar International built by HAL fitted with Agave radar. Twelve built
Jaguar International IS	Indian deep-penetration strike aircraft version supplied by BAe (thirty-five) and HAL (sixty-nine, plus twenty planned)
Jaguar International IT	Indian conversion trainer version supplied by BAe (five) and HAL (ten, plus seventeen on order)
Jaguar GR.1 (Interim)	Sixteen RAF GR.1s loaned to the Indian Air Force. Fourteen were returned, of which one was supplied to Oman
Jaguar T.2 (Interim)	Two RAF T.2s loaned to the Indian Air Force, one later going to Oman

B(0).2 203 of 20 Squadron of the SOAF (Royal Air Force Of Oman) taxies in at Thumrait. (Rolls-Royce)

JI004 ('Jaguar Interim') one of sixteen RAF GR.1s loaned to the Bharatiya Vayu Sena *(Indian Air Force) in July 1979, where they were used to re-equip 14 Squadron at Ambala. (BAe)*

Maritime Jaguar JM252 of 6 'Dragons' Squadron, Indian Air Force, with Agave nose radar and BAe Sea Eagle anti-shipping missile on the fuselage centre-line. (IAF)

Although there were no European buyers, the Jaguar International was successfully sold to four overseas countries. In September 1974, a month after two undisclosed customers for the Jaguar were announced (Oman and Ecuador, which each placed orders for twelve Jaguars), the Jaguar International was publicly launched at the Farnborough Air Show. XX108 was fitted out especially for the occasion with a mock-up of the Agave radar nose and a whole host of weapons options. Oman placed an order for ten single-seat Jaguar S(O).1 aircraft and two Jaguar B(0).2 two-seaters for the *Al Quwwat Al Jawwiya Al Sultanant Oman*, or Sultanate of Oman's Air Force (after 1990, SOAF, or Royal Air Force of Oman). British Aerospace Dynamics also won a contract to supply the Rapier SAM system to Oman, and other orders were for ground radar and communications equipment. The first two aircraft (202/G-BEET and 2004/G-BETB) were displayed at the 1977 Paris Air

Jaguar FAE302, the second of ten Jaguar International ES single-seat versions of the S to be delivered to the Fuerza Aerea Ecuatoriana *(Ecuadorian Air Force) in 1977. (BAe)*

Jaguar International SN, one of thirteen single-seaters built for the Nigerian Air Force. (BAe)

Show, the first deliveries of the aircraft to SOAF beginning in March 1977. All twelve aircraft, which were powered by the Adour Mk 804 engine, had been delivered to the Middle East state by spring 1978, when they began equipping 8 Squadron at Thumrait. Later, the unit moved to Al Masirah.

In mid 1980 Oman repeated the original order for twelve more Jaguar Internationals to re-equip 20 Squadron at Al Masirah, and these were all delivered by late 1983. (Later the Jaguars returned to Thumrait when ROAF BAe Hawks were stationed at Al Masirah.) These differed from the first batch in the single-seaters having uprated Mk 811-26 engines, and the two-seaters Dash-26 series engines. SOAF Jaguars were fitted with the Ferranti LRMTS nose for the strike/attack role and were configured to carry air-to-air missiles for their secondary role of air defence. The first single-seaters were fitted with overwing launchers for the Matra 550 Magic AAMs, while the second delivery batch had adapted outboard underwing pylons to carry the AIM-9P Sidewinder. When the Tornado F.3 replaced the Jaguar in the air defence role, the Jaguar's primary role became close support and strike. As in the case of RAF Jaguars, Oman's surviving fleet of sixteen

GR.1 XX765 was used by the Royal Aircraft Establishment (RAE) (later Defence Research Agency, DERA) as a flying test-bed for the Active Control Technology (ACT) systems programme. Both cannon ports were faired over and the glazing in the nose blanked off, and the aircraft featured a fly-by-wire (FBW) system, which was the first flown anywhere in the world on 20 October 1981 by BAe senior test pilot Chris Yea at Warton. The FBW control system replaced the conventional mechanical units and control rods. XX765 was retired from test-flying in 1984. (BAe)

single-seat and three two-seat Jaguars received '96' and '97' upgrades, together with FIN 1064 nav/attack systems and the GEC Marconi thermal imaging airborne laser designator (TIALD) system. Rolls-Royce is currently engaged in a programme of activity designed to extend operations of the Jaguar in Oman until at least 2010. Thirty-five of the Jaguar's Mk 811 Adours are being put through a mid-life upgrade, which effectively breathes new life into the engine for an additional 1,200 hours. Once the engines have been upgraded at the East Kilbride facility in the UK, they are then shipped to Oman and run in an open-air test facility. Thumrait is the focal point for the Adour engine maintenance. It serves both the Mk 811s and Mk 871s that power the single-seat Mk 203 Hawks used in the air defence role and the Hawk Mk 103s that are used for advanced pilot training; one of the roles initially given to the Omani Jaguars.

Ecuador, meanwhile, acquired ten single-seat ES models and two EB two-seat trainers, all of which were delivered to the *Fuerza Aérea Ecuatoriana* (FAE, Ecuadorian Air Force) by October 1977. As with the RAF and SOAF Jaguars, Ecuador also retained the LRMTS nose and the Marconi-Elliott NAVWASS equipment, and the aircraft were fitted with overwing missile launchers for carrying the Matra 550 Magic AAM and powered by Adour Mk 811 engines. Ecuadorian Jaguars no doubt took part in the border wars with neighbouring Peru that flared up in 1981 (Paquisha Conflict) and early 1995 (the Condor War, or 'Alto-Canepa' War), until the signing of a peace treaty in October 1998 ended hostilities between the two countries. By mid-1991 only seven single-seaters and one two-seater remained from the original order, and three ex-RAF Jaguars were acquired as replacement aircraft. Today, only four single-seaters remain in service at Base Aérea Militar Taura, near Guayaquil, with *Escuadrón de Combate 2111 Jaquares, part of Ala de Combate 21.*

In July 1983 Nigeria ordered thirteen single-seat 'NS' and five two-seat 'NB' Jaguar Internationals. Deliveries survived a military coup in December 1983, and all the aircraft had arrived by 1985. The Jaguars were soon withdrawn from service as an economy measure.

It is in India that the Jaguar International has realized its sales potential, where 160 aircraft were selected to replace the English Electric Canberra B(I)58 and Hawker Hunter FGA.56A in *Bharatiya Vayu Sena* (Indian Air Force) service. The order resulted in October 1978 after the Jaguar beat off the very best competing designs, which included the Mikoyan-Gurevich MiG-23 *Flogger*, Sukhoi Su-20 Fitter and (of course!) the Dassault Mirage F.1 to emerge the winner of the DPSA (deep-penetration strike aircraft) competition. The successful design had to be capable of low-level penetration and hit targets 300 miles inside hostile territory. Equally importantly, the aircraft had to be available off the shelf and the bulk of the order had to be produced under licence in India. With an export deal worth £1,000 million, BAe reached agreement with the MoD to

Adour engine on the move. RAF GR.1/T.2 and Armée de l'Air *A/E production models were powered by two Adour 102 turbofans, and then in 1998 it was decided to proceed with the upgrade of the Adour 104 engines to Mk 106 standard. The 104 experienced hot spots in the jet pipe caused by unregulated mixing of air and fuel, which could lead to fire in the engine bays and even the loss of the aircraft. The purpose of the upgrade was to reduce the number of problems per flight hour with the Adour Mk 104 from six to two. The hot-spot problem was particular to the Mk 104, whereas the phenomenon is not as problematical on the Mk 811, which powers the export version of the Jaguar. (Author)*

Adour engine maintenance on the Jaguar was simplified by their location towards the end of the fuselage and removable access panels and standing. Engineers could easily reach the power plants from ground level or the occasional 'assist', as shown here. About 87% of a front-line squadron is composed of ground crew and five aircraft trades: 'fairies' (avionics), electricians (leckies), riggers (airframe), 'sooties' (propulsion) and 'plumbers' (armourers). They have to operate in all weathers and climes, from the desert heat of Arizona to a freezing fog-bound night in Lossiemouth. As the Jaguars neared the end of their operational career the engineering personnel's days seemed to be filled with endless updates to quite an old aircraft. Putting this into perspective, an engineering officer said, 'You are unlikely to buy a Morris Minor in 1973, drive it reasonably carefully for several years, give it a couple of major overhauls, then decide it would be much better with a GPS system, some racing seats, a fairing here and there, a 16-valve engine and some formation lights now, would you?' (Author)

Sooties working on the Jaguar's Adour engines in the engine shop at RAF Coltishall on 10 June 1999. (Author)

supply an initial batch of eighteen Jaguars (sixteen GR.ls and two T.2s) loaned from RAF stock. A further forty Jaguars (thirty-five Jaguar International IS single-seaters and five IT two-seaters) would be built at Warton, equipped with the overwing pylons for Matra Magic AAMs, uprated Mk 811 engines and the BAe reconnaissance pod, with the remaining 120 constructed by HAL (Hindustan) in Bangalore. Despite political infighting in India and more than one attempt by the French government and Dassault to overturn the decision, the deal was honoured and all the aircraft were eventually delivered to the IAF.

In February 1979 the first four of the twelve IAF officers selected to fly the Jaguar joined Course 29 at 226 OCU RAF Lossiemouth to convert to the type. The first of the ex-RAF (Interim) aircraft left for India in July, where they joined 14 Squadron at Ambala and replaced Hunter FGA.56As. In the summer of 1981, 5 Squadron (the 'Tuskers') at Agra became the second Canberra unit to re-equip with the Jaguar when it re-formed at Ambala, initially with a small nucleus of officers and men drawn from 14 Squadron. The 'Tuskers' were the first unit to receive Jaguars built specifically to the IAF's standard of preparation, which included uprated Adour 804E engines, with 27% more combat thrust than the original Adour 102s. Besides the strike role common to all Jaguar units, the 'Tuskers' also assumed a reconnaissance role, initially using BAe-supplied pods. They later standardized on Vinten pods. The 'interim' Jaguars were returned to the UK as promised, after the initial Indian-built production aircraft were issued to 5 and 14 Squadrons at Ambala in mid-1981. The first batch of forty new aircraft powered by the Adour Mk 804 were delivered to India between 5 March 1981 and 6 November 1982. All were fitted with the NAVWASS, which eventually would be replaced by the indigenous DARIN (display attack and ranging inertial navigation) developed at the Aircraft & Systems Testing Establishment in India. The next forty-five aircraft (including ten ITs) were assembled in India from kits supplied by SEPECAT, and were powered by the more powerful Adour Mk 811 engine and equipped with the DARIN system as standard. The first Indian-assembled Jaguar (JS136) flew on 31 March 1982. That summer the first HAL-built Jaguars were issued to 27 Squadron (the 'Flaming Arrows') at Bangalore, where they replaced the unit's Hunter FGA.56As. In October 1986 16 Squadron (the 'Cobras') at Gorakhpur converted to the Jaguar from the Canberra. By now the Jaguar in

IAF service was known officially as the *Shamsher* (a Persian word whose literal translation is 'Sword of Justice'). In July 1988 5 Squadron participated in Operation *Pawan*, the Indian Peacekeeping Force operation in Sri Lanka. In the early days of the operation the Tuskers flew long-range reconnaissance missions, launching from bases well inside peninsular India, overflying Jaffna and then returning to India, often at night. The squadron was on alert to carry out strike missions as well, particularly during the withdrawal of the IPKF, but it was stood down without having to use its weapons in anger.

The next Jaguars built in India were a batch of thirty-one single-seaters. Included in the last batches were eight Jaguar International IM maritime strike aircraft, which differed from the IS in having nose-mounted Thomson-CSF Agave radar and the capability to operate the BAe Sea Eagle anti-shipping missile. These first of these aircraft flew in 1985 and were delivered to 6 Squadron (the 'Dragons') at Poona (now Pune), near Bombay (now Mumbai) (one of the IM aircraft was lost during development trials) during 1986–93, whereby they replaced the unit's Canberras. In 1998 fifteen additional Jaguar IS aircraft were ordered, but these were cancelled a year later. In 1993 this order was revived and is believed to have included four more IM versions. All fifteen aircraft had entered service by the end of 1999. A further seventeen Jaguar ITs were delivered from 2002.

In April 2006 it was announced that Hindustan would build twenty more two-seat training versions of the Jaguar. Jaguar production in India is expected to continue until 2007, and the type will remain in service beyond 2010. There is a need to replace the Sea Eagle anti-shipping missile. The majority of strike Jaguars have received phased upgrades, which has included replacing the NAVWASS on the BAe-built aircraft and DARIN on the HAL aircraft with a new system, including an inertial navigation system-ring laser gyro with embedded global positioning system (GPS) receiver. The BAe aircraft have also been fitted with the MIL-STD 1553B databus unit for conformity with HAL-built aircraft. A digital map generator developed by HAL at Korwa reads onto a new head-down display (HDD). A centralized threat-warning system, including a new Indian-built radar-warning receiver, has also been incorporated. The upgraded Jaguar first flew in 2002, with the first aircraft being delivered to 5 Squadron late in 2002. The Rafael Litening laser target designation pod will be adopted for widespread use by the fleet.

JAGUAR GR.1B

In June 1994, the Chief of the Defence Staff, Sir Peter Harding, prompted the raising of an urgent operational requirement (UOR 41/94) to give ten Jaguar GR.1As and two T.2As a laser designation ability that could be employed quickly, especially in Bosnia. Ferranti (later GEC Ferranti) had been involved since 1973 in the development of a laser designator to enable an aircraft to direct laser-guided bombs (LGBs) onto the target. This culminated in the production of a thermal imaging airborne laser designator (TIALD) pod, which had been under flight development on a Buccaneer at RAE Farnborough since early 1988. To permit day and night operation under varying weather conditions, TIALD was equipped with thermal imaging and a TV camera, which were mounted in a pod carried beneath the aircraft. The designator was integrated into the aircraft's navigation and attack (nav/attack) system to enable it to be directed and controlled, and the thermal or visual images were recorded by the infra-red recce recorder in the aircraft. Before TIALD, the RAF's ability to use LGBs depended on designation of the target by a manually controlled laser marker. This was operated either from a ground-based designator, as was used in the Falklands conflict, or from the air; in the latter case, the marker equipment was fitted to a Buccaneer and controlled by the navigator. Although Tornado GR.1A aircraft employed it successfully during the Gulf War, there were several limitations to this system. The main one was that the navigator needed to see the target visually, thus limiting its use to good weather by day. Additionally, it could not be integrated with a modern nav/attack system. Also, having located the target, the navigator had to track it visually – not easy in turbulence or if the aircraft was taking evasive action.

TIALD had been trialled for the Tornado aboard Jaguar T.2A XX833 'NightCat', one of a number of aircraft used by the DERA (which in April 1995 became the Defence Evaluation and Research Agency) for passive night-attack studies. XX833 had originally been delivered to RAE Farnborough on 8 April 1988 for laser modifications. These included a new HUD, the MIL STD 1553B databus and a new head-down display (HDD). The aircraft then flew with an underwing GEC-Marconi podded ATLANTIC (airborne targeting low altitude thermal imaging and cueing) Type 1010 FLIR system to test procedures and monitor the aircraft's other arrangements, such as presenting an image onto the HUD and HDD. The NightCat later flew with an 'A-Model' TIALD pod, which was subsequently removed and rushed to the Gulf for urgent operation in Operation Granby.

In the event, UOR 41/94 was achieved mainly by using and modifying the equipment already being trialled for production, and the TIALD pod was fully integrated into the Jaguar's avionics systems and harmonized with the INS, being mounted on the aircraft centre-line station, where fewer obstructions obscured the field of view. As well as the interface for the TIALD equipment (using as MIL-STD-1553B databus), it was inside the cockpit that the new toys were most obvious to those familiar with the 'old machine'. Improved navigation equipment and cockpit displays, including a Marconi FD 4500 A4 wide-angle HUD, were installed. The 1:1 ratio wide-angle head-up display and associated up-front controller replaced the peculiar 5:1 geared version of old, and with the new HUD came the capability to display a multitude of real-time information. To enable TIALD operation in a single-seat cockpit a HOTAS (hands on throttle and stick) arrangement was created by using stick tops from Tornado F2s and hand controllers from scrapped Harrier GR.3s, HOTAS functions reducing time spent 'head in cockpit' dealing with navigation button-pressing and weapons-aiming facilities. Out went the microfilm-fed moving-map display, and in its place a head-down display consisting of a Marconi PMD with GEC symbol and digital map generators from the Tornado GR.4 upgrade programme was fitted. This unit, which later became known as the MPCD (multi-purpose colour display) could display a digitally generated map or the image seen through the newly acquired TIALD pod by displaying TV/IR imagery in video-style format. The FIN 1064C taken from Tornado and Harrier stocks improved navigational accuracy and allowed automatic target acquisition by the TIALD tracker. To record TIALD imagery Vinten dual video recorders were installed. In its 'designator' role the Jaguar also carried a Phimat AN/ALQ-101 (V)-10 jammer pod and two 264-gallon (1,200-litre) fuel tanks. The rear warning radar was uprated to 'Sky Guardian' 200-15 standard. While it was designed for daylight operations during the mid-1990s, trials were undertaken to make the Jaguar fleet compatible with night-vision goggles (NVGs). All twelve TIALD aircraft were delivered to Coltishall within twelve months, the last arriving in spring 1997. Modifications to

Jaguar pilot wearing the helmet-mounted night-vision goggles (NVGs), which contain light-intensifying tubes to amplify electromagnetic energy in the visible and near infra-red part of the spectrum. The NVGs have a field of view of about 40 ft. Early sorties in fast jets were flown using 'Generation 2' light tubes, which required a small amount of moonlight to provide enough light. Jaguars of II (AC) Squadron at Laarbruch were involved in much of the NVG work. The NVGs proved particularly suitable for their role of tactical reconnaissance, where the ability to see the area around the aircraft in detail is more important than seeing a considerable distance ahead of it, as is required for attack flying. NVG training included taking off from an unlit runway, flying a low-level route with targets through a variety of terrain, from hills to flat plains, landing back on the unlit runway and then even taxiing back around the airfield in the dark. During a major NATO field exercise in Germany in 1988, two Jaguars were permitted to fly at low level at around midnight over the exercise area of a US Army reinforcement exercise. On analysis of the IRLS after landing, the PIs identified preparations for river crossings at two of the sites, and provided the commanders with an assessment of when it would be complete; it was then attacked by Tornadoes at 3 a.m. 'We did not even know we had been recce'd,' one American officer was heard to say, 'we just heard a noise in the dark.' (Author)

GR.1B XX729/EL of 6 Squadron with a GEC Marconi thermal imaging airborne laser designator (TIALD) system on the centre-line. Behind is XZ362/GC of 54 Squadron with a 1,000 lb (454 kg) laser-guided bomb on the centre-line and a 41 Squadron Jaguar carrying a 1,000 lb free-fall bomb. Both are armed with overwing-mounted AIM-9L Sidewinders. XZ362/GC crashed in Alaska on 24 June 1996 during Exercise Cope Thunder. Flight Lieutenant Whittaker struck the tops of trees on a lightly wooded ridge rolling out of a turn twenty miles from Eielson AFB, near Fairbanks, and he ejected. Whittaker ejected from a Jaguar a second time on 3 September 1998, when he banged out of XZ108. (Rick Brewell)

Jaguar 97 cockpit (Author)

cockpit lighting and capability to use the exterior station-keeping lights were subsequently fitted to the majority of the fleet.

JAGUAR T.2B

T.2A XX835 and T.2A XX146 were modified under UOR 41/94 (see above) to serve as airborne TIALD instructional aircraft, which in time of war were to serve as laser designator aircraft.

JAGUAR 96 (GR.3)

Following on from the success of the original GR.1B and T.2B programme, a further two-stage upgrade was introduced to bring the remainder of the Jaguar fleet up to the same standard. As far as the Jaguar was concerned, MoD had only to pay for the upgrade work, and not the design, making it cheaper to add capability to Jaguar than to any other front-line aircraft, to the extent that the Jaguar's out-of-service date was delayed twice. The programmes took on added importance when delays in the Eurofighter Typhoon programme pushed back the retirement date of the Jaguars from operational service so that they would have to remain viable for a longer period than originally thought. The first phase of the upgrade programme was known as 'Jaguar 96' (the second phase – 'Jaguar 97' – bringing all the aircraft to a common standard) was applied, as these were the scheduled dates for their service entry. These modifications included the full list of *Granby* modifications and the modifications introduced on the GR1B/T.2B. Once all these modifications had been incorporated, the designation of the Jaguar became GR.3 and T.4. The upgrades changed the Jaguar from a low-level strike and reconnaissance aircraft to a medium-level platform capable of employing precision-guided munitions (PGMs). Much of this change was brought about through the efforts of Wing Commander Pete Birch, the Jaguar upgrade project officer (JUPO). His 'Jaguar 96' standard introduced a databus into the aircraft avionics architecture; a network that connects the aircraft's 'black boxes'. 'Jaguar 97' really furnished this network with up-to-date equipment.

Jaguar 96 used the MIL-STD-1553B databus, making the aircraft compatible with smart weapons, even though the majority of aircraft could not use them, and each was wired for TIALD, if not compatible with the podded system. The wide-angle HUD used on the Jaguar GR.1B was installed. The excellent Ferranti FIN 1064 INAS, which allowed the Jaguar to be operated accurately and reliably at low level, was updated by integrating a GPS receiver and the BASE terrain profile matching system (TerProm) to give outstanding accuracy and performance with weapon aiming and navigation: no more excuses for missing any targets! An in-built ground proximity warning system (GPWS) also utilized the digital terrain elevation database (DTED) of TerProm, warning of an impending collision with either granite or significant man-made obstructions. All the new hardware was linked by a 1553 databus, and imagery from both the HUD and TIALD could be recorded onto S-VHS compact video-cassettes for debriefing purposes. A digital map, the symbol generator and processors being built onto one computer card acquired from the C-130J Hercules programme, were installed in some of the Jaguar 96 aircraft. On the ground, planning a sortie could now be done on the Jaguar Mission Planner (JMP), a PC-based system using a similar database to that of TerProm. It allowed pilots to choose very careful routes through known Surface-to-Air Missile threat areas and minimize aircraft exposure in hostile territory. XX738, the first Jaguar 96, which flew for the first time in January 1996, was delivered to RAF Coltishall in March 1997. Not all Jaguar 96s were of a single standard, some being compatible with TIALD and others with the recce pods, while the rest, depending on the configuration of the aircraft upgraded, could use all of these systems. Full clearance for the Jaguar 96 was gained in February 1998.

JAGUAR 97 (JAGUAR GR.3A)

The main aim of Jaguar 97 was to give each aircraft the ability to use TIALD and podded reconnaissance systems and to slave the TIALD system to a GEC-Marconi/Honeywell helmet-mounted sighting system (HMSS). For the pilots the HMSS and the data link (IDM) were the key capabilities of the GR.3A, both of which made the Jaguar unique in the RAF. The IDM transmits information between up to eight aircraft and a ground station known as a 'Termite'. A forward air controller (FAC), who moves with ground forces and calls in air strikes, can send coded targeting information directly into the Jaguar's navigation system. Not only is this a great improvement in efficiency but it also means that the FAC transmits far less on the radio and is therefore less vulnerable to enemy direction finding. The IDM also transmits present position (PP) data around the network. If he wishes, the pilot will see the position of the other members of his formation on his moving map in the cockpit almost continuously, so the pilots are better placed to look after each other while on a mission.

The HMSS fitted to a standard HISL Alpha lightweight flying-helmet incorporates a tiny projector that projects a varying combination of crosses, circles and squares onto the inside of a pilot's visor, in front of his right eye. This removes the need for the pilot to 'look down' into the cockpit while operating the TIALD pod. HMSS can also be used in the air-to-air role to point the Sidewinder AAM missile towards an enemy aircraft and also to designate points on the ground. It is this second facility that is especially important to pilots. Most contemporary exercises and operations rely heavily on medium-level close air support (CAS). CAS is the FAC calling air strikes onto enemy positions. If the FAC needs to call in medium-level CAS, he talks the pilot's eyes onto the target by using features on the ground; woods, lakes, railways, road junctions. Once the pilot and FAC are sure that they are talking about the same position, then the FAC can clear the pilot to attack the target; a procedure routinely used in Afghanistan and Iraq. A Jaguar pilot could dispense with much of the talking. Once the FAC has sent a target over the IDM, it would be a matter of seconds before the pilot was looking at the target. Conversely, if a pilot saw something of interest, he could designate it and the aircraft computer would derive a latitude, longitude and height for that position. This target could be sent to another Jaguar, to the FAC or to anyone with an IDM on the network.

Jaguar 97 also had the ability to use the Paveway III laser-guided bomb. Another enhancement was the fitting of the common rail launcher (CRL) on the overwing Sidewinder pylon. In the cockpit the MPCD was replaced by a GEC-Marconi portrait-format active matrix liquid crystal head-down display (AMLCD), with twenty-eight multi-function soft keys and excellent sunlight glare rejection. The AMLCD is better able to show the digital moving map and TIALD imagery, as well as other flight information than the MPCD. The Jaguar 97 also had a fully integrated Jaguar mission planner (JMP). The route planned on the JMP is downloaded to the aircraft using a data transfer cartridge. Multiple routes can be loaded to the cartridge, giving the aircraft navigation

The GEC-Marconi/Honeywell helmet-mounted sighting system (HMSS). For the pilots the HMSS and the data link (IDM) were the key capabilities of the GR.3A, both making the Jaguar unique in the RAF. (RAF)

system access to well over 1,000 waypoints. The information can be displayed on the AMLCD, showing the track lines, waypoints and targets, as well as timing and heading information. The NVG-compatible cockpit included new filters, electro-luminescent floodlights and replacement panel illumination. The first Jaguar 97 (XZ3990) flew on 4 August 1997, and the type gained its military aircraft release on 14 January 2000. Single-seater Jaguar 97s became GR.3As, and two-seaters T.4As, which did not have the ability to use the HMSS.

The final element of the Jaguar improvement programme was the award of a mid-1998 contract by the Jaguar and Canberra integrated project team (IPT) to upgrade the Adour 104 engines to Mk 106 standard. The earlier engine experienced hot spots in the jet pipe, caused by unregulated mixing of air and fuel, which could lead to fire in the engine bays and even the loss of the aircraft. The purpose of the upgrade was to reduce the number of problems per flight hour with the Adour Mk 104 from six to two. (Though increased thrust was not the prime reason for the upgrade, re-engining produced a 5–6% increase in the thrust available to the aircraft, leading to improved airfield performance.) The hot-spot problem was particular to the Mk 104, whereas the phenomenon is not as problematical on the Mk 811, which powers the export version of the Jaguar. The Adour Mk 106 is based on the dry section of the Mk 871 used in the Hawk and USN Goshawk and the Mk 811 afterburner unit used on the export Jaguars. Compared to the Mk 104, it has a modified fairing to smooth the air/fuel flow in the jet pipe, and clamps to restrict the fuel injection in critical areas of the pipe. Although the total number of Jaguars that would use the new engine was not expected to exceed sixty aircraft, 122 engine conversion kit sets were manufactured to cover operational requirements until the end of service date and a number of spare engines at a cost of £105 million. This figure included four development Adour Mk 106s, which were produced for engine testing and flight trials. BAe Systems at Warton flight tested the new engine in Jaguar GR.1A XX108 (S1, the first production single seater for the RAF). Phase 1 trials, involving a Mk 106 in one engine bay and the baseline Mk 104 in the other, began in July 2000, and were followed by a pair of Mk 106s built to slightly differing standards being fitted and flown. Slight problems in the jet pipe were remedied by Rolls-Royce before Phase 2 began in July 2001, when two full production Mk 106 engines were used. Flight testing was completed in November 2001, and EPA.1 (engineering production aircraft 1, GR.3 XZ400) was delivered to RAF Coltishall on 24 January 2002. The last of fifty upgraded single- and two-seater aircraft were returned to service early in 2005.

E22 7-PI of 1ième Escadrille, Escadron de Chasse 2/7 'Argonne', *in 1993. (Gary Parsons)*

CHAPTER FIVE

The Armée de l'Air

It is a straightforward aircraft of great reliability and it handles extremely well. Operationally speaking, it complies exactly with the French Operational Requirements, which called for medium- and low-altitude performance. It meets the short take-off and landing requirement, although this has tended to complicate the design somewhat. At the same time it is capable of high speeds, good manoeuvrability at low altitudes, an extensive range and supersonic capability. Like all prototypes, there have been problems but these are now cleared up and the aircraft is OK.

Général d'Armée Aérienne, Claude Grigaut, Chief of
the Air Staff, speaking in 1973

Renowned for its ruggedness and relatively straightforward maintenance, especially in combat theatres in former colonies in Africa in the 1970s and 1980s, and in 1991 in Kuwait, and then over Bosnia-Herzegovina, *Armée de l'Air* pilots have taken Jaguars to war on several occasions. At its peak in the mid-1980s, the *Armée de l'Air* operated nine squadrons of fifteen Jaguars each, or 135 aircraft, the remainder being stored at the Chatendun Centre as reserve stock and attrition replacements. Originally it was intended that the Jaguar would have a reconnaissance role, possibly as a replacement for the Mirage IIIR, with a revised nose section fitted with a camera suite. However, sixty examples of the Mirage F1CR-200 were eventually selected for this role, and the Jaguar was reduced to having a more limited reconnaissance capability, fitted with a RP36P camera pod on the aircraft centre-line. On 24 July 1974 a Jaguar A of CEAM at Mont de Marsan flown by Capitaine M. Gauthier made the first live drop of the French AN52 free-fall nuclear weapon in Operation *Maquis* over the Mururoa Atoll in French Polynesia. For the nuclear role, the Jaguars would have been configured with a centre-line AN52, two RP36 fuel tanks on their inner wing pylons and two Phimat pods on the outer wing pylons.

Throughout the 1970s and early eighties some French Jaguar units also took part in exercises in Africa. In 1975 three Jaguars flew a 'proving trip' to the Republic of Djibouti, a former French colony and a mainly desert country on the Gulf of Aden. In 1976 four Jaguars refuelled by a Boeing C-135F tanker[24] and accompanied by a Transall C-160F twin-engined turboprop transport, deployed to Libreville to take part in Operation *Abidjan* with Gabon. In January 1977 another four Jaguars deployed to the Ivory Coast for Exercise *Bandama* after flying to Senegal in Operation *N'Diambour*. French Jaguars also took part in Exercise *Estuaire* in Gabon, and *Mangrove* and *Murene* in Togo. Late in 1977 French Jaguars carried out their first operational deployment to Dakar in Senegal to

A54 11-RT of 2ième Escadrille, Escadron de Chasse 3/11 'Corse', *touching down at RAF Coltishall. The SPA69 badge of* Rencontre de chat *(cat's face) is worn on the starboard side of the tailfin. (Author)*

help counter Algerian-backed Polisario Front guerillas carrying out attacks in the former French colony of Mauritania. The aircraft took part in Operation *Lamentin*, but two of *EC 3/11*'s Jaguars were shot down in December 1977 and a third was lost on 3 May 1978 during a fourth strike against guerilla positions before Mauritania relinquished its territorial claims and the guerilla war ended.

Late in April 1978 *EC 3/11*'s Jaguars were detached to the airport at N'Djamena (formerly Fort Lamy), the capital of Chad, in north-central Africa, to take part in Operation *Tacaud* against Libyan-backed Frolinat guerrillas. Once part of French Equatorial Africa, the land-locked country gained independence in August 1960. It was torn by civil wars and was the scene of repeated intervention by Libya to the north. In 1973 Colonel Muammar Gaddhafi, the Libyan leader, annexed the 62-mile (100 km) wide by 621-mile (1,000 km) long Aouzou strip in northern Chad that was believed to contain the impoverished

A-36 71A of 2ième Escadrille, Escadron de Chasse 3/7 'Languedoc', *at Mildenhall on 26 August 1978. On the side of the tailfin is the* Chardon de Lorraine *(Lorraine Thistle) red and white pennant. (Tom Trower)*

country's only mineral resources. This area was also used to provide bases from which Libyan forces could support Chadian rebels. On 31 May 1978 a Jaguar was shot down by a SA-7 *Grail* SAM, and a second aircraft was lost on a reconnaissance flight on 8 August. On 23 August a third Jaguar was lost in a collision and a fourth was destroyed on 14

A74 7-NA of 1ième Escadrille, Escadron de Chasse 4/7 'Limousin', *at RAF Coltishall on 8 April 1989. On the tailfin is the* Aigle *(eagle) insignia. (Tom Trower)*

HIGH SPEED BOOM

An Armée de l'Air *Jaguar being refuelled from a C-135F before a bombing mission into Iraq. Note the side-by-side bomb carriers under the Jaguar's wings, which differed from the RAF method of carrying them on tandem beams. (French Air Force)*

A157 11-EN of 2ième Escadrille, Escadron de Chasse 1/11 'Roussillon', *at RAF Coltishall, 26 July 1989. On the tailfin is the* Masque de comédie *(mask of comedy). (Tom Trower)*

October. Despite the intervention by French troops supported by the Jaguars they could not affect the outcome, and all French forces had withdrawn by May 1980. Early in 1981 Colonel Gaddhafi announced that Libya and Chad would be united, but after yet another civil war rebel forces were routed and the Libyans asked to leave the country in November 1981. Two years later the rebel forces in the Libyan-annexed Aouzou strip, aided and armed by Libya, advanced and made substantial gains, but the battle swayed to and fro and finally Gaddhafi had to commit his air force. Chad's obsolete aircraft were no match for the Libyan Mirage, MiG and Sukhoi jets, so France was again asked to intervene.

Finally, on the night of 10/11 August 1983, French paratroopers crossed into Chad from Cameroon and secured N'Djamena Airport, which was to be used to stage *Manta*, a full-scale French military operation to oust the insurgents from Chad. By 19 August four Jaguars, part of *Air Manta*, the air component assigned to the large French tri-service force, were based at Libreville Airport in Gabon. Four more Jaguars, three C-135F tankers and two Breguet Atlantic Comint/Sigint aircraft of the *Aéronavale* were based at Bangui M'Poko Airport in the Central African Republic. Lack of fuel in Chad delayed operations from N'Djamena until 21 August, when four Jaguars, four Mirage F1C-200 interceptors and a single C-135F tanker began operating from the airport. For operations in Chad most of the Jaguars were from *EC 4/11 Jura*, but crews were rotated frequently and came from other FATacs (*Force Aérienne Tactique* (French tactical air command). The objective of Operation *Manta* was to establish a 'red line' in the middle of Chad along an east–west axis from Sudan to Niger to prevent the Libyan-backed rebels moving southwards through the country. For a time the French forces asserted their presence without actually engaging in combat with the rebels. On 2 September 1983 the Jaguars 'buzzed' Libyan-backed guerrilla forces that were attacking Oum Chalouba. Two days later, when it was feared that the fighting might led to a confrontation between French and guerrilla forces, two Jaguars and a C-135F tanker were dispatched north of Arada in the 'red line' in another show of strength.

The undeclared war quietened down for a while, but when on 24 January 1984 the guerrillas took the garrison at the town of Ziguey and made twelve Chadian soldiers and a Belgian doctor and nurse hostage, French forces had to act. On the morning of 25 January two Jaguars of *EC 4/11 Jura*, escorted by two Mirage F.IC-200s and supported by a C-135F tanker, were dispatched to find the 21-mile guerrilla convoy, which had left Ziguey and was heading back to the safety of the 'red line'. The convoy was discovered near Torodoum, and SA-7 *Grail* surface-to-air missiles were fired at the aircraft, but none found their target. A French Army Gazelle helicopter destroyed one of the vehicles with a HOT missile, and then the Jaguars and Mirages attacked. One of the Jaguars, which was in a tight banking turn when it was hit in the main hydraulic system by 23 mm gunfire, crashed, and Capitaine Michel Croci, the pilot, died when he ejected too close to the ground. The remaining aircraft strafed and stopped the convoy, despite one of the F.IC-200s also being damaged by gunfire. Capitaine Croci was posthumously awarded the *Légion d'honneur* in February 1984. As a result of the incident additional forces, including more Jaguars and Mirages, were sent to N'Djamena, and Solenzara Air Base in Corsica was placed on alert for possible operations against Libya. A second Jaguar was lost on 16 April 1984 during a probing flight sixty-two miles (100 km) north of the 'red line', when Commandant Bernard Voelckel flew into a sand dune near Faya Largeau. Five months later France and Libya agreed on a mutual withdrawal of forces from Chad, despite the occupation of the northern part of Chad territory by Libyan-backed forces. The French withdrawal, code-named Operation *Silure*, began in September, and the Mirage F1C-200s and the Jaguars left during the first week of October. The last of the French forces left from N'Djamena on 7 November 1984, but within a few weeks Libyan and East German military personnel began building a military airfield at Ouadi-Doum in northern Chad, 186 miles (300 km) north of N'Djamena. The base was completed in October 1985 and accommodated Libyan MiG-21 and MiG-23 tactical aircraft, and

A54 of 1ième Escadrille, Escadron de Chasse 1/7 'Provence', *at RAF Mildenhall in May 1992. On the tailfin is the SPA15 insignia* Casque de Bayard *(Bayard's helmet). (Author)*

Jaguars of 2ième Escadrille, Escadron de Chasse 2/7 'Argonne'*, with E25 nearest, at Mildenhall Air Fête, June 1993. EC 2/7's SPA48 insignia* Tête de coq *(cock's head) is applied to the starboard side of the tailfins. (Author)*

bristled with Soviet-built radar systems and SAM missile sites and AAA batteries.

On 10 February 1986 the Libyan-backed rebels, supported by armed SIAI-Marchetti SF.260WL Warriors[25] and Libyan Air Force transports and helicopters, went on the offensive south of the 'red line' once more. At this time twelve Jaguar As, four Mirage F1C-200s, three C-135F tankers, six Transall C-160F transports and two Dassault-Breguet Atlantic ASW aircraft for use as airborne command posts were in position at Bangui M'Opoko Airport ready to strike at Ouadi-Doum. Operation *Épervier* ('Sparrowhawk'), as it was code-named, began on 16 February when eight Jaguars escorted by Mirage F1C-200s, refuelled by C-135F and guided by the Atlantics in a five-hour round trip, were dispatched to attack the airfield. Six of the Jaguars each carried eighteen Thomson-Brandt BAP-100 runway-cratering munitions beneath the fuselage, a

A137 11-EM of 1ième Escadrille, Escadron de Chasse 1/11 'Roussillon' *(Gary Parsons)*

E11 of 1ième Escadrille, Escadron de Chasse 2/7 'Argonne'*, taxiing out at North Weald in March 1994. (Author)*

E38 7-PI of 2ième Escadrille, Escadron de Chasse 2/7 'Argonne'*, in Desert Scheme at RAF Lakenheath in May 1994. (Author)*

E7-PF of 2ième Escadrille, Escadron de Chasse 2/7 'Argonne'*, taxiing at RAF Lakenheath in May 1994. (Author)*

E40 of 2ième Escadrille, Escadron de Chasse 1/7 'Provence'*, at RAF Coltishall, 10 August 1998. On the right-hand side of the tailfin is the* Croix de Jerusalem *(Cross of Jerusalem). (Author)*

Barracuda ECM pod, a Phimat chaff dispenser, a tailcone flare launcher and a 1,200-litre (244 gal) tank under each wing. Two more were armed with 400 kg (882 lb) retarded bombs instead of BAP-100s. After refuelling from the tankers at 16,400 ft (5,000 m), cruise altitude being limited by the heavily laden Jaguars, the strike went in at low level and completely surprised the Libyan defenders. Crossing the Ouadi-Doum runway at a 17-degree angle relative to its axis and releasing their BAP-100s in a single pass, the Jaguars put the airfield out of action for several days and all aircraft returned safely. Less than twenty-four hours later a Libyan Air Force Tupolev Tu-22 *Blinder-A* supersonic bomber dropped three bombs on the single runway at N'Djamena Airport, putting it out of action for heavy-lift aircraft for several days. On 27 March a Jaguar crashed soon after take-off from Bangui Airport, and the pilot ejected safely, but the aircraft hit a school, killing twenty-one people, including many children and injuring thirty others.

On 7 January 1987 ten Jaguars escorted by Mirage 5Fs and Mirage F1CR-200s attacked radar installations at Ouadi-Doum with MARTEL (missile anti-radar television) missiles. Gradually the Chadian Army pushed back the insurgents, and in 1987, with further support by Jaguars and Mirages, the enemy forces were routed. Twenty-three Libyan aircraft were captured on the ground, and the war was over, although Jaguars and transport aircraft remained on station at Djibouti ready to help stamp out any further trouble.

Plans to modernize the Jaguar fleet at the beginning of the 1980s with upgraded engines and a new avionics suite based on the Sagem INS were shelved, and with the ending of the Cold War the Jaguar force was reduced by three squadrons.

The French Jaguars' biggest test came in 1990, when the *Armée de l'Air* deployed twenty-eight Jaguar As to the Gulf region as part of Operation *Daguet*, the French contribution to *Desert Storm*. France was the largest user of the Jaguar in the Gulf War, the first sixteen aircraft being sent to Al Ahsa Air Base near Hufuf, eighty miles south-

Jaguar A 7-HP of Escadron de Chasse 3/7 'Languedoc' *at RAF Coltishall in 2001. EC 3/7 disbanded at Saint-Dizier on 30 June 2001. (RAF Coltishall)*

west of Dhahran, in October. Twelve more Jaguars arrived in early January 1991. Eventually thirty-five Jaguars were deployed to the region, although twenty-eight were operational at any one time.

The *Armée de l'Air* Jaguars lacked the sophisticated equipment such as FIN 1064 and LRMTS fitted to RAF Jaguar GR.ls. Standard fit was a Thomson-CSF CILAS TAV 38 laser rangefinder carried under the nose. However, the Thomson-CSF ATLIS (automatic tracking laser illumination system) laser-designator pod could be carried on the centre-line station in place of the 264 gal (1,200-litre) RP36 fuel tank. This self-contained precision weapon delivery system could be used very effectively in tandem with the Aérospatiale AS 30L missile. French Jaguars had no provision for carrying overwing Sidewinder missile launchers as used by RAF Jaguars. They had to rely on a combination of the internal DEFA 553 cannon, with 300 rounds of ammunition[26], a single Matra 550 AAM or a Matra Phimat or Bofors BOZ-103 chaff/flare pod and a Dassault Electronique Barracudaor, Barem or Remora wide-band ECM detector/jammer pod. A 56-cartridge Alkan 5020/5021 conformal chaff and flare launcher was also fitted beneath each wing root, and sometimes an 18-cartridge Lacroix flare dispenser was carried in the tailcone in place of the drag-chute. The ECM fit included an internal Thomson-CSF TH RWR on the tailfin, and Thomson-CSF Caiman or Basilisk EW pods were carried. Pilots were issued with a hand-held GPS system to put inside the cockpit of each Jaguar. Apart from the Aérospatiale AS.30L (L for laser) missile, *Armée de l'Air* Jaguars also carried the Matra/Thomson Brandt BLG 66 Belouga 640 lb (290 kg) grenade-dispenser weapon for dispensing 66 mm grenades. (Later, when missions were changed to higher altitudes, the Belouga system, which was principally for low-level operation, saw only limited use.) Also, 'slick' 250 lb (113 kg) and 500 lb (226 kg) bombs could be carried on twin side-by-side carriers on the inner wing pylons. Alternatively, Thomson Brandt BAP 100 (*bombe accélérée de penetration 100 mm*, or 100 mm anti-runway bombs) (or a RP36P reconnaissance pod) on the aircraft centre-line, Thomson-Brandt BAT-120 (*bombe d'appui tactique 120 mm*) anti-armour bombs and LR-F1 non-reloading launchers containing 68 mm rockets each or Matra R-3 l00 mm unguided rockets could be carried. Near the end of the Gulf War, twin SAMP BLG 450 laser-guided bombs were carried.

The *Armée de l'Air* and RAF Jaguars were assigned daylight operations only, but at first the French government limited the former to one mission per day and none were to be flown into Iraq. Unlike their RAF counterparts, French Jaguar pilots were tasked to streak in at low level where the threat from AAS and shoulder-launched missiles was formidable. The first mission by French Jaguars went ahead on 17 January 1991, when twelve aircraft attacked a Scud missile site at Ahmed Al Jaber Air Base in Kuwait with AS.30L missiles and Belouga aerial grenade canisters dropped from 100 ft (30 m). The French aircraft were bracketed by intense cannon fire, shoulder-launched SAMs and AAA, and four of the Jaguars were damaged. One was hit in the starboard engine by a shell, and a shoulder-launched SA-7 Grail missile, which set the engine on fire, blasted another. The pilot nursed the aircraft to the US base at Jubail, and landed safely, but the Jaguar had to be returned to France. An AAA shell passed through the canopy of another Jaguar and the pilot's flying helmet, which grazed his scalp, but he was able to make it back to Al Ahasa, where he received immediate treatment while still in the cockpit.

Next morning another twelve Jaguars, in three groups of four, attacked a munitions dump at Ras Al Quilayah on the coast of Kuwait, nineteen miles (30 km) from Kuwait

Jaguar A 7-HO of Escadron de Chasse 1/7 'Provence' in June 2005. EC 1/7 was the last French Jaguar unit, and it converted to the Rafale that same year. (Armée de l'Air)

City, at medium level this time. The site consisted of hangars surrounded by concrete blast revetments, some of which had been designed to house MM-39 Exocet sea-skimming missiles captured from the Kuwaiti Navy during the Iraqi invasion. Four of the Jaguars carried laser-guided AS.30L stand-off missiles reconfigured for medium-altitude delivery, and these were aimed at storage hangars in the dive from 4,000 ft (1,220 m), and at a range of seven and a half miles (10 km). The other eight Jaguars dropped 250 lb (113 kg) bombs from 15,000 ft (4,570 m). Ras Al Quilayah was attacked again on 19 January, and was to have been attacked a third time on the 20th, but the mission was recalled because of severe thunderstorms in the area. Another mission planned for 21 January was also a victim of the weather, but on the 22nd six Jaguars attacked Iraqi vessels with AS.30L missiles. On 23 January eight Jaguars bombed artillery positions with 250 lb bombs. On 24 January attacks on targets in Iraq were finally permitted, and the Jaguars bombed mechanized units of the Republican Guard. Two days later six Jaguars supported by Mirage F1CR-200s of the *33ème Escadre de Reconnaissance* at Al Ahsa, using their Cyrano IVM-R radar and Uliss-47 INS to provide accurate navigational data, attacked an Iraqi divisional command post and artillery positions in southern Kuwait. The Jaguars

continued operations with attacks on sites at Tallil, Shaiba and Jalibah, firing AS 30L missiles against bridges, and finally hitting battlefield targets as the deadline for the ground war approached. By the end of the war the French Jaguars had flown 615 sorties in 1,088 flying hours. During these strikes the Jaguars had launched sixty-two AS30L missiles and had made 185 'contacts' with Boeing C-135FR tankers of the *93ème Escadre* at Riyadh. The Jaguars began returning to France on 5 March.

Further cuts in Jaguar numbers were made following the Gulf War, and sixty Jaguar A and Es were allocated to the three units of the *7ème Escadre* at St Dizier, with the remainder being placed in storage or sent to ground training units. Jaguars participated in Operation *Aconit*, as part of the UN's joint Operation *Provide Comfort* over Iraq, policing the no-fly zones. This was followed by Operation *Crécerelle* over Bosnia, which began in April 1993 as part of the *Armée de l'Air* contribution to enforce UN Resolution 781 and the air exclusion zone. The Jaguars' main role was to provide an all-round bombing capability as well as reconnaissance over Bosnia-Herzegovina. In June 1994 the French formed part of the UN humanitarian effort in the beleaguered African country of Rwanda, when Jaguar As and ten Mirage F1CR-200s, supported by C-135F tankers, were based at Kisangani Air Base near Goma to provide reconnaissance and air support to ground troops.

Dassault Mirage IVP of Escadron de Reconnaissance Stratégique 1/91 'Gascogne', Jaguar A154 7-HO of Escadron de Chasse 1/7 'Provence', with a MATRA 1000 kg laser-guided bomb on the centre-line and a TAV-38 rangefinder under the nose, and Dassault Rafale-B 304 330-EB of the Centre d'Expériences Aériennes Militaires (CEAM) on 23 June 2005, when EC 1/7 flew the last French Air Force Jaguar sortie. (Armée de l'Air)

CHAPTER SIX

Operation *Granby* and the Gulf War, 1991

The Gulf War could not have been won without air power. Within the grand coalition, the RAF's contribution was substantial. During the campaign, the RAF deployed 158 aircraft and 7,000 personnel to the region. A total of 6,500 sorties were flown during the six-week war, of which 2,000 were offensive missions into Iraq and Kuwait by Tornado GR.1s and Jaguars . . . . The achievements are seemingly endless and were brought about by total commitment, great endeavour and no small amount of personal courage. The end result was a highly effective air campaign which paved the way for a swift and decisive land offensive, proving conclusively the immense reach, flexibility and speed of reaction associated with air power.

Air Marshal Sir Andrew Wilson KGB AFC

Following the Iraqi invasion of Kuwait, thirteen Jaguars at Coltishall were given an overwash of 'desert-sand ARTF' (alkaline removable temporary finish) and despatched to the Gulf on 11 August 1990. Each aircraft carried a Westinghouse AN/ALQ-101 (V) jamming pod and a Phimat chaff dispenser on the outer wing pylons, two Tracor AN/ALE-40 flare dispensers under the rear fuselage and three external fuel tanks. Four of the aircraft were fitted with a BAe recce pod on their centre-line stations. Not all of these aircraft were ideal for operations in desert conditions, and they were regarded as an interim measure until a second, more highly modified batch were prepared for deployment to the Gulf. (RAF Coltishall)

GR.1 XZ372, part of the initial deployment to Oman, 12 August 1991, refuelling from a Victor tanker of 55 Squadron from RAF Marham. During the Gulf War the Victors played an invaluable role, as Mike Rondot recalled: 'We used in-flight refuelling on about half the missions, always with the Victors. They were brilliant, they were always there, they never failed to turn up and they were always in the right place, at the right time, with the right fuel. We just used to pitch up, get in behind them, take our fuel and go away, not a word being said on the radio unless they were in thick cloud. Even then we could get very close using air-to-air TACAN [tactical air navigation], but if you couldn't find them, you had to talk.' (RAF Coltishall)

When Iraq invaded Kuwait on 2 August 1990 and the Saudi Arabian government requested assistance, air power was the only instrument at the disposal of the British government that could get to the Gulf in time and with sufficient force to deter any further aggression by Saddam Hussein. Because of this the RAF was from the outset at the forefront of the British effort, and remained so throughout hostilities. The RAF's contribution to air power in the Gulf – in both crisis and conflict – was second only in importance to that of the United States of America. Within forty-eight hours of the Defence Secretary Tom King's announcement that the government was sending large-scale forces to the Gulf in Operation *Granby*, a squadron of Tornado F.3s arrived in Saudi Arabia, and two hours later they flew their first operational sortie. First word of a possible Jaguar GR.1A deployment from RAF Coltishall came on 8 August. Immediately, the Norfolk station began to generate thirteen aircraft and prepare more than 300 personnel for a rapid move to the Middle East, though at this stage the final destination was unknown. Hectic activity followed during the next forty-eight hours, with all Coltishall personnel working extremely hard to prepare the deploying squadron for possible Gulf operations. The three resident Jaguar squadrons had a rapid-deployment role within NATO, and as such were well practised in the art of swift reaction, and the station's

Jaguar GR.1 taxies out at Muharraq for the aircraft's first big strike of the war.
(via Dave Bagshaw)

Squadron Leader Dave Bagshaw steps down from XX962/X on 8 January 1991, having just completed his 4,000th hour on Jaguars with a 1 hour 20 minute air interdiction flight during Exercise Fish Barrel. *He went on to fly twenty-three missions, including five bombing operations during the Gulf War, when missions flown were code-named after cricketing terms such as* Batsman, Longstop, Bowler *and* Wicket. *The artwork for XX962/X was originally an Arabian woman with two left feet and a white shield with red cross painted by Paul Robins, which was augmented on the starboard side by* Viz *magazine characters the* Fat Slags. *(via Dave Bagshaw)*

previous hard training was now paying off. Operational requirements dictated that the detachment, which would be commanded by Wing Commander Jerry Connolly, OC 6 Squadron, was to be made up of more pilots and ground crew than a normal Jaguar squadron, so the decision was made not to send a single numbered squadron but to make up the unit with personnel from the whole wing at Coltishall. Additional support was provided by crews from 226 OCU at RAF Lossiemouth.

All thirteen Jaguars (a dozen were destined for the Gulf, the thirteenth – XX766 – would remain at Coltishall as a spare) were given an overwash of 'Desert Sand ARTF' (alkaline removable temporary finish), reportedly designed for low-level operations by Philip Barley at the Royal Aircraft Establishment. The desert-pink paint arrived shortly

GR.1 XZ106 armed with four 1,000 lb bombs on tandem beams below each wing, with AIM-9L Sidewinders above and Phimat and ALQ-101 (V) jammer pod at Muharraq during Operation Granby. *(MoD)*

before midnight the day before the Jaguars' departure. It was all hands to the wheel, including the employment of Air Training Corps cadets at summer camp. Remarkably, ten aircraft were sprayed in less than five hours. Pale blue roundels were painted below the cockpits and black serial numbers applied to the rear fuselage. At first, the horde of media representing local, national and overseas interests at the press briefing on 10 August refused to believe that these sandy-coloured weapons of war had not been hidden away until they were shown the

A Jaguar armed with Sidewinders and bombs on the aircraft centre-line taxies out at Muharraq past a Tornado in its hangar. (via Dave Bagshaw)

spray equipment in No. 3 Hangar.

Each aircraft carried a Westinghouse AN/ALQ-101 (V) jamming pod and a French-built Philips-Matra Phimat chaff dispenser on the outer wing pylons, and two Tracor AN/ALE-40 flare dispensers under the rear fuselage. Nine of the thirteen Jaguars were standard GR.1As and carried three external fuel tanks – a 264 gal (1,200-litre) fuel tank on each inner wing pylon and one on the centre-line. (The two inboard wing pylons at first limited the weapons load to a pair of 1,000 lb (454 kg) retarded bombs or 582 lb (264 kg) Hunting/BL753 cluster-bomb weapons under the fuselage.) Four others were fitted with a BAe recce pod on their centre-line stations. All of these aircraft were not ideal for operations in desert conditions, and they were regarded as an interim measure until a second, more highly modified, batch was prepared for deployment to the Gulf. The final decision to move came on 10 August, with the start being scheduled for the morning of the 11th. The destination was then expected to be Oman, although confirmation was still required. (Their actual location would be Thumrait in the southern desert of the Sultanate of Oman, to join the growing number of Coalition aircraft participating in the US-led Operation *Desert Shield*. The training missions with the Omanis would be of great benefit to the RAF pilots, many of whom had not experienced flying in desert conditions.) While intensive training in theatre continued, the pace at Coltishall also ran into overdrive. Amid a flurry of media coverage, XZ263, piloted by Squadron Leader Alex Muskett, was the

GR.1 XX733/R at Muharraq armed with AIM-9L Sidewinders and a Westinghouse ALQ (V)-101 jamming pod and bombs on a tandem beam on the port outboard pylons. (via Dave Bagshaw)

first of the freshly painted *Pink Panther* Jaguars to taxi, and the formation departed Coltishall in four waves for a direct flight, with air-to-air refuelling from Victor tankers, to Cyprus. Wing Commander Jerry Connolly recalls:

They all arrived on time, just after the last of the Tornado F.3s had departed from Cyprus on their way to Saudi Arabia. In the meantime, the airlift of ground crew and equipment from Coltishall commenced using Hercules transport aircraft. On the morning of 13 August all the Jaguars departed Cyprus for a non-stop flight to Thumrait. On this leg we were supported by VC 10 tanker aircraft. All aircraft arrived on time and without incident to be greeted by the ground crew that had already arrived and the host RAF Oman (RAFO) personnel. Thumrait airfield is about forty miles north of the coastal town of Salalah. The base was home to two RAFO operational squadrons, one flying Jaguars and the other Hunters. We were well received by our Omani hosts, who made all their operational facilities available to us. The base is relatively small, and our unexpected arrival, along with 2,000 US personnel, meant that domestic accommodation was at absolute premium. The result was that most of the detachment personnel had to live in conditions not quite up to those we are used to in the UK. However, the amount of work that lay before us did not leave too much time to dwell on such matters!

Throughout this period a constant stream of transport aircraft were arriving at the base laden with the equipment and people that were required to bring the squadron up to operational readiness. Within a couple of days, the detachment, which had now taken the unofficial name of the *Desert Cats*, was holding an operational alert posture, conducting operational flying and ground training and was over 400 strong. Plans and procedures were devised to ensure that we could readily fly operational missions to the Saudi/Kuwait border should the Iraqi forces move into Saudi Arabia. Although the base was some way from the potential battle area, operational missions were quite feasible, yet the surrounding area afforded the perfect arena for operational flying training.

The days soon turned to weeks, and with the expectation of a few tense periods, it became apparent that Iraq did not intend to move any further down the Gulf. However, we continued apace with our training programme and refined our tactics to cater for this very different operating environment. Probably most notable were operations in very hot temperatures. We arrived in Oman at the hottest time of the year; daily high temperatures were often in excess of 45C. We rewrote the aircraft operating manual and all the detachment personnel had to learn how to cope with such high temperatures, yet still get the job done. Good personal care and adherence to the advice given by the medics resulted in not a single case of sunburn or heat exhaustion but some excellent suntans! A final note on this subject is that the maximum temperature we recorded during this period was 70C one lunchtime in the field kitchen!

The long process of waiting was now under way and the UK force build-up was moving ahead with much vigour. The HQ in Riyadh reviewed the disposition of forces, and as a result it was decided to move the Jaguar squadron north to Bahrain [to Muharraq International Airport to allow the Jaguars to become fully integrated into the Coalition command structure, while Tornado GR.1s from Germany took

Flight Lieutenant Pete 'Frog' Tholen back from a mission. Left is Squadron Leader Dick Midwinter. Alex Emtage has his back to the camera. Note the AIM-9L Sidewinder missile stencilled beside the two black bombs below the cockpit. Two Sidewinders were fired in anger and one accidentally by the JagDet during the Gulf War. (via Dave Bagshaw)

Warrant Officer Mick Cartwright drew the line at foul language painted on the bombs, but this did not prevent the lineys coming up with some excellent gallows humour about 41 Squadron 'landscape gardeners' and the like. Mick got a message off himself, pointing out to Saddam how he had screwed up Christmas, New Year and possibly Easter. It was delivered by Flight Lieutenant Dave 'Footy' Foote at the second attempt. (Mick Cartwright)

Jaguars taxi in at Muharraq after a bombing mission in Kuwait. (via Dave Bagshaw)

Mission completed! Squadron Leader Alex Emtage moves to shake the hand of Squadron Leader Ted Stringer after his first mission in Buster Gonad and his Unfeasibly Large Testicles, *which Flying Officer Paul Robins painted on the nose of XZ118/Y after he was approached by Jaguar pilot Flight Lieutenant Steve Thomas.* Buster Gonad *was one of several* Viz *magazine characters that were painted on the Jags by Paul Robins, whose choice of paint was largely restricted to red, black and white, so other colours had to be acquired in the back streets of Bahrain. (via Dave Bagshaw)*

their place at Thumrait] to join a Tornado squadron that was already there. Thus, some two months after the move into the Gulf, the *Desert Cats* had to pack their bags and move the whole operation yet again. However, mobility is an integral part of our lives and this move was a rapid and unqualified success. It was also unique in that the total airlift was provided by the USAF air transport squadron at Thumrait,

a great success for co-operation between the Allies. The move was completed in four days and throughout the squadron maintained its alert posture and continued flying training.

Life in Bahrain was quite different. From the operational viewpoint we were more fully integrated into the Allied command and control structure on a daily basis. From the domestic viewpoint life could not have been more different. The spartan accommodation in Thumrait gave way to a comfortable hotel [the Diplomat] with all modern facilities. It took some time for most of the *Desert Cats* to get over the culture shock! However, the

GR.1 XZ356/N with BAe recce pod at Muharraq. The aircraft carried the wing commander's pennant of the 'Boss', Wing Commander William Pixton AFC, and the Mary Rose *nose art was painted by Chris Froome. (via Dave Bagshaw)*

Squadron Leader Dave Bagshaw flying XX725/T, which carried the Viz *magazine character* Johnny Fartpants, *painted on the forward fuselage by Paul Robins. The final bomb log registered sixty-four 1,000 lb bombs and thirty-six CBUs dropped and a CVR-7 rocket cluster. (Mike Rondot via Dave Bagshaw)*

continuing threat from Iraq and the intransigence of Saddam Hussein were ever present factors in our daily lives, so we continued to carefully practise and rehearse our flying and ground operations as the days crept towards the UN deadline.

Much happened since those heady days in early August! However, from the very outset, RAF Coltishall and the Jaguar force proved that the rapid projection of air power could play a most vital role in the deterrence of potential aggression. We shall never really know whether Saddam Hussein intended to move further into the Gulf States, but our ability to respond rapidly, in concert with our Allies, undoubtedly made him reassess the situation. We were, and still are, very proud of the real contribution we made to the international condemnation of naked military aggression.

On 27 October the first of the dozen Jaguars arrived back at Coltishall, where another twelve aircraft and twenty-two pilots[27] of 41 (Composite) Squadron, commanded by Wing Commander William Pixton AFC, were waiting to fly out to Oman as roulement. The twelve aircraft had been modified to what became known as the *Granby* Stage 3 Upgrades, and the rapid modification was to become one of Operation *Granby*'s most

GR.1A XZ358/W Diplomatic Service *reflected in a rain-soaked Muharraq. (Mick Cartwright)*

remarkable features as far as the RAF was concerned. The official name of the modification programme was 'Fast Track', although those on the ground soon realized the change of name to 'Operation Goalpost' was more appropriate – because the size kept changing! The Jaguar Detachment (JagDet)'s aircraft had Adour Mk 104 engines modified for greater thrust and improved hot-weather performance after they had been engineered for higher turbine temperatures (from 700 to 725 °C). The ARI-18223 RHWR was upgraded to 'Sky Guardian 200-13PD' standard to improve detection capability and identify scanning pulse-Doppler radars at long range, and a Vinten colour HUD video recording facility was installed in place of the mono wet film system.

The offensive capability, which comprised two internal 30 mm ADEN cannon with 150 rounds each, was increased when all the aircraft were fitted with overwing missile pylons, reportedly obtained by the MoD from the SOAF, to permit the carriage of Sidewinder AIM-9L missiles. This feature was first incorporated in former RAF aircraft supplied to India but was not previously applied to the GR.1A version as used by the RAF. Weapons stations, which would normally have been used to carry the AIM-9, were occupied by a Westinghouse ECM pod (port outer) and a Phimat chaff dispenser (starboard outer). The AAM modification had been trialled on XZ385 of 54 Squadron at A&AEE Boscombe Down in September 1990, and within a week had been approved for use by the Jaguars in the Gulf.

The 41 (Composite) Squadron aircraft were also fitted with the revised AN/ALQ-101 (V)-10 noise/deception jammer, which uses a ventral gondola to increase the pod's capacity and detection frequency coverage, and Phimat chaff pod and twin Tracor AN/ALE-40 flare dispensers. AN/ALE-40 had been modified to fire Type 118 and M206 flares, which burn hotter and longer, and the firing configuration was modified to permit the firing of flares even with the undercarriage in the 'down' position. Other new innovations included a Mk XII Mode 4 IFF and a Magnavox AN/ARC-164 *Have Quick* frequency-hopping UHF in place of the little-used stand-by UHF system to complement the standard ARI 233 15/4 set. A larger single UHF T-shaped blade aerial replaced the twin homing VHF aerial arrangement mounted behind the canopy. The wing leading edges were treated with SWAM (surface-wave radar-absorbent material), and RAM (radar-absorbent material) tiles were fitted to the engine intakes to help reduce their radar cross-section. All the Jaguar windscreens were treated with a coating of gold film to help minimize radar detection, while the forward warning panels and the meter hanging from the bracing strip were deleted to improve pilot visibility. While the overall colour of the aircraft remained 'pink', the serial numbers were now white. Seven of these aircraft[28] arrived at Muharraq on 23 October and five more[29] on 2 November. Aircraft such as XZ358/W *Diplomatic Service* and XZ356/N *Mary Rose* were tasked with pre- and post-strike reconnaissance, using the standard BAe Dynamics Series 401 infra-red linescan system (IRLS) reconnaissance pod, but with its vertical linescan unit replaced by an F126 survey camera. XZ106/O was fitted with a lightweight Vinten 18 Series 600 LOROP (long-range oblique photography) pod designed for recce tasks from medium level, which had been hurriedly cleared for service, as the RAF urgently needed a stand-off reconnaissance capability.

During the autumn of 1990 a series of United Nations resolutions were passed imposing sanctions on Iraq in an attempt to persuade Saddam Hussein to withdraw his forces peacefully. The diplomatic effort culminated in UN Resolution 678 authorizing

A heavily armed F-14A Tomcat of VF-41 'Black Aces' with an AIM-54C Phoenix long-range AAM below the fuselage centre-line, from the nuclear-powered Theodore Roosevelt *(CVN-71) photographed on 23 January 1991 by RAF Squadron Leader Mike Rondot from his 41 Squadron Jaguar, XZ358,* Diplomatic Service, *near Faylaka Island, ten miles east of Kuwait City. (Mike Rondot)*

'use of all necessary means' to evict Iraqi military forces from Kuwait after a deadline set for 15 January 1991. In the meanwhile, the Coalition forces commenced their work-up period, which for the Jaguars entailed regular low-flying exercises. During a formation join-up manoeuvre in the desert in Qatar, 100 miles south of Bahrain, on 13 November Flight Lieutenant Keith Collister of 54 Squadron was killed when his GR.1A (XX754) flew into a low ridge 87 ft above ground level. On 27 November Jaguar pilots Flight Lieutenant Dave Foote and Squadron Leader Dave Bagshaw and 41 Squadron engineering personnel led by 53-year-old Warrant Officer Mick Cartwright landed at Bahrain in a Hercules at 03.00 hours, having left Coltishall on a typically balmy Norfolk day on the 26th. A few months earlier he had been flown back from Bergstrom AFB, Texas, where he had been among those comfortably installed as 41 Squadron's Jaguars were pitching their recce skills against the Americans and Australians in RAM 90 (Reconnaissance Air Meet). He had returned to Coltishall after a night stop at Gander while an engine on the Hercules was changed, and then to Lyneham, followed by a bumpy ride back to Norfolk in a minibus. The long flight to Bahrain was no less uncomfortable, with everyone trying to settle down on para seats along the left side of the Hercules, as Cartwright recalls:

Footy gave me two yellow pills which he said would knock me out all the way to

Bahrain, but I decided to take them after the Akrotiri refuelling stop, where I wanted to introduce Steve Farrow to the Sergeants' Mess following his promotion. After Akrotiri I took my pills. They worked! Someone shook me awake. 'Are we here already?' Of course we weren't. The Herc had a radar problem and we were back in Akrotiri. But Baggers, who also took two yellow pills, remained out of it throughout the wait.

Soft-spoken and bewhiskered 54-year-old Squadron Leader Dave Bagshaw was born on 28 February 1937 in Flin Flon, Northern Manitoba, the eldest of nine. His first active tour with 41 Squadron terminated in September 1979 when he was posted back to the OCU at Lossiemouth, becoming at the same time the Jaguar display pilot for 1980. In July 1984 Baggers began his second tour on 41 Squadron at Coltishall. He regularly flew the Jaguar on exercises in Norway, as well as many other locations, including Nellis, Nevada, for *Red Flag*, and occasionally to Canada and Cold Lake for *Maple Flag*. On 29 November Baggers flew the first of his twenty-nine sorties in the period up to 10 January 1991. On 31 December he received an AFC in the New Year Honours List, and on 8 January he set a record that is unlikely to ever be beaten when he logged his 4,000th hour on the Jaguar. Mick Cartwright continues:

At Bahrain it was the usual routine with everyone running around like headless chickens. A quick briefing and then to the hotel, our home for as long as it took. It was a grand establishment called the Diplomat. We had been told that there would be no more roulements, so we were there until the job was done. I reflected that this was not what we had been training for over the last six years. It was considerably warmer than the Arctic and my accommodation was unusually palatial. And if things got serious, we stood a better chance of survival here than at Bardufoss. Lying on my king-size bed I thought it best to accept the situation philosophically. The handover from 6 Squadron was straightforward and we took up the challenge. December continued much the same as November, with lots of flying and constant

moving around until we arrived at three fixed operating sites: hangar (Chris Tracey), airport (Tony Tagg) and parade ground (myself), each with four aircraft. It was a system which served us well. During this period we were inundated with gift parcels and cards, all of which had to be acknowledged. Some were particularly touching, especially

Bombs dropped by Squadron Leader Mike Rondot exploding on the target in Kuwait. (Mike Rondot)

those from the local schools around Coltishall. One card arrived showing a picture of an attractive lady with very little on, asking if she could write to somebody. I handed it to one of my electricians, and one thing led to another. To the best of my knowledge, they are still married! December 2 was Scud Sunday. I was in Ops with Wing Commander Jerry Connolly, OC 6 Squadron, and all the station hierarchy for the morning briefing, listening to all the gloom and doom about Tornado serviceability. Our twelve aircraft were all fine, as always. The door opened and a Regiment guy poked his head in and informed us that the Iraqis had launched a Scud missile. All eyes turned to the front but nothing was said. A few minutes later, the same chap came in again and said another Scud had been launched. Eyes front again, response much the same as before. I looked across at OC 6 Squadron: 'Shouldn't we be doing something?' I asked. From that moment, action. We returned to the flight line with instructions to arm and make ready. Warrant Officer Vern Watkin and 6 [Squadron] offered their help but I thought no – if we can't cope, we shouldn't be here. All aircraft were soon up and ready, armed to conform to the mission profile of low level. All the pilots were strapped in and waiting. OC 6 Squadron told me that the situation was not as serious as we first thought but we were to go ahead, treating it as real. Boss [Wing Commander William Pixton, OC 41 Squadron] arrived in the early hours of 3 December. I met him for breakfast,

JagDet at Muharraq during Operation Granby. *Front l-r (sitting): SENGO; Phil Goodhall; Henry Bradshaw (GLO); Flight Lieutenant Pete Livesey; Major Pat King (GLO1), Flight Lieutenant Dave Foote; Wing Commander (later Group Captain) William Pixton; Squadron Leaders Ted Stringer; Mike Rondot and Dave Bagshaw AFC. Middle Row (standing): Squadron Leader Chris Allam; SQUINTO; Flight Lieutenant Mike Seares; Toby Craig; Steve Thomas; Steve Shutt; Squadron Leader Dick Midwinter. Back Row: Intelligence officer; Mark Hopkins; u/k EWO; Roger Crowder; Squadron Leader Mike Gordon; Bob Neilson, Ops Officer; Pete 'Frog' Tholen; Craig Hill; Nick Collins; Simon Young; R.M.J. 'Dick' McCormac; Alex Emtage. On wall, Malcolm Rainier. (via Dave Bagshaw)*

Jaguar GR.1 with a single CBU on pylon. In the foreground are Roger Crowder and Mike Rondot by the nosewheel, Mal Rainier at the top of the ladder and Alex Emtage at the bottom of the ladder. Pete Tholen is flanked on his right by Bob Neilson, Ops Officer, Steve Shutt and Craig Hill. Far right is Wing Commander William Pixton. (via Dave Bagshaw)

gave him a full briefing as I saw it and then we both enjoyed our omelettes and went our separate ways: him to bed, me to work. The first major change following Boss's arrival was the dropping of the low-level missions in favour of medium level. The pilots cheered up immediately.

William Pixton, or 'Billy P' as he was known, would encourage debate about tactics and would consult all pilots, listen to their arguments and then reach his decision, based on those arguments. It was decided that medium-level missions would offer better protection from the threat of AAA and shoulder-launched SAMs on combat missions. As well as friendly fighters there was SEAD (suppression of enemy air defences) provided by USAF EF-111A Ravens jamming Iraqi radars, while F-4G *Wild Weasels* were ready to engage any SAM site that showed signs of launching. There was also a constant commentary on SAM/MA threats and enemy fighter activity by E-3 Sentry AWACS and EC-130E ABCCC (airborne battlefield command and control centre).

With the decision to change to medium level, the retard tails on the 1,000 lb (454 kg) bombs were replaced by free-fall fins. The Hunting BL755 cluster-bomb unit (CBU), which can only be delivered effectively from low level, was replaced by the Bristol Aerospace (Canada) LAU-5003B/A pod containing nineteen CRV-7 2.75 in. (7 cm) high-velocity rocket projectiles. The CRV-7, which underwent proving trials in the UK in late 1990 and was cleared for operational use, was used from the outset. The pod and nineteen rocket projectiles, which can be fired singly or in a 'ripple', has a total weight of just 530 lb (240 kg), and aircraft carried two of the pods per mission. Because of its high speed of around Mach 4, CRV-7 is accurate over ranges of 6,000 metres, but a hurried integration with the Jaguar's weapons-aiming computer resulted in inaccurate deliveries and it was temporarily withdrawn from the inventory. (Ferranti provided rewritten software within two weeks and CRV-7 was soon reinstated.) As an interim measure the American CBU-87 Rockeye II cluster-bomb, which unlike BL755 could be released from the new operating height above 10,000 ft (2,626 m) was introduced with effect from 29 January, although it was too long for more than one to be carried on a twin-carrier beam. Flight Lieutenant Alex Emtage recalled, 'It's really quite vicious. Excellent against troops; excellent against soft-skinned vehicles, ammo storages if they are not that hardened, petrol stores and that sort of thing. I wouldn't like to be anywhere near it when it went off.' (It was not long into the war before a single fuel tank was attached under the fuselage and twin carriers fitted to the inner pylons to allow the weapons load to be doubled.) Most bombing missions were flown thus: the weapons fused for air burst, impact or delayed action. Paveway II laser-guided bombs were also trialled for use by the Jaguar, but they were not carried during the war.

Squadron Leader Chris M. Allam, one of the new arrivals in November who had

Artwork for XZ364/Q Sadman, *with Saddam Hussein getting the boot, was inspired by Douglas Bader's Hurricane of 242 Squadron at Coltishall in the Second World War, which showed Hitler getting a kick up the rea A replica of this Hurricane was unveiled in July 1989 on a roundabout near the guardhouse at the Norfolk station Paul Robins began sketching the design on the Jaguar la at night under torchlight, and at daybreak he and Chris Froome filled in the lines with colour. With forty-seven bomb symbols,* Sadman *had the highest sortie rate of any RAF aircraft in Operation* Granby, *dropping ninety-six 1,000 lb bombs and forty-one CBUs, and firing thirty-eight CVR-7 rockets. (via Dave Bagshaw)*

been told to expect a detachment of six months, had soon settled down and worked hard to learn from the pilots who had been flying in the Gulf for three months.

We learnt how demanding flying over the desert is at extremely low levels, brushed up our air-to-air refuelling skills and took part in numerous exercises with other

Squadron Leader Dave Bagshaw and Flight Lieutenant Pete Livesey, the pilots who flew recce, in front of XX733/R at Muharraq towards the end of the Gulf War. The artwork showing 'Baggers' in the cockpit of a pink Spitfire was the personal favourite of Paul Robins, who painted it over a four-day period during the final week of the Gulf War from sketches he had prepared earlier in the campaign on scraps of paper. The creation was finished only thirty minutes before the cease-fire was declared. Initially Robins's idea was to have an archetypal moustachioed RAF pilot leaning out of a biplane. (via Dave Bagshaw)

Diplomatic Service, *which was painted on the nose of XZ358/W, got its name from the Hotel Diplomat in Muharraq where the JagDet personnel were accommodated during Operation* Granby. *Six black 'SLR camera' silhouettes denoted reconnaissance missions flown. XZ358 also dropped twenty-two 1,000 lb bombs and four CBUs. (via Mick Cartwright)*

Jaguar GR.1 XZ367/P originally had a caricature called Debbie, *which was painted by Paul Robins and named after the wife of David Albert Hall, a member of the JagDet engineering team. It was replaced later with a white rose painted by Chris Froome. (via Mick Cartwright)*

JagDet line-up at Muharraq. The tail far right is XZ364 XZ364/Q Sadman. *Next left is XZ356/N* Mary Rose, *then XX962/X, followed by XZ118/Y* Buster Gonad and his Unfeasibly Large Testicles, *XZ119/Z* Katrina Jane; *XX733/R* Baggers *and XZ367/P* White Rose. *(via Dave Bagshaw)*

Bomb log on the side of XX748/U. The stencil of the Sidewinder top row fourth from left has 'Oopps?' on the fin. (via Mick Cartwright)

Coalition air forces. Life was not all hard work. Bahrain is a most cosmopolitan island, allowing them all to relax fully when away from work. Christmas came and went with us all hoping that diplomacy would resolve the impasse. As the UN deadline of 15 January approached we reduced our flying commitment, allowing pilots to become fully familiar with the numerous documents and plans associated with operations. This cutback on flying allowed the engineers and support staff to prepare the aircraft. It also meant that the squadron was fully rested should the worst happen. During the last few weeks prior to the UN deadline we introduced into RAF service the Canadian CRV-7 rocket, with most pilots having the opportunity to fire a few training rounds on King Fahd Weapon Range in Saudi Arabia. Much time was also spent discussing tactics. Discussion on all tactical matters was encouraged, based on the premise that no one has a monopoly on good ideas, and many of the younger pilots showed fine tactical thinking. Obviously the major discussion point was of low- or high-speed operations. Initially, we thought we would fly at low level, as this is how we had trained over the years and our aircraft and weapons were optimized for that role. We were, therefore, leaning towards the opinion that you fight the way you train. However, for targets in the KTO, we had to penetrate over the densely packed ground forces that Iraq had deployed. The devastating amount of AAA and small-arms fire that were ranged against us effectively ruled out the low-level option, and we therefore took the high-level

Bomb log and Arabian woman nose art on the port side of XX962/X. The Fat Slags *artwork was applied to the starboard side of the nose during the Gulf War. (via Mick Cartwright)*

choice from day one. Bonuses from this tactic were easier target acquisition and increased radius of action, and of course we also had the CVR-7 rocket, which is delivered from medium level.

The days slipped by; the tension increased as it finally sank in to most of us that we would probably be involved in some form of conflict. We ceased flying on the day before the UN deadline. The engineers prepared the aircraft with war loads: 1,000 lb bombs, CRV-7 rocket pods, AIM-9L missiles, full chaff and flare pods, and we all sat and waited, expecting the worst but hoping for a last-minute diplomatic solution. We felt should the need arise we were as ready as you ever can be to go to war.

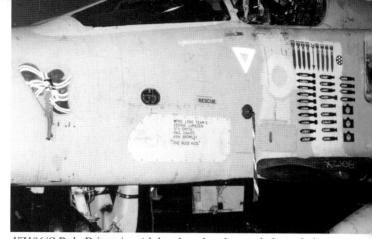

XZ106/O Rule Britannia *with bomb and rocket symbols, including a stencil of an AIM-9L Sidewinder (top row) marked 'Truck' because the pilot who accidentally fired it claimed he was aiming at an enemy vehicle! During the Gulf War an F-15 pilot locked onto a very low-level target, which he thought was a helicopter, travelling at about 100 knots, and fired a Sparrow. He followed the missile to observe results and to his amazement it homed onto, and destroyed, a car speeding down the Baghdad highway. His ground crew marked the kill by painting a car symbol on the side of his aircraft. The AIM-9L could home onto targets from any aspect, whereas the earlier models were effective only for stern attacks where the missile seeker head could lock onto the heat of the engine exhaust. (via Mick Cartwright)*

Then the war started. Warrant Officer Mick Cartwright, who had more than thirty-five years' service, recalls:

Here we go, I thought. I had never imagined it would come to this but we had to get on with it. I was nearly 54, with a year left to serve, and I realized that I was about to embark on something I'd remember for the rest of my life. Our first mission on the 17th was led by 'Strike' [Squadron Leader Mike Gordon], with Stevie

XZ375/S The Guardian reader *bombed up with four 1,000 lb free-fall bombs, one of which is suitably inscribed 'Chris's Crusher' by an armourer, at its parade ground dispersal at Muharraq. (via Mick Cartwright)*

T[homas], Roger [Crowder] and Mal [Rainier] completing the four-ship. I wished them all well with a handshake and a pat on the helmet, a gesture I tried to repeat on all the pilots' first missions.

The four Jaguar pilots were given an Iraqi army barracks in Kuwait as their target, with each aircraft carrying overwing AIM-9Ls with auxiliary fuel tanks being carried on the inner wing stations. This left only the centre-line hardpoint available for the carriage of two 1,000 lb free-fall bombs. (Within days, the configuration was changed, the underwing fuel tanks being replaced by tandem beams and the centre-line station devoted to the carriage of fuel, so that up to four 1,000 lb bombs could be carried in tandem pairs under each wing. Fusing options varied depending on the target, with airburst, impact and delayed action being employed.)

Squadron Leader Chris Allam had had a tense disturbed night's sleep, woken at 2 a.m. by aircraft getting airborne from Muharraq. Allam opened the curtains of his comfortable hotel room and saw reheat from Tornadoes on their first war mission. His thoughts ranged from 'Oh, Bugger' to the definitely unprintable. Allam decided that sleep now was impossible:

> We had all been briefed on the Air Task Order some days before the deadline expired. Even so I was surprised when I was woken on the morning of the 17 January to the sound of Tornadoes getting airborne on their first mission. I switched on the television to watch CNN. Already it seemed; judging by the news reports, that Iraq was on fire: surely no nation could survive this massive onslaught! The night raids had had their desired effect and Saddam Hussein would soon be surrendering. Relief, I would not be needed to fly. However, once at work, more realistic thinking took over.

Wing Commander William Pixton recorded in his diary on Thursday 17 January 1991 –

All the JagDet pilots pose for the camera on XZ364/Q Sadman *with its forty-seven bomb symbols denoting the highest number of missions of any aircraft in the Gulf War.*
(via Dave Bagshaw)

The JagDet returned to RAF Coltishall on 12 and 13 March 1991 at the end of the Leopard Trail from Iraq. Four aircraft, including XZ119/Z Katrina Jane, which returned in the first wave on the 12th, and XX115 (behind), which was part of the initial deployment to Oman, in August 1991, took off from Coltishall on the 13th to join up to make a full twelve-ship 'return'. (Author)

Squadron Leader Dave Bagshaw touches down in XX733/R on 13 March 1991 at the end of the Leopard Trail from Iraq and a stop along the way at Akrotiri in Cyprus. Five years later XX733 crashed on take-off at RAF Coltishall, on 23 January 1996, when Flight Lieutenant Greg Noble of 41 Squadron was killed. (Author)

XZ118/Y Buster Gonad and his Unfeasibly Large Testicles *returns to Coltishall on 13 March 1991. (Author)*

XZ367/P White Rose with its 18 ft (5.5 m) diameter brake 'chute deployed after touching down at Coltishall. (Author)

Sadman *touches down at Coltishall on 13 March 1991 and deploys the 'chute. (Author)*

Day 1:

War has broken out. I can't believe it! It's 04.00 local and Kuwaitis are in the foyer of the hotel watching CNN – like an insomniac football crowd! Got to work at 04.15. Air Raid warning Red, NBC state Black – soon All Clear. Tornadoes are on their second wave. 1st wave all returned to base safely. Shortly afterwards I hear that all the second wave aircraft have returned to base safely – so far no RAF losses.

Jaguar pilots quite excited at the prospect and we wait our turn keenly – some more than others. 3rd Tornado wave gets airborne – still no Jaguar tasking. I am holding four Jaguars on 30 minutes readiness for combat search and rescue (CSAR), four on 30 minutes ground alert close air support (GCAS) and four on 60 minutes GCAS. CNN in the briefing room is like the Ben Hur epic.

1st Tornado lost. It looks as if they got out but the mood in the Squadron has changed – much more subdued. I am offered the first Jaguar tasking by Riyadh – and told I have a choice whether to accept or not! This is an unbelievable and unexpected responsibility. It dawns on me that the fate of the Jaguar pilots rests largely on my shoulders – wibble. With some trepidation I accept the CAS tasking, give it to Squadron Leader Mike Gordon's four-ship (Flight Lieutenant Steve Thomas, Flying Officer Mal Rainier and Flight Lieutenant Roger Crowder) – they are the ones holding the 30-minute GCAS slot – and go off to worry.

Squadron Leader Chris Allam continues:

It was just like a tactical evaluation, I thought, as I sat listening to the electronic warfare officer's (EWO), Intelligence Officer's (IO) and ground liaison officer's (GLO) briefs. With the other members of my constituted four I went through the air task message, which had details of our mission. We were to standby on 30-minute ground alert for close air support (CAS). We planned and briefed the mission, went to the aircraft and put them on state and then returned to the Squadron Operations room to await the message to go. We were all immensely relieved when the first Tornado mission arrived safely back at Bahrain. Hopefully our mission would go equally as well. After about six hours on ground alert my mission was stood down, the tension was lifted, jokes were told and we are soon on our way back to the hotel. It was only after we have been back at the hotel for some time that we learned that one of the Jaguar missions has been launched into the Kuwait theatre of operation. They had all successfully bombed the target but better still all had returned safely.

William Pixton had watched their IFF squawk out and back on the local Rapier's secondary radar kit, but he was unable to tell if all four were returning until they were within VHF range. Relieved, he wrote, 'They're all safe. After they land it's like "Top Gun". All our troops come out to greet the returning pilots – an emotional moment. End of Day One. Everyone OK. TOTAL JAGUAR SORTIES: 4.'

Squadron Leader Chris Allam concludes:

That evening we all gathered in the Boss's room in the hotel to congratulate the pilots on their successful mission and they in turn passed on lessons learnt from the mission: 'Don't go around for a reattack on the target; Don't go below 10,000 ft, otherwise the anti-aircraft artillery fire becomes intense.' No, they hadn't been threatened by the Iraqi Air Force. All they had heard from the airborne warning and control was 'Picture clear!' It seemed that the decision to fly at high level was correct, so we would continue like that at least for the next few missions.[30]

On Friday 18 January Wing Commander William Pixton and his four-ship of Flight Lieutenant Pete 'Frog' Tholen, Ted Stringer and Nick Collins flew the first Jaguar bombing mission. Pixton wrote:

Our primary target is 'out' due to bad weather so we end up after a Republican Guard outfit just west of the Kuwait/Iraq border. With the weather this bad I can, quite legitimately, bring 'Team Tab' home – but could you return from Mission-1 still fully bombed up? I call up the AWACS and offer our services. The AWACS comes back immediately: 'We've got a fast FAC who needs some help from fighters carrying Mk 83s [Jaguars carrying 1,000 pounders, nearly].' The word 'help' is just too emotive to ignore.

XX748/U passes the 41 Squadron hangar as it taxies by at RAF Coltishall on 13 March 1991. (Steve Jefferson)

Flight Lieutenant Stevie Thomas, pilot of XZ118/Y Buster Gonad and his Unfeasibly Large Testicles*, receives a hero's welcome from his wife at Coltishall on 13 March 1991. (Steve Jefferson)*

The AWACS controller puts us in contact with the FAC, who is flying an OA-10. We check-in on his frequency and he's quick to tell us: 'I've been in the target area once already and it's a bit thick with Triple A and SAMs, but never mind.' Never mind is not the phrase I would choose – is he attempting British understatement for our benefit? He goes on, 'I've got some targets for you. I'll run in from the west. I'm going to descend until I break cloud – how far out are you now?'

The plan is for the FAC to enter the target area from the west, fire a smoke rocket at the selected target and pull-off into cloud and head back west. We should break cloud a few seconds later from the south and bomb the marked target – simple. Now thirty-odd miles into Iraq, with about ten miles to run to target, we are flying at

Eight of the Desert Pink Jaguars at Coltishall on 13 March 1991, with XX962/X Fat Slags *nearest the camera. (Steve Jefferson)*

25,000 ft in pairs trail, wingmen in close formation. I start to wonder what the hell I'm doing here and I haven't thought of a good answer when it's time for us to start descending. Pete calls and asks, incredulously: 'Are we going down?'

'Affirm.' What else can I say? I've talked us into this and I can't think of a dignified way out. If the FAC is happy to return to the target area it can't be all that bad – can it?

At that moment the FAC must have broken cloud, down at 10,000 ft, because the radio was immediately jammed out by his transmission: 'Abort. Abort. Abort.' And then again, more urgently: 'Abort! Abort! Abort!' There is some tension in his voice as he reports, 'Be advised, I was getting AAA shot at me!'

We are still descending, passing 12,000 and going to break cloud at any moment. I now know that it's time for us to leave, and quickly. We have reached the FAC's inertial position of the target and I tell him that we are going to live jettison our weapons. Feeling that a small amount of sense had returned to my cockpit I call Pete: 'Frog, pickle 'em off.' We don't break cloud and the bombs fall somewhat north of the target's inertial position.

So far it hasn't entered my (tiny) mind that if the FAC was taking fire then someone might shoot at us too. Then I hear the three words that threatened to be my undoing: 'Boss triple A.' I look over my shoulder at Pete and a football-sized yellow 'something' flies vertically between our aircraft and explodes above and between our fins. I brake hard up and right to get away from what I realize is particularly hostile fire. Almost immediately I lose Pete in the cloud. In my haste to escape this rather inhospitable piece of airspace my normal consideration for my Number 2 has deserted me. Ditto my feather-light aircraft handling. I have selected full dry power, rolled into the turn

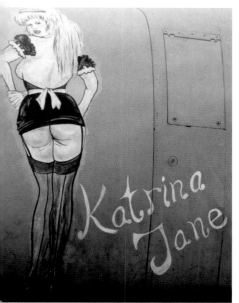

XZ119/Z Katrina Jane. *In the Gulf* Katrina Jane *was flown by Flying Officer (now Group Captain) R.M.J. 'Dick' McCormac, Flying Officer (now Squadron Leader) Mal Rainier and Flying Officer (now Squadron Leader) Nick Collins. (via Mick Cartwright)*

and pulled – HARD. Just to increase my adrenaline flow the RWR tells me that a number of threats are taking an interest in my progress. The extra flush of adrenaline makes me pull even harder and I succeed in pulling off just about all of my aircraft's energy. I am now much lower and slower than I want to be, on my own and still some thirty miles the wrong side of the border.

My alpha-warner warbles insistently, confirming my aircraft's lack of energy, but despite this clearly recognizable warning I am unable to reduce the back pressure – such is the power of fear. I know I need to turn right and to climb, and my right hand moves the stick to the right and hard back but I am unable to apply anything other than full control inputs, regardless of the complaints of my aircraft. Eventually, with the stall-warner going off and the RWR alarm (real or imagined) sounding, I realize that I am in deep trouble and seriously close to losing control of the aircraft. Forty miles ago I should have said, 'Sorry, the weather's not fit – we'll come back tomorrow!' But he needed help, and this was my Mission-1. Stupid!

At last common sense penetrates the fog in my mind and I decide to get rid of the tanks in the hope that this will improve the aircraft's performance – they are 'drop' tanks, after all. I also considered using the burners. They increase the IR signature, but in cloud? I use them. At the same time my brain re-engages with my right hand and gives the aircraft back a bit. At last I stagger up to 20,000 ft and head for home. I hear the other three members of my formation crossing the border while I still have ten miles to go and I realize with relief that they at least had enough sense to 'fly the aircraft'.

Whether we hit anything when we dropped our bombs, I'll never know. What I do know is that my first encounter with the enemy frightened me almost senseless. I will never forget looking at that yellow globe and wondering what it was, and I will always be amazed by how long it took me to register that it was AAA, and by the strength of reaction once realization dawned. I've been a combat-ready Jaguar pilot for years – but today for the first time, I understand what it means.

End of Day Two. Everyone still OK. TOTAL JAGUAR SORTIES: 11.

Better weather on 19 January resulted in the first full day's operations for the Jaguars, and twenty sorties involving four separate missions were scheduled. The first was launched at 04.25 hours with an eight-ship attack on SA-2 SAM and AAA sites. One of the pilots in this formation was Flight Lieutenant (later Group Captain) Mike Seares, who was flying his first ever Jaguar operational mission. Two days earlier he and fellow Jaguar pilots had all gone out in a buoyant mood to greet the first eight-ship as they returned. But as Seares was to recall:

The smiles were soon wiped from our faces when we realized that two of the aircraft had fired their air-to-air missiles and two were without their centre-line fuel tanks. Had they got involved in some incredible dogfight just off the coast of Kuwait? Beads of sweat were now emerging on our foreheads as we realized that tomorrow we were up for the same thing. They'd survived, though, so why shouldn't we?

Our mission was led by Flight Lieutenant Stevie Thomas; QWI, hard man and just the sort you wanted up the front to instill confidence in us more junior types. We were to attack a SAM-2 site in the Kuwait theatre of operations (KTO), a mad mission if you applied Cold War logic to it, as we were going in at medium level and there was no chance of us climbing above the missile engagement envelope. Anticipation and nervous trepidation hung over the briefing like a cloud, but now that we were ready it was just a case of wanting to get the job done.

We outbriefed with some last-minute intelligence and a pat on the back from the GLO, Pat King, then wandered out to the aircraft dispersed behind concrete revetments at Muharraq International Airport, our new home in Bahrain. My walkround checks were a little more thorough than usual and the four 1,000 lb bombs hanging from the tandem beams on my inboard pylons got a very close inspection. As I strapped in, though, and started my left to rights it became readily apparent that this jet was very unserviceable and was going nowhere. To cries of 'I just don't believe it' and 'not today of all days', I rushed for the spare, cursing the fact that I'd just lost all my extra walk time and was now in a complete rush to make the check-in. I briefed the liney to do the externals and make sure all the pins were out as I strapped in and fired up as quickly as I could – just the way you want it on your first operational mission, I don't think. Still, there was no time for worry now, and as we taxied out I was as fully focused on what lay ahead.

Stevie called, 'Keeper 01 ready for take-off' and Air Traffic enquired as to how long we would be away – no answer was the reply for obvious reasons as we got airborne and departed to the north. There was rather too much cloud around for my liking, and as I led the back four up the transit corridor we went IMC at about 10,000 ft with only the air-to-air tacan as our friend, in ten-second pairs trail as an eight-ship. This definitely wasn't what we had practised day to day on the work-up, but this was war and it would surely get better as we approached the KTO. The word from the front was that we would press on to the target area, descend to a minimum of 15,000 ft and if we didn't get sight of the ground, RTB. We checked in with AWACs, were declared 'sweet' and continued in eerie silence towards Kuwait.

As we crossed the border into enemy territory I made sure all my weapon switches were live and glued my eyes to the radar warning receiver. 'Time to descend', called Stevie and down we went, breaking cloud at exactly 15,000 ft. What were we to do now? How can we do a dive attack if we're not supposed to go below 15,000 ft? Well, no time for thoughts like that and as I scanned the ground looking for the familiar circular shape of the SAM-2 site, I incredibly saw one right 2 o'clock at about eight miles. Letting Mike Rondot, my wingman, know where the target was I tipped into the attack, releasing my stick of weapons at about 9,000 ft, a perilously low height considering the target could shoot back.

It was now every man for himself as I became aware of bombs going off north and south of my position, and tracer fire was everywhere, highlighted by the poor light conditions prevalent below the overcast skies. For some reason I desperately wanted to get back into cloud, in the vain hope that it offered me some protection from the forces below. We now had eight separate Jaguars, in cloud, heading as fast as possible towards the safety of the Saudi border – thank God for big sky theory. As our heart rates slowed we joined back up for the recovery into Bahrain; laden with the mixed emotions of euphoria at surviving and concern at what we had just done. As the authorization sheets logged, one aircraft ['X', flown by Squadron Leader Mike Gordon] suffered minor flak damage but otherwise no harm done. We, however, were somehow much wiser as to what an operational mission was all about and the kind of dangers we faced, which weren't always attributable to the enemy. Six weeks and 617 missions later I'm pleased to say we had all survived to tell the tales.

All eight Jaguars returned safely at around 08.45 hours. A second four-ship formation, which would be led by Squadron Leader Allam, waited for the call to arms, which would come ten minutes after the eight-ship formation landed back.

> The day followed the same routine as the first. We were on 30-minute alert for CAS. We did not expect to be launched. Then from our tasking authority in Riyadh a flash message. They had a mission for us to Iraq, time over target in two hours. Mayhem. Maps were found, thoughts were gathered, then the automatic routine took over. We were ready to go, final brief from the GLO – people wished us luck, we in turn tried to smile, not really showing how we felt. The engineers had prepared the aircraft. More good wishes. A final walk around the jet, all the pins were out. A final nervous chat with the ground crew helping me to strap in – then a smile and he was gone and I was on my own. I went through the mission in my mind, reminding myself of the lessons the pilots learnt the day before and telling myself that I wouldn't make the same mistakes. Almost before I was ready it was time to start engines: no problems there, as usual – the Jaguar was fully serviceable. Check-in time arrived; everyone was on frequency, serviceable and ready to go.
>
> Once airborne I carried out operational checks to make sure all the aircraft systems were working. The electronic countermeasures pod self-tested, lighting up the rear warning radar, chaff was fired from the Phimat chaff dispenser and the flares came out from the ALE 40-flare dispenser. I checked in the formation with the AWACs: lots of friendly voices with the best information from our controller being 'Picture Clear' – no Iraqi aircraft airborne. We continued northwards climbing to high level. As we approached the border we were handed over to our assigned ground control agency. He told us the weather was poor in the target area but he was able to give us an alternative target in Kuwait where the weather was suitable for our mission. The weather improved as we crossed the border. ECM pod was in automatic mode, weapon switches were made live and the RWR started to light up, indicating all manner of systems, some friendly, some not. I took in some of this information, then the target area was approaching – weapon aiming selected,

XZ118/Y Buster Gonad and his Unfeasibly Large Testicles, *showing the imaginative artwork and bomb log, which has a plan view of a Sidewinder with the inscription 'SWM x 1'. The CRV-7s were marked in two ways, either a plan view of the LAU pod, or, as here, a circular cross-section with white rockets inside.*
(via Mick Cartwright)

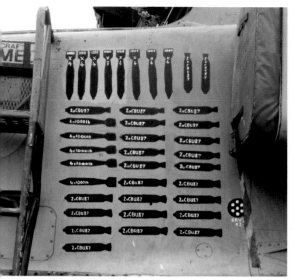

Bomb log on the port side of XZ119/Z Katrina Jane. *(via Mick Cartwright)*

find the target and into the dive. I seemed to be in the dive for an eternity, in reality only seconds – and then the weapons were released and I started to climb away. No time for proper battle damage assessment, but my bombs appeared to have exploded in the area of the target. Back over the Gulf I had time to think clearly. I checked-in the rest of the formation – they were all there, weapons delivered. In no time at all we were taxiing in at Bahrain. Smiles, handshakes and congratulations all round, nobody was thinking that we might have to do this again tomorrow. Back to the Squadron Operations room. Debrief the mission with the GLO, EWO and IO and then back to the hotel for the squadron nightly debrief. So ended my first day of operational flying.

The third formation of four Jaguars, led by the Boss, took off at 09.10 hours and attacked more AAA batteries before returning safely. Squadron Leader Allam led the fourth and final four-ship mission after a change of aircraft to the ones used earlier in the day, and they took off at 12.55 hours to attack more AAA batteries. Chris Allam, Craig Hill, Steve Shutt and Dave Foote all returned safely at 14.05 hours.

Mick Cartwright recalls:

The reality of what we were doing soon came home, with a Tornado lost on each of the first three nights, but we settled down very quickly to a routine: two shifts, twelve hours on, twelve off, a week of days and a week of nights. The night shift quickly became a week of rest. The day shift would do their utmost to rearm and clear all snags before we came in, which enabled 90% of the night men to be back in the Hotel Diplomat by 19.00 hours. At Coltishall I had been told that my manpower was set at around 200 men, but I wasn't allowed to pick who I wanted from 54 Squadron. 'Don't worry about it,' I was told, 'you won't go short.' Technically everyone blended very well. Whereas 6 Squadron had my personnel, 41 finished up with technicians from Lossiemouth to Wildenrath and the battle-damage team from Abingdon. These chaps were excellent, carrying out in-theatre mods on two aircraft per evening and, more importantly, bringing 41's and 6's battle-damage kits up to spec. This became the pattern, with minor battle-damage repairs needed on only two aircraft. The lads worked hard and they accepted their responsibilities willingly. Some were barely eighteen years old yet they performed to the highest standards, only to be ignored when the plaudits were handed out. Mike Rondot mentioned to me, quite rightly, that the windscreens on two aircraft were a bit ropey, but I was reluctant to change them in theatre. I spoke often with my OC Eng at Coltishall, Wing Commander Peter Dye. Well into the conflict he asked me to consider the roulement of the Jaguars, so we drew up a suggested programme based on hours and on which aircraft were the biggest pain in the backside. I sent the info down the tubes to Peter and a copy also found its way to HQ in Saudi. Soon afterwards we got a terse reply from some chairbound engineering wonder stating that they would decide which aircraft were rotated, and when. The fact that we knew every inch of our charges didn't seem to come into it.

Our twelve Jaguars gave no trouble whatsoever throughout the whole conflict and we did not replace one engine. Weapon loads were known twenty-four hours in advance, so when the aircraft returned everything was ready to upload. Indeed, the guys got so adept it was alarming – not the place for establishment turkeys. I drew the line at foul language painted on the bombs, but this didn't prevent them coming up with some excellent gallows humour about 41 Squadron landscape gardeners and the like. I got a message off myself pointing out to Saddam how he had screwed up Christmas, New Year and possibly Easter. It was delivered by Footy [Flight Lieutenant Dave Foote] at the second attempt. The sorties were always two four-ships in the morning followed by two four-ships plus two recce in the afternoon – mostly bombs but occasionally rockets. The lads were most concerned about their charges. When Shutty [Steve Shutt] diverted, I remember the look on his mechanic's face when he did not return with the rest of the four-ship. When he did finally arrive, having refuelled at some godforsaken place, the young airman couldn't contain himself. 'Where the hell have you been?' he blurted out. Shutty proffered his regrets and promised it wouldn't happen again. I pointed out to the lad that you don't normally talk to flight lieutenants like that.

'This ain't normal, sir', he glowered.

Throughout the short conflict the primary role assigned to the Jaguars was battlefield air interdiction (BAI). One or two missions were made against targets in Iraq, but before *Desert Sabre* and the start of the ground war the Jaguars' main operational axis was the area south of Kuwait City, which was very well defended by AAA. Targets included SAM and AM sites, SY-1 *Silkworm* SSM batteries, coastal and inland fixed and mobile artillery pieces, Astros multiple rocket launchers, armoured columns, barracks, storage facilities and at least one airfield. Once *Desert Sabre* began and the Allied advance turned into a rout, JagDet's main area of operations soon moved up to the area north of the Kuwaiti capital, and from thenceforward missions were mainly directed against the Iraqi Republican Guard. Kuwait and Iraq were divided into 'kill zones', and primary and secondary targeting instructions were passed from the Coalition headquarters in Riyadh on the day before the mission was to be flown so that planning and preparation could begin. Then the mission data was fed into the Ferranti FIN1064 digital nav/attack system. The pilots on standby would receive a final intelligence update from the ground liaison officer (GLO), and a five- to ten-minute brief on the target area (with emphasis on the defences) before it was time to walk.

The majority of the twenty-two pilots in JagDet were given attack tasks, with twenty pilots being organized into 'constituted fours'. Two of the Jaguars were normally configured for reconnaissance operations, and their primary objective was to take pre-strike pictures of target areas as a supplement to satellite imagery in the planning process.

On reconnaissance missions one of the Jaguars carried a Vinten LOROP (long-range oblique photography) pod and the other a standard BAe pod with an F126 survey camera in place of its vertical linescanner. This was because while the LOROP imagery offered remarkable resolution, its narrow field of view and lack of a data matrix made results difficult to determine, so comparison with F126 imagery was made to enable RIC (Reconnaissance Interpretation Centre) personnel to achieve satisfactory results. The aircraft completed thirty-one sorties in twenty-one separate reconnaissance missions. Squadron Leader Dave Bagshaw AFC and Flight Lieutenant Pete Livesey, the 'recce specialists', almost invariably operated as a pair, although Baggers flew some solo reconnaissance sorties, usually latching on to a four-ship for extra protection. During the Gulf War five of his twenty-four missions were bombing operations.

Generally, aircrew flew a four days on/one day off routine, with the flight schedule being arranged to permit a 48-hour interval between each duty period. Thus, following a day off a constituted four would return to action on the afternoon wave, flying as the second element of an eight-aircraft group. On the next day, they would have responsibility for planning and leading the afternoon wave, again of eight aircraft. After this, they would operate as the second element on the following morning's early raid before ending up as lead element on the morning of the fourth duty day. With this mission completed, they would then have a 48-hour break before resuming the cycle. A typical flying day required JagDet to mount two eight-aircraft attack waves, for a total of sixteen sorties. After each mission the pilots would go to debrief, which often lasted longer than the mission itself, since it invariably included electronic warfare analysis, study of HUD videos, discussion of RWR indications and notification of visual identifications of SAM and MA sites to the GLO. This level of activity was sustained for most of the campaign, apart from weather disruptions or the very occasional technical problem.

As the war progressed [continues Squadron Leader Chris Allam], it became clear that, apart from an occasional sortie, the Iraqi Air Force was not going to pose a major threat. This meant that we could continue to fly at high level, although we consistently refined our tactics in the light of operational experience. It also became obvious that we needed a cluster-bomb that could be delivered from high level. Excellent work by the support staff in Riyadh and the UK meant that we had the American CBU87 within two weeks of asking. Similarly, computed weapon aiming was necessary to guarantee hitting a target on the first pass with the CRV7 rocket. Again, good work by the engineers, support staff and the Ferranti company meant that a new flight programme for the weapons-aiming computer was available by the first week of February.

So our tasking and flying settled down into a routine: four days on, one day off. Our targets included Silkworm anti-ship missile sites, SAM sites, and artillery and weapon storage areas. The squadron had been reinforced by pilots from the OCU, bringing our total strength up to twenty-two pilots. We had also started to fly reconnaissance missions, initially for our own benefit, but once we had proved the Vinten LOROP pod we were tasked by Riyadh usually for pre-strike photography of our target areas to aid planning and target acquisition.

The days passed by as the relentless air bombardment continued against the Iraqi forces. The ground forces started their offensive and we found ourselves flying

Jaguar GR.1 XZ356/N, which carried the wing commander's pennant of the 'Boss', Wing Commander William Pixton AFC, at Coltishall on 13 March 1991. Chris Froome painted the Mary Rose *nose art. (Steve Jefferson)*

missions deep into Iraq in support of it: these missions required us to complete multiple AAR brackets but such was the speed of the ground forces' advance that we often found they had over-run the target area before we could get there!

On 26 January the Jaguars made a highly successful dawn attack on an SY-1 Silkworm coastal anti-ship missile battery in Kuwait, as part of preparations for an amphibious landing. Although the much-publicized potential assault by the US Marine Corps was a deception, it would have gone ahead had the Coalition's ground thrust deep into Iraq misfired. On 29 January Jaguars again attacked Silkworm sites using the CBU-87 cluster-bombs for the first time. On 30 January, when the Jaguars destroyed an artillery battery north of, and a command bunker south of, Kuwait, Wing Commander William Pixton AFC and Flight Lieutenant Peter 'Frog' Tholen destroyed a 1,120-ton Polnochmy-C-class landing craft. Pixton recalled:

The AWACS was telling us that the picture was clear, so there were no enemy fighters in the area. We almost set up an academic range pattern on the ship. It will sound terrible, and my professional counterparts at home will probably have a fit

XX962/X with the Fat Slags *artwork on the starboard side of the aircraft. (Steve Jefferson)*

but we did two passes ripple-firing CRV-7 rockets and four passes 30 mm ADEN guns each, when normally we would never consider reattacking in a high-threat environment.

On 31 January the Jaguars attacked artillery in southern Kuwait. On 1 February two Jaguars diverted from another mission to attack a ZSU-23/4 flak vehicle in south-east Kuwait with cluster-bombs. On 3 February the Jaguars raided ammunition dumps south of Kuwait City and dropped 1,000 lb (454 kg) air-burst bombs successfully on six Iraqi artillery emplacements on Faylakah Island ten miles (16 km) off the Kuwaiti coast. On 5 February, with Iraq's Navy virtually destroyed, SuCAP (support combat air patrol) and the associated CSAR (combat search and rescue) operations ceased after forty-eight sorties (twenty-three missions). Mostly these missions, which typically were three to four hours' duration and required air-to-air refuellings, involved pairs of Jaguars armed with bombs, rockets and cannon, which maintained a CAP while they orbited waiting for 'trade' (like the famous CAB ranks of Typhoons in the Second World War). Bombing of the Republican Guard intensified during the second week of February, while on the 12th the campaign against Iraqi communications was supported by a mission against a pontoon bridge constructed to replace one knocked down by LGBs a few days before. The final phase of the Jaguars' war brought individual artillery pieces into the target lists, an early success being destruction of five Astros multi-ramp rocket launchers on 13 February. Once the land war began on 24 February, Jaguars operated exclusively north of Kuwait City for the remaining three days of war.

Squadron Leader Mike Rondot, flight commander of 6 Squadron, was attached to 41 Squadron during the Gulf War. He recalls:

One of the very few good things to come out of the Gulf War was the opportunity

Squadron Leader Dave Bagshaw's logbook with the highly prized 4000 hours Jaguar and Arabian Gulf Aero Club *Velcro badges. (Author)*

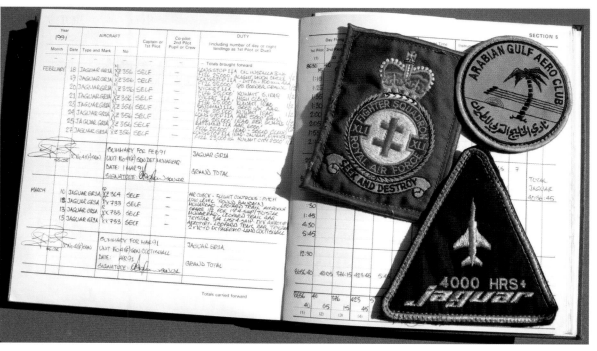

for the much-maligned Jaguar to finally lay to rest many of the ill-founded rumours and bar-stories about its ability to go to war and sustain an effective strike rate in a hostile AAA and SAM environment. The bare facts are that twelve aircraft flew 618 operational sorties in forty-two days without loss. Two were damaged by AAA fire, necessitating battle-damage repairs at Bahrain, but both were ready to fly again within a few hours. A small team of engineers and ground crew were able to present twelve serviceable Jaguars every day for weeks on end without drama. Armourers were able to rearm the aircraft between missions quickly and simply. The phrase 'clockwork mouse' springs to mind, but the bottom line is that when eight Jaguars were needed for a mission Warrant Officer Mick Cartwright was always able to provide eight and four spares.

I flew twenty-nine combat missions and only once took a spare jet. The engineers and armourers did a fantastic job but the aeroplane was rugged, dependable and serviceable. We gave them a pretty good workout in the air. The Jaguar has always had one throttle setting – full power, with reheat available for maintaining speed in a turn – but we thrashed the engines really hard. The Adour 206 was tweaked to run at a higher temperature and give a bit more power and we used it all. You have to understand that the Jaguar was built to fly at 420 knots with a full warload at low level. It would go faster – I have flown a Jaguar to 700 knots indicated – but in the Gulf temperatures with four 1,000 lb bombs, loaded guns, two Sidewinders, ECM suite and external fuel, the Jaguar needed afterburner to get anywhere near a respectable speed for going to war. Anything below 600 knots at low level in the Kuwait theatre of operations would have been suicide and we simply could not achieve it in military power without afterburner. More importantly, in a hostile area known to be full of heat-seeking SAMs it is not a good idea to fly around in afterburner. My opinion has always been that low-level tactics are good fun in peacetime but if I have to go to war I want to learn from the Vietnam experience and be a high-level dive-bomber. The Gulf War reinforced that view in the most dramatic manner. We were very well prepared for the ultra-low-level attack mission. Most of the twenty pilots we started with were very comfortable flying at 20–30 ft above ground level at 450 knots. Some were able to fly lower than that but 450 knots is painfully slow when compared to an aircraft like the AJ37 Viggen, which cruises at 650 knots and is steady as a rock at 50 ft at that speed. Take a Jaguar up to 650 knots and it's a very special event – not for the faint-hearted – whereas I have flown the Viggen at 650 knots in military power and felt quite safe and comfortable at 30 ft.

The Jaguar would have been just as reliable and serviceable flying the low-level mission, but luckily for us common sense prevailed at the eleventh hour and we switched to medium-level tactics, dive-bombing from around 20,000 ft where we were above most of the heat-seeking IR SAMs. It takes years to train a pilot to fly safely at ultra-low level but only one or two sorties to turn a low-level pilot into a capable dive-bomber, so we were ready to go when war was declared on 17 January 1991.

Virtually every mission we flew had dedicated SAM suppression and you felt like you had minders all the way, with air defence stuff roaming about, clearing the skies. We used in-flight refuelling on about half the missions, always with the

Victors. They were brilliant, they were always there, they never failed to turn up and they were always in the right place, at the right time, with the right fuel. We just used to pitch up, get in behind them, take our fuel and go away, not a word being said on the radio unless they were in thick cloud. Even then we could get very close using air-to-air TACAN, but if you couldn't find them, you had to talk.

We had all sorts of targets, mainly in Kuwait and southern Iraq. Barracks, storage depots, artillery, SAM sites, coastal defence missile sites, troop emplacements, installations on airfields, things like that. We were attacking targets in the area with the heaviest concentration of known Iraqi defences. So, while we felt sorry for the guys flying deep-penetration missions into Iraq, or for the A-10s down at 8,000 ft over the open desert, looking for tanks, they had a lot of respect for what we were doing.

We did hit our targets. The Jaguar was brilliant as a dive-bomber. We could barrel roll into a 60° dive with four 1,000 lb bombs on board from 30,000 ft and get a good laser-locked aiming solution to allow us to pickle the bombs right on target and recover from the dive without going below 10,000 ft. At those dive angles the bombs go in like darts so some very good hits were achieved.

The attack gunsight videos make interesting viewing. Few would have believed a Jaguar could haul a weapon load up to 34,000 ft and cruise at Mach 0.99; or that it could snap out of a 60° dive without breaking something, but I've seen it – I've got the film. We pushed the aeroplane way outside its flight envelope, we overstressed it, flew it supersonic with full external stores, overtemped the engines and gave the airframe a real beating, but the twelve jets remained stubbornly serviceable and just soaked it up.

As a final tribute to the machine and Mick Cartwright's team of engineers, we flew the jets non-stop from Bahrain to Coltishall after hostilities ceased – a flight of 8 hours, 35 minutes. And guess what? All twelve ran like clockwork mice all the way home.

Squadron Leader Chris Allam concludes:

Suddenly it was all over – the Iraqis agreed to a ceasefire.[31] Everybody is happy and sad at the same time; pleased that the war is over but sad that we had needed to use force to get the Iraqi Army out of Kuwait. We are also proud that we have played a small but successful part in the Coalition air offensive. We could not have done it on our own but were dependent on the support of other Coalition forces – Wild Weasel and EF-111A Raven jamming aircraft, F-14 and F-15 fighter support and of course, AWACs. However, I like to think that our success was due in no small part to our normal training. Although we did not fight the way we had trained, practising for the 'worst case' scenario, the low-level war, we were able to switch to high-level tactics fairly easily. This, with the good fortune that was denied our Tornado colleagues, meant that we flew 618 sorties without loss and only suffered minor battle damage to three aircraft.

My final thoughts are best summarized in the words spoken by one pilot after his first mission over Kuwait: 'Just off target there was a lot of flak. It's the first time I have ever seen tracer coming up at me. It was the longest minute of my life, I can tell you.'[32]

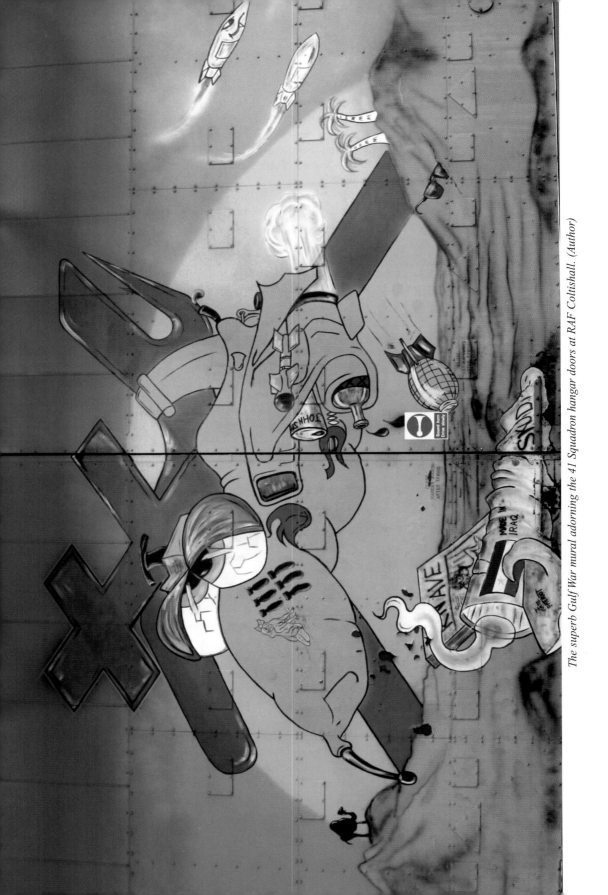

The superb Gulf War mural adorning the 41 Squadron hangar doors at RAF Coltishall. (Author)

CHAPTER SEVEN

Warden and *Grapple*

The chances of being shot at on the average sortie were high, as Saddam Hussein's air defence personnel were active and looking to bring down an expensive American or British jet.

Tim McLean, a pilot on 6 Squadron

After the ceasefire in the Gulf War the Jaguars returned home to Coltishall to a heroes' welcome, but soon another detachment was being prepared to fly back to the Gulf region. Saddam Hussein had begun attacks against the Kurdish population in the mountainous regions in the north of Iraq bordering Iran, Turkey and Syria, which resulted in massive refugee problems for those three countries. The UN responded by establishing a safe haven and security zone for the Kurdish people. An area of Iraq above 36 degrees North was also designated an air exclusion zone to Saddam Hussein's Air Force. To ensure compliance with the UN resolutions, a Coalition Task Force comprising the USA, UK and France was formed to patrol the area, primarily to discourage Iraq from infringement but also to respond in the event of any flagrant disregard of the UN edict. Turkey agreed to join the Coalition force for Operation *Warden*, as it was called, and operations were to be conducted from the Turkish Air Force base at Incirlik. The USAF provided the air defence and fighter-bomber role, shared with the Turkish Air Force, while the UK and

Sign of the times at
RAF Coltishall.
(Author)

GR.1 XZ398/A of 41 Squadron in 75th Anniversary colours refuelling from VC 10 tanker ZA149 of 101 Squadron. (Mike Rondot)

France provided tactical photographic and reconnaissance cover, as the USAF did not have this component in Europe. The UK committed eight Jaguar GR.1A aircraft and France a similar number of Mirage F1CR-200s, both dedicated to observe and record Iraqi military activity within the exclusion zones. The Jaguar GR.1A was selected as the most suitable aircraft, as their BAe and Vinten VICON LOROP pods recorded their imagery on film, unlike the Tornado GR.1A, which used video cameras.

The UK commitment was formed during August 1991 under the command of Group Captain John Morley. The eight Jaguars were drawn from all three squadrons at Coltishall and were painted in the now familiar 'desert-pink' scheme. Although 41 Squadron was the only Jaguar unit dedicated to photographic reconnaissance, both 6 and 54 Squadron pilots had been trained to undertake this role, with each squadron providing aircrew and ground crew on a two monthly rotation. The first four aircraft departed Coltishall on 4 September, followed by the remaining aircraft five days later. No.41 Reconnaissance Intelligence Centre (RIC), plus support personnel and equipment, were flown out to Turkey by C-130 Hercules aircraft. In addition, the VC 10 tankers of 101 Squadron, which supported the initial deployment of the Jaguars in their non-stop flight, were to remain in theatre to provide air-to-air refuelling cover for the duration of Operation *Warden*.

The Jaguars, generally operating in pairs, one armed with CBUs, a second configured for reconnaissance, were required to overfly regularly all known military sites and photograph the activities to provide constantly updated intelligence. Targets included Iraqi troop concentrations, air defence sites, military airfields, at least five of which were located within the no fly zone, railway terminus, barracks and vehicle parking areas. All the targets were located within Iraqi territory and were potentially hostile. Therefore the Jaguars carried defence packages consisting of overwing-mounted AIM-9L Sidewinder missiles, 30 mm Aden cannon and an electronic countermeasures suite that included the Phimat chaff/flare dispenser and an ALQ-101 jamming pod on underwing hard points. Periodically the recce pod was replaced by 1,000 lb bombs to demonstrate to the Iraqis that the Coalition was ready and willing to respond with force if needed. The Mirage F1CR-200s invariably performed their recce task in the mornings, while the Jaguars flew slots later in the day. The location of each target to be photographed was carefully plotted on large maps to determine their exact positions. The number of aircraft required to perform the mission was also determined by the quantity of subjects that needed to be photographed, although the normal sortie rate saw the Jaguars working in pairs, with up to six aircraft flying per day. Missions usually lasted two hours and were flown with support packages provided by USAF F-16s or F-15s, defence-suppression F-4G Phantoms and ECM-jamming EF-111 'Spark Varks', or USN EA-6B Prowlers and tanker support.

It was with a certain amount of trepidation that Tim McLean, a pilot on 6 Squadron, stepped onto the tarmac at Incirlik Air Base, near Adana, in the southern reaches of Turkey:

The long, and slightly painful, Hercules flight from RAF Lyneham had given me ample time to consider what was in store in the forthcoming weeks. Within a few days the years of training I had undergone would be put to the test, as I would fly over hostile Iraqi territory for the first time. The chances of being shot at on the average sortie were high, as Saddam Hussein's air defence personnel were active and looking to bring down an expensive American or British jet.

I was welcomed by a couple of my fellow squadron members, Graham Duff and Andy Millikin, who quickly showed me the ropes and handed me an obligatory beer. The weekend would be available to acclimatize and read up on the extensive orders, rules of engagement and standard procedures that had to be understood, and of course signed for, before taking to the air. The amount of information to be

Wing Commander William Pixton DFC AFC, Boss of 41 Squadron, flying GR.1 XZ398/A. (Mike Rondot)

assimilated was daunting, to say the least. There was also the chance to socialize with the squadron ground crew, and it was here that I first saw the camaraderie that I will always remember from my time on operations with 6 Squadron. Although everybody was relaxed and made the most of the excellent facilities at the base, it was evident from the start that there was a focus beyond what is seen on the standard training deployment. With that focus the entire squadron was brought closer together, making for an excellent work and social environment.

Monday morning saw us rise at 04.30, which was a most pleasant 02.30 UK time if the body had not quite adjusted its circadian rhythms. The main briefing room was large to accommodate crews from over forty aircraft. The amount of assets employed on each mission was awe-inspiring for one who had not been in this environment before. Crews from Airborne Warning and Control, Tankers (UK and US), Electronic Intelligence platforms (*Rivet Joint*), Electronic Warfare Jammers (US Navy Prowlers), Offensive Counter Air (F-15Cs), Suppression of Enemy Air Defence (F-16s) and Emergency Defence Suppression (F-l5Es) were all in attendance. No.6 Squadron's Jaguar pilots were also there to brief on the Reconnaissance plan for the day. Good for morale was the presence of the Combat Search and Rescue (F-16s and Pave Low Helos) personnel who would he

On Friday 7 February 1992 Squadron Leader Dave 'Baggers' Bagshaw AFC flew his last sortie in a Jaguar when he flew in XZ101 in formation from Coltishall with his brother Lieutenant-Colonel John 'Baggy' Bagshaw flying a CF-18 Hornet. 'Baggy' had arrived the day before from CFB Baden Söllingen, and joined his brother and the Boss of 41 Squadron, Wing Commander William Pixton DFC AFC, who flew XZ398 in the formation. Altogether Baggers accumulated a total of 9,660 flying hours, 4,200 of which were on the Jaguar. (Chris Bennett)

Desert-pink GR.1 XZ114/FB and another Jaguar from RAF Coltishall form an airborne honour guard to welcome LB-30 Liberator AM927 N12905 Diamond Lil *of the Confederate Air Force to Norfolk on 10 June 1992 after the wartime bomber flew to England from Fort Worth, Texas, via Canada, Iceland and Prestwick, Scotland, to visit the UK as part of the USAAF Fiftieth Anniversary celebrations. In 1943 US 9th Air Force Liberators operated from the North African desert and were painted the same colour, although the Americans christened the scheme 'titty pink'. (Mike Rondot)*

responsible for defence and pick-up of any downed airmen.

The aims for the day were covered along with the important logistics of managing to get those forty aircraft out and back from Incirlik in good order. Expansions were made on the air tasking order and the crews then cleared off for individual briefs. It was here that the Squadron Intelligence Officer, Judith Graham, updated the political and tactical picture, and the sortie-lead covered the Jaguar specific details. Particular attention was paid to 'Green Lanes', which were lines of least resistance to vacate the Iraqi airspace in case of fighter launch. The time available was more than sufficient, which was a marked contrast to the training environment of home. It was then that we donned the flying equipment, which could prove crucial if one was unlucky enough to end up on Iraqi soil 'sans Jaguar'. The combat survival waistcoat contained everything but the kitchen sink, and the loaned pistol was also reassuring (as to whether it could repel advancing hordes was debatable). After being dropped off at the hardened aircraft shelters we were able to pre-flight the jets and check the various systems that would be required for each mission. Updates were broadcast on the package common frequency and, if there were no late injects, were spooled up and the long taxi commenced.

It is hard to describe how I was feeling as I joined the long queue of aircraft with

GR.3A FD Of 41 Squadron with a lightweight Vinten 18 Series 600 LOROP (long-range oblique photography) pod on the aircraft centre-line. (RAF Coltishall)

T.4 'EV' in sub-zero conditions. (RAF Coltishall)

their strictly choreographed take-off times: an edifying wave from the pilot of a heavily armed F-15 Eagle saw us onto the active runway and away. The long transit to the eastern part of Turkey enabled us to check and double-check our aircraft and to picture build from the various radio transmissions of the formations ahead of us. The nerves were starting to settle and concentration was brought to bear on the hours ahead. Fuel was taken from an RAF VC 10, final checks completed and the Iraqi border beckoned. It was surprising how mountainous the terrain was but this was soon left behind as we conducted a circular route over the desert area to the north of the 36th Parallel. The reconnaissance pod was pre-programmed to take footage of certain targets as requested by higher command. The frequent radio transmissions advised of anti-aircraft fire in a host of areas, but I have to admit that I saw nothing to alarm. It was only minutes later that we flew back into Turkish airspace ready to refuel and reconfigure our jets for further runs. These were duly completed and a westerly heading taken up for Adana. Once on the ground the tapes were taken from the reconnaissance pods for exploitation by the Intelligence community. Sortie duration for the Jaguars could be as much as five hours, with the Offensive Counter Air F-15s closer to seven, which made for some long days.

The mission flows, with time, could become routine. However, there is no doubt that the near certainty of being shot at and the knowledge of what could await if Iraq was via parachute counterbalanced this. The sorties flown, while on 6 Squadron, as part of *Northern Watch* will remain with me for a long time. The knowledge that the squadron did its part, in protecting the Kurds of northern Iraq from an oppressive regime for such a sustained period, is reward for the extended periods away from home and some heart-in-mouth moments. The feeling of comradeship with the 6 Squadron members that served in Turkey is also something I will always value.

The personnel of 41 Squadron were the first to deploy on Operation *Warden* during the late summer of 1991, and they were the last of Coltishall's squadrons to participate prior to being replaced by the Harrier force in April 1993.

Two months earlier, on 22 February, twelve Jaguars of 6 Squadron departed Coltishall for the Italian Air Force base at Gioia del Colle in southern Italy, when Coalition forces were once again tasked to support an international operation. *Deny Flight*, for which the UK's participation was known as Operation *Grapple*, was designed to help maintain the

GR.3As XZ103/FP and 'FT' of 41 Squadron with a BAe recce pod and a cluster-bomb unit respectively. For many years the squadron flew with the BAe recce pod that used enough F95 wet film cameras to provide 180-degree coverage. The 'barge', as it was affectionately known, served with distinction in many theatres, including the 1991 Gulf War and regular visits to Norway. The result of the BAe pod ageing and the occurrence of more modern technology saw the development of the Jaguar replacement recce pod, or JRRP. This later became the joint reconnaissance pod (JRP) as the new pod was introduced to operational service in the summer of 2000. The JRP featured a smaller housing, making it easier for the Jaguar to carry. It contains either two electro-optical line scanning cameras and a Vigil infra-red line scanner (IRLS) for low-level jobs, or a single EO camera in a swivelling nose for medium-level work. The IRLS also provided the aircraft with a night recce capability. The JRP has proved so successful that not only was it used operationally on the Jaguar but also on Tornado GR.4 and Harrier GR.7 aircraft – although without the same degree of integration and user-friendly simplicity. (RAF)

United Nations Protection Force (UNPROFOR) in Bosnia-Herzegovina in the former Yugoslavia. From thenceforth 6 Squadron shared the manning of the detachment with 54 and 41 Squadrons. The Jaguars at Gioia were representative of the Coltishall Wing, although with the application of a new colour scheme, ARTE light grey, designed for medium-level operations, the only method of determining squadron ownership of the aircraft was by the two-letter code on the tail and nosewheel door. The aircraft were fitted and prepared to Operation *Granby* standard, which included overwing AIM-9L Sidewinder launchers, Tracor flare dispensers, Phimat chaff dispenser and AN/ALQ- 101 ECM pod, and tweaked engines, with the only addition being an extra radio to allow for communications with in-theatre command and control agencies. Two of the aircraft (XZ364/GJ and XX720/GB) were permanently configured for 'wet film' photographic sorties; one with a LOROP (long-range oblique photography) pod (which was later substituted for the GP-1 pod) and the other with a BAe pod, which carried the F.126 general-survey camera. A reconnaissance intelligence centre (RIC) was set up at Gioia to handle wet film processing and subsequent interpretation. This information was then passed to the 5th Allied Tactical Air Force for future mission planning, particularly in the

VC 10 XV103 tanker of 101 Squadron
refuelling Jaguars in 1993. (RAF Coltishall)

GR.1 XX741 refuelling
from a TriStar C.Mk 1 of
216 Squadron. (RAF)

event of a close air support requirement. Unlike the Tornadoes, the Jaguars were tasked
during the daytime only, and they could fly anything between four and eight sorties a day,
including reconnaissance missions. The medium-level reconnaissance sorties were flown
with two or three aircraft with up to ten targets per sortie. One GR.1A flew as the 'photo-
ship' and the others, both standard GR.1As, acted as the 'stinger' to provide vital visual
cross-cover for any aerial SAM threats.

In July 1993 nine Jaguars left for Gioia Del Colle supported by thirty-six C-130 loads
of personnel and equipment. Flight Lieutenant (later Squadron Leader) Chris Hadlow,
fresh from the OCU, arrived at Coltishall a month later to find the 6 Squadron premises
deserted:

Five months later I stepped off the Hercules at Gioia, the newest combat-ready pilot
on the force. After a daunting theatre arrival brief and having attempted to navigate
my way around the SPINS, it was with some trepidation that I awaited my first trip.
My first trip came and went . . . six months later . . . I switched off my hotel

television having just watched the latest CNN analysis of the likelihood of the Serbs removing their artillery and tanks from the exclusion zone around Sarajevo. The Serbs had been in this situation some months ago and had capitulated.

Replete after another fine meal in the Hotel Suevo Restaurant, I drifted into sleep wondering whether tomorrow would be the day that I would actually drop my bombs after months of flying over the AOR.

Another sunny but hazy day dawned. Arriving at the JagDet accommodation on Gioia del Colle airfield, the daily intelligence brief unfolded. The Serb armour was still in place and the deadline was approaching. The flying programme had changed somewhat and I was now on R530 as No. 2 to Flight Lieutenant Dave Foote. We drew our weapons, gooley chit, deutchmarks, etc., and donned our CSWs and sat around. After a couple of hours, the phones and comms networks started to heat up. The Serbs had missed the deadline and there was talk of us launching to attack the Serb armour. Finally, the call came and the other pair on R530 was launched. At this stage Footey and I were champing at the bit, not wanting to he left out of the action. However, as the second 'alert' pair I felt we would not be required. An hour later we moved to cockpit readiness and then unbelievably it happened, we were scrambled. The front pair had been frustratingly held off and had run out of gas, and with no tanker available we were launched. We set off towards the gate, my leader barely visible in the thick haze. After the twenty-minute transit we reached the gate, and my aircraft was prepared. 'Crest, Magic 40 return to base, target has already been attacked.' An A-10 had already strafed the target and the Serbs had started to withdraw their armour.

This was an atypical day on Operation *Deny Flight*. Most days involved a 60:40 split of CAS and Recce and we worked a regime of six days 'on', two 'off'. Periods of RS were not uncommon and these involved much sitting around waiting for nothing to happen. This is not to say there were not moments of excitement. I remember assisting an FAC who was under attack, with repeated high-dive passes overhead the enemy's position. The fact that this guy lived to fight another day gave meaning to our efforts.

Perhaps the most exciting moment of our time over the former Yugoslavia was due to the vagaries of the Jaguar fuel system. One day after AAR our intrepid aviators flew up to Tuzla in the far north-east of the AOR to conduct a CAS sortie. Due to the nature of the mission the magnetic indicators that informs you if the fuel drop tanks are feeding or NOT were not checked, or gave an erroneous indication. Therefore relying on the detotalizer clicking down throughout the sortie, our intrepid aviator left Tuzla with what he thought was minimum fuel to get back to Italy. It rapidly transpired that he had 2,000 kg less than he thought. This fuel was trapped in his drop tanks and was not available at all, leaving him with around 300 kg! Faced with only one choice, he diverted into Sarajevo. Although run by the French UN peacekeepers, this was by no means a first-choice diversion. In fact it was never briefed as one. Welcomed by the French and donning a flak jacket, our intrepid aviator helped to 'hide' his aeroplane behind some lorries. After a sumptuous dining-in night, courtesy of the French, our pilot helped to sweep the snow off his aircraft and carried out a gravity refuelling from the Hercules that flew in to assist. After a low departure and zoom climb into cloud, the aeroplane was

Even in times of conflict the RAF is expected to show the flag on ceremonial occasions,
especially on Battle of Britain Day each year. 'A square full of Jaguars' quite rightly won for
Sergeant G. Card, of HQ Strike Command, the Best Battle of Britain 50th Anniversary
Photograph of 1990. (Crown copyright)

GR.1 XZ357/FK of 41 Squadron over Bosnia in 1994. (RAF Coltishall)

GR.1A XZ109/EN of 54 Squadron over Bosnia. (RAF Coltishall)

GR.1A XZ356 of 6 Squadron, which has swapped its desert pink scheme used in Operation Granby, *when it was 'N'/'Mary Rose', for all grey, taxies out for take-off with a BAe recce pod on the centre-line. During Operation* Warden *XZ356 was named* Marshall Connolly, *after Wing Commander (later Group Captain) Jerry Connolly. In the distance is an Ilyushin Il-76 long-range transport. (RAF Coltishall)*

escorted by two F-18s out of the AOR and back to Italy.

Pilots were rotated to Gioia del Colle throughout 1994, while back at Coltishall station life, exercises and other duties had to fit in with the detachments to Italy. Wing Commander Tim Keress recalls the events of 1994:

Fireworks heralded the start of the New Year in the town square of Gioia Del Colle. No.54 (F) Squadron was approaching the end of its first two-month deployment to Italy in support of Operation *Deny Flight*, providing air cover for United Nations in Bosnia. While the local Italian community celebrated the New Year in style, turning their towns into passable copies of Sarajevo on a heavy night, squadron personnel were somewhat more restrained as by 05.00 the next morning they would be on standby at the local airfield, ready to react to a call for close air support over Bosnia. Nevertheless the Italian celebrations were a sight to behold! New Year's Day turned out to be typical of those of the previous two months; no fireworks but eight operational sorties flown over towns that are now household names, such as Sarajevo, Goraide, Mostar and Tuzla.

Gioia Del Colle airfield sits on a 1,000-ft-high plateau in the Puglia region of southern Italy. In summer the weather is fine but in winter low cloud and heavy rain are common; even snow is not unknown. However, this year 1 January was relatively fine and good enough on 'Sausage Side' for all sorties to be successful. Six aircraft carried out simulated attacks on real artillery positions and two aircraft performed photo reconnaissance using high-powered optical cameras. By 5 January 54 (F) Squadron had flown many sorties over Bosnia, and after two months in theatre handed the commitment to its sister squadron from RAF Coltishall. With Christmas in the UK still to 'celebrate', the return home by VC 10 was welcomed by all of the 120-strong detachment.

However, after a well-earned two-week break, the squadron's personnel were well refreshed, and the pilots were champing at the bit to revive those skills that had been precluded by Bosnia operations, in particular low-level flying, weaponeering and air combat. These targets are the bread and butter of Jaguar operations, as the aircraft was designed to get to its target low and fast, its economical engines give it a fine range and its Ferranti navigation and weapons-aiming sub-system give pin-point accuracy for weapons delivery.

Nevertheless, the home routine did not last long. At the end of February aircraft, pilots and thirty ground crew departed for Florennes in Belgium to participate in the NATO Tactical Leadership Programme. This small but highly valued four-week detachment features participants from all NATO nations, flying a variety of aircraft in different roles. Having studied the theory and learnt about all factors that can affect modern-day air operations, the aircrew exercise and practise tactics with a view to flying as part of increasingly large 'packages'. In the meantime, the ground crew support the deployed aircraft but also have the opportunity to see how their NATO colleagues operate. Ultimately, the exercise results in a better understanding of the problems that each nation has, and most importantly gives everyone an insight into the problems, challenges and advantages of operating as part of a multi-national force.

Meanwhile, back at Coltishall, plans were well under way for the next squadron deployment overseas, this time to Bardufoss, an airfield located inside the Arctic Circle in northern Norway. So it was that in early March much of the remainder of 54 (F) Squadron, together with an element from Coltishall's reconnaissance squadron and a number of squadron support personnel, deployed with eight single-seat Jaguar GR1As and a two-seater to take part in Exercise *Arctic Express*, a major NATO exercise. The deployment marked a first for the Jaguar Force, 54 (F) Squadron being the first 'attack' Jaguar squadron to deploy to Norway. In the past, this commitment had fallen to 41 (F) Squadron operating primarily in its declared reconnaissance role. In this instance, however, 41 (F) Squadron was deployed to Gioia Del Colle and was thus unable to take part in Exercise *Arctic Express*. A number of its personnel, not immediately necessary for support in Gioia, accompanied 54 (F) to provide expertise in operating in arctic conditions and to allow continued training for subsequent exercises in Bardufoss. Operations in temperatures as low as minus 26C (at which a bare hand will freeze to metal) were a new experience for the majority of the pilots and ground crew, but it did not take long to 'learn the ropes'. The pilots perfected the art of landing on ice-covered runways and honed their low-flying skills over the spectacular valleys of northern Norway, providing air support and reconnaissance for NATO ground troops engaged in the exercise.

In addition, the squadron participated in a fire-power demonstration, delivering twelve 1,000 lb bombs on a single pass on the Seterrneon bombing range, as well as carrying out HE strafe attacks. Meanwhile, wearing their bulky Arctic clothing, the ground crew perfected operations from hardened aircraft shelters in this unusual and hostile environment. During the free time available, the majority of squadron and support personnel took full advantage of the excellent skiing facilities available, with many enjoying the sport for the first time. Miraculously very few injuries were experienced and all were able to walk off the VC 10 when it returned to Coltishall at the end of the month! For many, however, the overriding memory of the detachment was the sight of the Northern Lights, which appeared in the clear Arctic skies on a number of occasions. By now members of the squadron were turning their thoughts to preparations for the next deployment to Gioia Del Colle to participate again in Operation *Deny Flight*. Priority turned from the combat-ready work-up of new pilots, who had arrived from the Jaguar OCU at Lossiemouth, to refreshing flying skills necessary to operate over Bosnia. The pilots concentrated their efforts on 'medium-level' operations, often working with forward air controllers, who were themselves preparing to deploy into the Yugoslav theatre. Live weapon training took place, including the delivery of CRV 7 rockets and laser-guided and free-fall bombs. However, this time the Bosnian deployment was not to be for all; a small contingent of 54 (F) Squadron personnel was to deploy to Alberta, Canada, to take part in Exercise *Maple Flag*. This yielded the requirement for those pilots who would be participating in the exercise to practise flying down to 100 ft in specially designated areas around the United Kingdom. This demanding challenge enabled the pilots to hone their ability to pass undetected under the low-level radar coverage that would be an intrinsic part of any future major conflict, and prepared them well for an exercise where just such a scenario would prevail. While the pilots were getting to grips with a variety of flying environments the ground crew were particularly busy producing sufficient aircraft in the necessary fit.

The months leading up to the second deployment to Italy passed quickly. But in the event, the squadron's departure for Gioia was delayed by two days due to the siege of Gorazde and the associated UN ultimatum, which was due to expire on the day of the planned handover from 41 (F) Squadron. As a result, the detachment left Coltishall by VC 10 on 29 April and Jaguar operations recommenced the next day. The tempo of operations had increased somewhat since the previous deployment, with tasking for eight CAS and two reconnaissance sorties each day. Regular periods of readiness remained, frequently commencing at 4 a.m. and lasting for much of the flying day. The need to maintain serviceable aircraft in a condition ready to react at short notice while still fulfilling the operational tasking was certainly a challenge to the ground crew. The format of the operational sorties remained much as it had been, with armed aircraft operating in pairs at medium level under the control of tactical air control parties. By now, however, greater emphasis was being placed upon the use of airborne FACs in the shape of pilots of US Marine Corps F-18s and USAF A-10s, who talked our pilots' eyes onto targets. This system works well, as the FAC has the same perspective of features on the ground as the Jaguar pilot. Reconnaissance operations had also changed, with the introduction of the Vinten LOROP camera. With its greater magnification and upgraded electronics, this camera gives a quantum jump in the clarity of the end product and consequently a marked improvement in the intelligence that can be derived from it.

On the ground the engineers operated a 'split' shift system, ensuring that rectification and preparation work could be carried out over a 24-hour period. Thankfully, the Jaguar's excellent serviceability meant that long nights of rectification work were mercifully few. In practice, the oncoming shift arrived at work after lunch, completed the flying day and then rectified any faults before standing down until required for the next morning's flying programme or readiness commitment. After lunch the following day, the cycle began again but this time for the other shift. This proved to be a popular system, for, although the duty phase demanded hard work, the twenty-four hours off allowed personnel to take full advantage of their time in the local area and thus return to work fully refreshed. In high temperatures the cumulative effects of working a week of days or nights on the efficiency and morale of those involved can be significant. The shift system ensured a reasonable leisure period for ground crew even if the tactical situation required that weekend leave be cancelled. After all, there was always the possibility that the situation on the ground in Bosnia would require a higher rate of Jaguar flying. Consequently, it was essential that aircraft availability was maximized throughout the flying day. Any aircraft returning from a mission with a fault received very prompt attention, allowing it to be made available at the earliest opportunity. This placed great demands on the skills and ingenuity of the engineers, and an exceptionally high level of availability was maintained throughout the detachment. Operation of aircraft carrying live weapons yielded many potential hazards both in the air and on the ground, and personnel safety, as ever, was a major priority. Although live weapons were not called upon, the detachment armourers were kept very busy removing and replacing bombs, bullets and missiles so that rectification

GR.1 XZ398/A of 41 Squadron and GR.1A XZ112 of 54 (F) Squadron in striking 75th Anniversary blue and yellow chequer scheme. XZ398/A was painted in 75th Anniversary colours in 1991, the squadron having been formed at Gosport on 14 July 1916. The aircraft featured an all-red spine and tailfin, with the squadron's double-armed cross crest applied to the centre of the fin. Equipped with F.E.8 fighters, the squadron flew to the Western Front in October 1916 and was stationed initially at St Omer. Permission was granted to allow the squadron to incorporate the cross, which forms a part of the arms of St Omer, and it is surmounted with the squadron crown and Roman numerals representing the squadron number superimposed. (Mike Rondot)

work could be safely accomplished.

Throughout the detachment, tension in Bosnia remained high, and on 2 May, the third day in theatre, the operational HQ at 5 ATAF in Vicenza, Northern Italy, tasked three Jaguars to be re-roled into an anti-shipping fit. The chosen weapon was the CRV 7 rocket, and the aircraft re-role, which included the removal of bombs and underwing fuel tanks, fitment, filling and testing centre-line fuel tanks and preparation and loading of the rocket pods, was achieved in minutes rather than hours. In the event, the situation which had led to the call for these weapons was defused and the squadron was not required to use them in anger; however, the exercise had proved the flexibility of the Jaguar and professionalism of squadron personnel.

It is worth mentioning that all squadrons that deployed to Gioia were fully supported by resident detachment staff, who provide administrative, domestic and some second-line engineering support; their assistance is invaluable. Furthermore, the hospitality and good nature of the resident Italian squadrons have helped the 'UK outpost' integrate with the airfield and local community. At home, too, personnel at RAF Coltishall ensure that the Jaguar squadrons maintain their

GR.1A XX767/GE of 54 (F) Squadron taking off from RAF Coltishall on 9 December 1994. (Tom Trower)

capabilities and provide support in many forms, from assistance to families to rectification beyond the resources of the deployed squadron.

Despite the periods of excitement, life at Gioia Del Colle developed a routine. The weather was certainly kinder than it had been throughout the squadron's first stay, and temperatures of 32C were commonplace throughout the second half of the detachment. Leisure time was not unknown, with Rome and Naples close enough to allow short visits. In addition, most of the squadron personnel developed the ability to survive on Italian roads, considered by some to be more dangerous than flying over Bosnia. Also many people discovered that Italian food is not just Spag

GR.1 XX737/EE of 6 Squadron and XZ361 of 41 Squadron taking off from RAF Coltishall. XZ361 had previously served with II (AC) Squadron. During Operation Deny Flight *over Bosnia a 41 (F) Squadron Jaguar became the first RAF aircraft to drop a bomb in anger over Europe since 1945. This attack was carried out against a Bosnian Serb tank and resulted in the tank being severely damaged. In August 1995 the Harrier Force relieved the Jaguar wing of its responsibility to Operation* Deny Flight. *(RAF Coltishall)*

Bol and Pizza! But time away from work was not entirely given up to leisure: the squadron's SNCOs took the opportunity to embark on a programme to raise funds for sporting equipment for a school in an extremely poor district of Naples. In doing so, they raised in excess of one million lira. Meanwhile, the squadron football team enhanced relations with the local community with numerous football matches, underlining the detachment spirit aptly described by the old adage, 'work hard and play hard'.

Even with the rigours of Gioia and a forthcoming Canadian deployment, life at RAF Coltishall went on. A party of about thirty squadron personnel remained behind to act as a contact point for families and to assist in preparations for a visit to the station by HM the Queen and HRH the Duke of Edinburgh. It was immediately after the Royal Visit that members of the squadron departed for Cold Lake by TriStar of 216 Squadron. Exercise *Maple Flag* is just one of a number of large exercises which are held in particularly high esteem by RAF aircrew because they provide a unique opportunity for the whole squadron to fly in large 'packages' of aircraft against realistic targets and ground-threat simulators and against a state-of-the-art air threat. This was to be the squadron's third participation in successive years, but with the Bosnia commitment only a limited number of 54 (F) Squadron personnel could participate. The numbers were boosted by a small number of additional pilots who joined the detachment from the Jaguar OCU and from Coltishall's Ops Wing. The squadron's engineering team was supplemented by personnel from Engineering and Supply Wings.

The exercise was very successful and highly productive; the Jaguar held its own against ground-based surface-to-air missile-guidance radars and the American Aggressor F-16 aircraft. As ever, lessons were learnt and low-level tactics improved and updated. The detachment ended on 10 June, and the pilots returned to Gioia shortly thereafter. On 22 June the Operation *Deny Flight* commitment was again handed to 6 Squadron, and 54 returned to Coltishall having accomplished 100% of its tasked sorties.

After a month at home, the squadron suntans were beginning to fade, but 20 July saw the arrival of one of the year's high points, the NATO Squadron Exchange. Every year each squadron is given the chance to exchange with a counterpart in NATO. In 1994 the squadron was lucky enough to exchange with 330 Squadron of the Hellenic Air Force based at Nea Anchlios on the Aegean coast of Greece. Because of the distance involved and the shortage of air transport, it was decided that this was to be a 'simultaneous' exchange, with 330 Squadron deploying four F-16 aircraft and forty personnel to Coltishall, while 54 (F) Squadron deployed five Jaguars to Greece with nine pilots and forty ground crew. The aim of the exchange is for us to see how our allies work and for them to see how we go about our business. Needless to say, both squadrons took full advantage of this opportunity. As a note of co-operation, the ground parties deployed by Greek C-130H Hercules and returned to their respective home bases aboard an RAF Hercules C.Mk 3, the latter offering a little more space for souvenirs! On a serious note, the excavating proved to be an excellent medium for the 'exchange' of ideas, and views, and lessons on operating procedures were learnt by both sides. The British weather certainly provided the Greek pilots with some novel experiences!

54 Squadron Jaguar 'GN' undergoing maintenance in a hangar at Coltishall in June 2000. (Author)

It was traditional for 54 (F) Squadron to deploy at least once a year to Denmark to take part in one of the major exercises that take place in that country. Unfortunately, in 1994 the deployment to take part in September's Tactical Fighter Weaponry Exercise was cancelled for financial reasons. To fill the resulting 'void' in the squadron's yearly plan, it was decided to carry out combat training on the Air Combat Manoeuvring Installation (ACMI) at Decimomannu in Sardinia. Thus it was that, just three weeks after the end of the squadron exchange, eight Jaguars flew to the Mediterranean again. The ACMI is, as its name implies, a facility geared to air-combat training. It is like a giant three-dimensional radar, which covers a large area of airspace off the coast of Sardinia. Aircraft flying in this airspace carry special pods, which down-link to a central processing facility at Decimomannu. The data is used to produce aircraft performance and a true 3D picture of air combat. Pilots are able to simulate firing missiles using real switchery, and the machine will calculate whether 'kills' claimed are valid. Many a pilot has had to eat his words when faced by the evidence in the ACMI debrief! Virtually any type of modern aircraft can be fitted to fly on the ACMI, and in the case of 54 (F)'s deployment the opposition comprised Dutch F-l6Cs, Italian F-104s, German Phantoms and the much-valued MiG-29, operated by the German Air Force. The sorties carried out by British Jaguars were short but there were a lot of them! Rapid turn-rounds in exceptionally high temperatures were the order of the day. However, this did not

GR.3A XX766 of 16 (R) Squadron taxiing at Coltishall on 19 September 2003. The two yellow crossed keys symbolize the key to day-and-night operations. (Gary Parsons)

stop the squadron from achieving all its task sorties, again proving the flexibility of the aircraft and the men who service them. Needless to say, the training value for the pilots was enormous and some of the debriefs became very heated! The Jaguar fared remarkably well against the opposition, and tactical awareness increased exponentially as the detachment progressed. The performance of the Jaguar against the MiG-29 was particularly heartening, and the ground crew took great delight in watching the engagements 'live' in the ACMI monitoring cabins. One of the favourite views was the pilot's cockpit view, and as the intensity of each fight developed it was a fascinating experience to be able to switch from cockpit to cockpit to glimpse the views of opposing pilots. As the detachment progressed, so did the complexity of the fight scenarios, with 'multi-bogey' engagements and degraded fighter control from the ground. All in all, it was a highly successful deployment, and the squadron's return to Coltishall on 2 September marked the end of a spectacular summer![33]

With the summer's activity over, it was time for a comparative rest at Coltishall; however, with Operation *Deny Flight* looming on the horizon yet again, operational low flying, real weaponeering and work with FACs formed the majority of the squadron's training. Moreover, with two new pilots to bring up to combat-ready status, the UK low-flying system was put to good use. The squadron's third deployment to Gioia Del Colle took place on 12 October at a time when tension was running high in Bosnia. Initially operations continued at a normal pace with a mixture of reconnaissance and CAS sorties. However, at the beginning of November the world's attention fell on the Bihac Pocket in the north-west of the country. The use of missiles in the surface-to-surface role against a UN-protected area caused particular concern. But it was the attack on 19 November against the town itself by two Orao[34] aircraft from Udbina airfield in the RSK that finally provoked a NATO air strike.

In response to a UN request, a NATO raid on Udbina was planned by the Dutch contingent using photographs taken by the Jaguars on previous reconnaissance sorties.

The raid itself was planned for 20 November, but it had to be cancelled because of high cloud over the target area. The following day a strike package of more than fifty aircraft was tasked to strike the runways and taxiways on the airfield from the direction of the Dalmatian coast. The package consisted of US, Dutch, French and RAF aircraft – including four Jaguars – and was supported by the airborne controllers in their E3 Sentrys, together with USAF EF-111A Ravens and USN EA-6B Prowlers in the ECM role. Two Jaguars of 54 Squadron, one of which was flown by Wing Commander Tim Keress, dropped 1,000 lb bombs on the airfield. The other pair was tasked to carry out post-strike bomb-damage assessment photographs using the long-range attack pod. Flight Lieutenant Chris Carder, one of the Jaguar recce pilots, recalls:

> Funny thing, it was meant to be my day off. I was going to play golf (we did six days on, two days off). I got a telephone call at about 08.30 telling me to come in. At briefing we were told that in the afternoon we would be raiding Udbina and I was to lead the Jaguar post-attack recce pair. Basically, I was to get post-strike BDA photos using the LOROP at a height above 15,000 ft, 4–5 miles off the target.
>
> We tanked from a TriStar on the way in. Tanker after tanker was stacked up to refuel the American F-16s and F-18s and French Mirages. It was a gorgeous day. You could see for miles. AWACS cleared the package to push through, and then we got specific clearance to go in. An F-18, relaying the clearance from AWACs to us, said, 'You are cleared to press. "Manpads" (man-portable shoulder-launched missiles) and triple-A are in the area.' If flak was heavy we could always get the pictures later, but there was only light triple-A. The raid went in and palls of smoke were rising from the airfield, which was at the base of a mountain. The wingy asked, 'What speed are you going through?'
>
> I said, 'As fast as I can get.'
>
> I couldn't look out that much. I had to maintain level height to get good pictures and was using the HUD. My back-up was there just to watch my six. That was it. I

XZ363/FO of 41 Squadron and XX720/GB of 54 Squadron taxi out for a sortie in April 2000. Each aircraft is fitted with four practice bomb carriers (CBLS 100) on the under-fuselage pylons. In 1990 XZ363/A was painted with red 75th Anniversary tail markings to commemorate the squadron's formation in 1915. (RAF Coltishall).

got the photos and we all headed back to Giola Del Colle. We didn't need the tanker on the way home.[35]

Tim Keress continues:

> The results of the attack are now history, but it was indeed a proud moment for the squadron to represent the RAF in the largest air operation ever undertaken by NATO. The following days saw the planning and even launching of similar packages. Again, the Jaguars provided reconnaissance support but no further bombs were dropped in anger. Amid the flurry of subsequent diplomatic activity the threat of immediate air strikes abated and, by the time that the squadron returned to Coltishall during the first week of December, tasking was back to normal.
>
> Following a welcome but brief rest, 54 (F) Squadron took to the skies once again in force over the UK, an invaluable and necessary opportunity to rekindle academic and tactical skills in the air, and to reacquaint the ground crew with the challenges of running a full flying programme. When it came, the Christmas break was welcomed by all, a chance to reflect upon a truly memorable year and to contemplate what 1995 would bring. Already the programme was filling, with the promise of exercises in the USA and Norway, a missile-firing camp at RAF Valley and a squadron exchange to Portugal. The Cold War might have been over but with so much instability in the world the squadrons had never been busier! Mobility and flexibility were the keys to the emerging role, and while life could be hectic, it certainly wasn't boring!

During *Grapple*, the Jaguar force had flown 3,000 operational sorties over Bosnia, culminating in more than 5,000 flying hours. Not a single Jaguar was lost due to enemy action during this time. However, one aircraft, XZ373/GE, was lost on 21 June 1995 during a training sortie while being flown by a USAF exchange pilot with 6 Squadron. After a successful ejection over the Adriatic Sea, the pilot was eventually rescued by a Royal Navy Sea King, which had been scrambled from the NATO base at Split. On 31 January 1995 6 Squadron left Gioia del Colle, and Operation *Grapple* air operations were taken over by the Harrier force from RAF Wittering. At Coltishall two TIALD Jaguars (XX962 and XZ725) and crews were put on 48-hour standby ready to deploy to Italy to designate for the Harrier GR.7s against Serb targets in Bosnia if and when required. No. 6 Squadron took over the standby commitment on 24 August 1995, and shortly thereafter Operation *Deliberate Force* began when an artillery shell exploded in a market square in Sarajevo. On 29 and 30 August the TIALD Jaguars were flown to Gioia del Colle by Squadron Leader Alex Muskett (XX725) and Squadron Leader Simon Blake (XX692) respectively. One of the Jaguars had a TIALD pod owned by GEC Marconi, and the other was borrowed from a Tornado squadron at Brüggen. Operations began on 30 August when the two TIALD Jaguars and four Harriers, each armed with a pair of 1,000 lb Paveway II LGBs, attacked an ammunition storage depot near Sarajevo. Altogether Squadron Leaders Muskett and Blake flew twenty-five operational TIALD sorties, guiding forty-eight PGMs onto their targets and acquiring a number of other targets for Harriers attacking with 1,000 lb iron bombs. In January 1997 the Jaguars returned to Gioia del Colle to take over the *Grapple* detachment from the Harriers, with 41 Squadron leading the way.[36]

In April 2001 41 (F) Squadron RIC returned to Incirlik in Turkey to support the Jaguar Wing detachment which had once again taken over the task of policing the northern No Fly Zone in Iraq, now called Operation *Resinate* (*North*). This was a busy period operationally as Iraqi air defence units became noticeably more hostile in response to Coalition air activity in the run-up to Operation *Telic* in early 2003. Two of 6 Squadron's pilots were decorated for their contribution to operations over northern Iraq. In November 2001 Flight Lieutenant James Head was the formation leader of a two-aircraft reconnaissance mission patrolling the No Fly Zone. As the Jaguars crossed into hostile territory on their first 'recce run', they were met with far higher levels of anti-aircraft fire than usual. Having observed AAA exploding close aboard, Head called his formation to take evasive manoeuvres and modified the planned route. Subsequently, a further ten concentrated AAA airbursts were seen close to the Jaguars. Despite this he calmly continued the run while ensuring that the updated threat was passed to all other Coalition aircraft. On returning to Turkish airspace and following air-to-air refuelling, he was immediately given a complex airborne re-task. After ensuring his new wingman was fully prepared, Flight Lieutenant Head calmly led the formation back into hostile territory for a second reconnaissance run. His actions earned the award of the DFC. The previous such medal awarded to a 6 Squadron pilot was to Warrant Officer M. Gelbhauer in 1946.

Flight Lieutenant Graham Pemberton, who completed six operational tours on Operation *Resinate* (*North*) patrolling the No Fly Zone over northern Iraq, received the Queen's Commendation for valuable service in the air. In November 2002 he was detailed to carry out a tactical reconnaissance sortie. Having crossed into hostile airspace, he spotted intense anti-aircraft artillery fire that was a clear threat to his formation and F-16 aircraft in the vicinity. Pemberton directed immediate defensive manoeuvres and positively controlled the F-16s, ensuring all aircraft avoided the artillery airbursts. Subsequently, it was revealed that this had been the heaviest day of hostile fire since the operation commenced. During his operational tours, Graham Pemberton played an important part in developing Coalition tactics and procedures.

International political wrangling forced the rapid withdrawal of the Jaguar force detachment from Turkey only days before operations began to topple Saddam Hussein. Ultimately, although the Jaguar force was not required to take any further part in the operation, the JRP and the RIC deployed to Al Jaber in Kuwait to support reconnaissance operations by the Harrier during the war. At the end of hostilities in 2003, JRP and GIES were redeployed to the Tornado GR.4 detachment located initially at Ali Al Salem in Kuwait and subsequently at Al Udeid in Qatar.

41 and 54 Squadron Jaguars and Armée de l'Air *Mirage 2000Cs in April 2000. A month later, on 31 May, XX745/GV (nearest the camera) was involved in a mid-air collision with XX832/EZ T.2A of 6 Squadron during a sortie over Scotland, and both diverted into Leuchars, Fife. XX832 suffered only slight damage, but XX745 received severe damage to the underside of the cockpit area, and it was returned to Coltishall by road, where damage was assessed as CAT 4. Next are XX720/GB and XZ363/FO, which was lost on 26 July 2001 during Exercise* Cope Thunder *at Eielson AFB, Alaska, during simulated ground attack. Flight Lieutenant Jason Hayes was killed. Then come XX729/EL, XX829/GZ, XZ367/GP (which flew in Operation* Granby *as* Debbie, *and later* White Rose) *and XZ103/FP. (RAF Coltishall)*

CHAPTER EIGHT

'Train Hard, Fight Easy'

Those Jaguars pose us problems! The RAF boys truly part the sand and shave the rocks – they have a nice aeroplane; they fly it aggressively and their low-level tactics are good – very good! They have got the hang of terrain-masking their Jaguars. Yes, they gave us problems . . . . We find them hard to acquire visually and when we do pick 'em up, they're surely no 'easy' kill. We've flown against the best . . . for my money your Jaguar boys are as good as any of 'em and better than most!

USAF Aggressor pilot during a debrief after a sortie
flown during Exercise *Red Flag*, February 1981

Jaguars regularly took part in exercises at the Air Combat Manoeuvring Installation (ACMI) at Decimomannu in Sardinia and in *Maple Flag* at Cold Lake in Canada and *Red Flag* in the USA. *Red Flag* is one of the best training environments in the world for aircrew, offering realistic combat scenarios four times a year at Nellis Air Force Base in Nevada. The concept for *Red Flag* evolved from the American experience in SE Asia, when the previous air-to-air kill ratio of 10:1 reached during the Korean War of 1950–53

GR.1A 'GJ' of 54 Squadron at Red Flag. In 1980 at Red Flag, 54 Squadron flew 137 of 141 tasked sorties and incurred only a single air-to-air 'shoot down'. In Red Flag 1981, 54 Squadron Jaguars 'shot down' two USAF F-15 Eagles. (RAF Coltishall)

Jaguar in white ARTE scheme at Coltishall on 25 March 1982. Defending NATO's northern flank was a prime function of the Jaguars of the Coltishall Wing, and annual deployments were regularly made to the Royal Norwegian Air Force Base at Bardufoss, in northern Norway, 120 miles inside the Arctic Circle. All the aircraft that took part were normally given the standard Arctic scheme, consisting of an 'overwash' of white ARTE, while the normal full-colour squadron markings were retained. (Author)

fell to a low of 3:1. Lack of realistic training was perceived as part of the problem, and in 1972 the Red Aggressors, an air-to-air combat force designed to simulate Soviet airpower, were created. The Aggressors' aim was to employ Soviet-style tactics against USAF aircrew, though it did not address the high losses sustained from SAMs and AAA, and so in 1975 Nellis Range began a transformation into a Soviet-style integrated air defence system. Later that year, the first *Red Flag* exercise began with US fighters only, but within two years the RAF was invited to join. RAF Jaguars first attended *Red Flag* in 1976, when eight GR.1s of RAF Germany (five of 31 Squadron and three of 17 Squadron at Brüggen) were ferried to the USA by tanker-qualified pilots of 41 (F) Squadron. During the period 17 January to 28 February pilots of II (AC), 41 (F), 17, 31 and 6 Squadrons flew as part of the 'Blue Force' at Nellis AFB, operating with F-4E Phantoms as part of the primary air-to-ground exercise, as well as taking part in large composite attack forces. In 1978 54 Squadron's Jaguars took part in their first *Red Flag*. In 1980 they were tasked to attack a Red Force convoy 100 miles (160 km) from base. Flying at high transonic speeds at very low level, the Jaguars arrived unopposed and undetected at the target, much to the surprise of the Red Force aggressors. The following year 54 Squadron's Jaguars returned to *Red Flag* and 'shot down' two USAF F-15 Eagles!

'The primary aim of *Red Flag*', says Major Pete Davidson USAF, who participated in four *Red Flag* exercises, hauling bombs on an F-16 to simulate striking targets deep behind enemy lines, 'is to prepare aircrew for their first combat sorties so that pilots can face the threat of an SA-8 SAM for the first time without the real Mach 3 projectile coming his way!' Davidson spent his first year in the UK attending the Joint Services Command and Staff College, where he adopted 'proper English as his second language'. After graduating he was posted to Headquarters Strike Command to 'fly' the North American Exercises desk as project manager for all North American exercises, including *Red Flag*. He continues:

Just as the name implies, *Red Flag* is a carry-over from the Cold War mentality of

XZ115 and XZ355/J of 41 Squadron in Arctic scheme camouflage in March 1990. XZ355 was previously one of a batch used by II (AC) Squadron, which disbanded on 31 December 1987 and re-equipped with the Tornado GR.1A. (RAF Coltishall)

large forces operating against large forces. The challenge in the new millennium is to adapt to the changing face of global warfare. Since we should train the way we fight, future *Red Flag* exercises will need to adapt to include long-range surgical strikes, peacekeeping missions, which minimize collateral damage, and procedures to counter cruise missile threats. The focus of *Red Flag* is strictly airpower, lots of it. Fighters, bombers, tankers, transport and stealth aircraft, jammers, airborne early warning and

GR.1 XZ103/FP of 41 Squadron taxiing with the brake chute deployed after landing at Bardufoss. (RAF Coltishall)

GR.1s of 41 Squadron over Norway, with the leading aircraft very effectively painted overall in 'blotched' Arctic camouflage. (via Dave Bagshaw)

electronic intelligence platforms, helicopters, unmanned aerial vehicles (UAVs) – to the tune of about eighty aircraft – and that is just the good guys. Throw in sixteen Red Force Aggressors (the enemy) and you're nearly at 100 aeroplanes. *Red Flag* is a tactical exercise in integrating and employing a large force package – exactly what inexperienced aircrew need to prepare themselves for their vital role in modern warfare.

What prompts the RAF to pack up its people and kit and send them thousands of miles to the arid Nevada desert? Maybe it is the location. After all, Nellis AFB is located just a few miles north of Las Vegas. But it doesn't take a rocket scientist to figure out that sending assets thousands of miles for a bit of adventure training at the blackjack or roulette tables will not pass an audit. Location is the key draw for *Red Flag*, not because of Las Vegas but because of the Nellis Range complex. The exercise airspace is situated in a sparsely populated desert

GR.1 XZ372/ED of 6 Squadron in Arctic camouflage scheme. (RAF Coltishall)

area in southern Nevada and covers 9,000 square miles – bigger than the skies over the whole of Wales and up as far as the Isle of Man. Even after the airspace is divided up into blue, red, and air-to-air-refuelling areas, there is still enough to allow AWACS and fast-jets to build a good radar picture. It means they have time to get their ducks in a row before the heat of the battle. Most exercise areas are half this size and just don't allow for proper training of the latest and greatest long-range missiles. Not only is the area immense, it is also varied, rising from flat scrub brush to 10,000 ft snow-capped mountain peaks. Here is where the 'mud-movers' (the ground-attack aircraft) and transport aircrew gain the maximum benefit. Training is simply outstanding in an area where you can traverse through mountain passes at 100 ft above the ground while evading enemy fighters and SAMs! Add in the clearance to fly supersonic attacking targets defended by a formidable array of threats, and you start to get the picture of why *Red Flag* is such good training value. But there is more.

Red Flag aircraft carry instruments that record their every move. The $58 million *Red Flag* Measurement and Debriefing System (RFMDS) allows directing staff to monitor the war safely as it unfolds and record all the data for further review.[37] We are talking serious data: airspeed, altitude, attitude, six-forces, manoeuvring and weapon releases, to name but a few. After each mock battle the players gather in the

GR.1 of 6 Squadron taxiing at Coltishall in July 1980. (Author)

300-seat main auditorium to review the war on two-storey-high projection screens. Here they thrash out who shot whom and assess the overall strategy, as well as who made it safely to their target and came back alive. Sometimes there are differing opinions as to how the war went, so the playback can be stopped and reviewed in explicit detail. The system can also be zoomed-in to scrutinize any allegations and ascertain the truth of a situation. For further clarification, the view can even be switched to look through the computer simulation of the cockpit of any aircraft.

Conditions at Nellis AFB can cause problems for both aircraft and their operators, and the 41 (R) and 54 (F) Squadron Jaguars got more than they had bargained for in August 1999. The extreme summer heat, coupled with the high-pressure altitude of Nellis, forced them to operate close to the edge of the aircraft's performance envelope. But being faced with challenging obstacles is the environment that service personnel thrive on. The Jaguar pilots were creative in adapting their flying profiles to optimize the aircraft's performance, complete their missions safely and get their bombs on target. But it was not just the pilots who had to be creative. The ground engineers found themselves grappling with the searing heat on the aircraft dispersal, and frequently had to adapt their operations to cope with the conditions. Continually flying the Jaguars towards the edge of their performance envelope also created problems, which meant the engineers had to work that much harder to keep them serviceable. There were occasions when their day shifts worked right through until 3 a.m. or 4 a.m. to get the jets ready for the

Jaguars of 41 Squadron on the line at RAF Coltishall in unseasonable spring weather early in 2000. (RAF Coltishall)

Jaguars of 54, 6 and 41 Squadrons from RAF Coltishall on 4 September 1998. Nearest aircraft is XZ396. Behind is XZ369/EF of 6 Squadron with TIALD pod, FK of 41 Squadron and GO of 54 Squadron. (RAF Coltishall)

next day's sortie. When I pressed them about how they felt about the long hours they all said that it was part of the job, which had thoroughly tested their operational mettle and was a great experience. I think I got straight answers from everyone because when I started prodding them for their impressions of *Red Flag* I didn't introduce myself – I was just another American asking dumb questions!

Recovering from America from a major exercise like *Red Flag*, as ten Jaguars of 54 (F) Squadron did in September 1999, is always an adventure, and the major obstacle to be overcome is the Atlantic Ocean. A number of assets had to be in the right places and serviceable before the start on Wednesday 1 September: the ten Jaguars in Bangor, Maine, one Nimrod for search and rescue cover, two VC-10 tankers, one Lockheed TriStar K.Mk 1 tanker, and everyone was ready to go. The plan was to head east for a refuelling stop in the Azores (five hours' flying time) and then complete the trip to Coltishall the following day. However, on the day of the trail to the Azores the original VC 10 was grounded with a problem at Nellis. It would get to Bangor on 2 September, but the trail needed to go ahead, so a spare VC 10 had to be flown out from the UK. This spare was a K.Mk 2, one of the smaller marks of VC 10, only carrying enough fuel for three Jaguars to cross to the Azores. And so the spare Jaguar had to trail across to the Azores with the VC 10 from Nellis a day later.[38] For the rest of the pilots it was a case of 'Kick the navigators and light the fires'. The first wave of three Jaguars, led by the Boss, got airborne, followed by their

Given RAF Coltishall's Polish history during the Second World War, it proved timely to host a visit in June 2000 during the 60th Anniversary of operations at RAF Coltishall, the last Battle of Britain fighter station to have been continuously used for fighter operations. Among the visitors were a single-seater and a two-seater Sukhoi Su 22 M4 Fitter-K of 8 Eskadra Lotnictwa Taktycznego (8th Tactical Fighter Squadron) at Miroslawiec Air Base. It was the first time that the Polish Air Force had landed at Coltishall since February 1947. (RAF Coltishall)

Jaguars of 41 (F) Squadron in flight with Swedish Air Force Saab 37 Viggens in May 2001. A year earlier the most northern Swedish Air Force wing, Norbotten, played host to five Jaguars of 41 (F) Squadron during the first bilateral operational training deployment to Sweden by an RAF unit. The aircraft deployed to Kallax air base near the northern town of Lulea following their participation in Exercise Snow Goose in Norway. Exercise Lone Wolf, named after the F21 Wing Saab 37 Viggen squadron which hosted the visit, involved around a hundred RAF personnel, who arrived anticipating temperatures well below freezing, with considerable quantities of snow. Unseasonably high temperatures meant that the weather was actually all too familiar, with rain and low cloud keeping the aircraft grounded for most of the week (RAF Coltishall)

VC 10. Thirty minutes later the second three-ship of Jaguars was airborne, this time followed by their TriStar. However, when the TriStar got up to flying speed and rotated to get airborne it managed to blow a hole six feet across and two inches deep in the Bangor runway. Until that was fixed there was no way that the third wave of three Jaguars and the second VC 10 could get airborne. It would take a few hours at least to repair, and so, due to daylight and crew duty time, there was no way those guys were leaving Bangor that day! Then the TriStar's refuelling system developed a problem, and despite many attempts by the Jaguars, was unable to give them fuel. The Jaguars diverted to Halifax, Nova Scotia, and the TriStar, after circling for hours waiting for the runway to be fixed, returned to Bangor, probably to apologize to air traffic control.

On Thursday 2 September the remaining seven Jaguars were ready to go, but they were not going to try refuelling from the TriStar this time because the VC 10 from Nellis was now available. All were in their cockpits, ready to start engines, when word came through that the Nimrod was now unserviceable. It would take at least two hours to fix, and once again this would take the Jaguar pilots outside crew duty time. It was quickly decided that the trail was not going that day after all, and since Bangor was going to close for Labor Day, the Jaguars and the VC 10 needed to fly to Halifax. The TriStar was no longer required due to the shorter distance involved, so the aircraft flew home to the UK. The three Jaguars already in the Azores trailed to Coltishall as planned. The four Jaguars from Bangor landed uneventfully but the VC 10 had an anti-skid system failure, burst a tyre and required an undercarriage leg change, which would not be ready until the Saturday. The three Jaguars that originally diverted to Halifax trailed to the Azores with their VC 10. After a four-hour 'faff' over a hydraulic leak in the nose of the VC 10, they continued to the UK with two of the three. The third Jaguar had a starting problem and was left in the Azores for a new starter motor, which would arrive on the Saturday with the last VC 10. Two aircraft arrived back at Coltishall late at night after the pilots had flown for nine hours that day.

Jaguars of 54, 6 and 41 Squadrons at Coltishall in January 2001. Nearest aircraft is XZ394/GN of 54 Squadron. Behind are XX637/EE, XZ396/EM and XZ372/ED of 6 Squadron. (RAF Coltishall)

On Saturday 4 September the remaining four Jaguars trailed from Halifax to the Azores. The 54 (F) Squadron ground crew on the VC 10 carried out the quickest change of a starter motor ever seen, and the spare pilot got in the aircraft to go as a five-ship to Coltishall. Unfortunately one of the other four now decided to catch his starter motor on fire, so only four made the trail. Since the one and only spare starter motor for the trail had already been used, it was decided to wrap the aircraft up and leave it in the Azores. All the ground crew jumped on the sweeper Hercules and flew back to Lyneham, where they got 'mucked about' royally. The last aircraft was flown back to the UK ten days later, after some fairly major work was required to get it serviceable. All in all, then, quite a smooth trail to cap an excellent exercise! The tanker crews told the Jaguar pilots that they

Wing Commander Mike Seares MBE, OC 6 Squadron, on 14 May 2004 in front of GR.3A XX112 with the colourful 'Flying Canopeners 1914–2004' commemorative tail at RAF Coltishall on 29 October 2003. Mike Seares graduated from flying training with HRH Major-General Prince Feisal Bin-al Hussein of Jordan in 1988 and joined 54 (F) Squadron; after flying in the Gulf War he became a QWI and flight commander on 6 Squadron. One of the youngest squadron commanders in the RAF, he assumed command of 6 Squadron in 2002. (Gary Parsons)

GR.3A 'EF' of 6 Squadron taxiing out at Coltishall on 12 August 2004. (Gary Parsons)

never expected Jaguar trails to go as planned because the aircraft were not very serviceable. On this occasion it was everything except the Jaguars that was broken. The only time they did not perform as advertised was in the Azores, but then, who could blame them?

On occasion the Jaguar squadrons have made trips to countries once hostile to Britain. In November 1996 a memorandum of understanding was signed between Britain and Egypt, which paved the way for the first RAF fighters since the Suez Crisis of 1956 to fly to Egypt, where they took part in Exercise *Jagged Sphinx*. On 29 November the Jaguars, aircrew and ground crews of 41 (F) Squadron, under the command of Wing Commander Chris Harper, together with support elements from RAF Coltishall, made the six-hour flight to Cairo West Air Base. XZ113/ED and XZ367/GP were painted in temporary sand camouflage, similar to that adopted by the Jaguar fleet during Operation *Desert Storm*. During their two-week deployment members of 41 Squadron were guests of 222 Tactical Fighter Brigade equipped with ex-USAF F-4E Phantoms. Approximately ninety sorties were flown, mostly combined air operations comprising up to ten Jaguars, 8 F-16s and 4 F-4Es ranged against a variety of targets, including HMS *Invincible*, which was operating in the region at the time. Other missions included air-to-air refuelling (AAR) with VC 10 tankers. The Egyptian Air Force, which until this time had little or no experience in the 'hose-to-basket' technique, took advantage of the tanker to practise AAR with their Mirage 2000s.[39]

In Germany the RAF remained on full alert and exercised regularly on the continent and further afield to remain at the forefront of the NATO deterrent. Defending NATO's northern flank was a prime function of the Jaguars of the Coltishall Wing, and annual deployments were regularly made to the Royal Norwegian Air Force base at Bardufoss, in northern Norway, 120 miles inside the Arctic Circle. All the aircraft that took part were normally given the standard Arctic scheme, consisting of an 'overwash' of white ARTE,

Jaguar GR.3A 'GB' of 41 Squadron in Arctic scheme at RAF Coltishall on 11 March 2005. (Gary Parsons)

while the normal full-colour squadron markings were retained. No. 41 (F) Squadron was the declared Arctic specialist in the Jaguar wing, although 6 and 54 Squadrons also regularly deployed to the inhospitable snowy wastes as part of their rapid deployment capability. Flight Lieutenant Dave Stephen of 41 (F) Squadron recalls:

> If the Cold War had ever turned hot, then it is most likely that 41 (F) Squadron, in keeping with the expeditionary nature of the Jaguar force, would have been tasked to provide recce and attack support to NATO's northern flank. In all probability, the manifestation of this would have been a rapid deployment, for the whole squadron, to RNoAF Bardufoss to fight the war from inside the Arctic Circle. For the uninitiated, Bardufoss is a small airfield in the north of Norway where winter temperatures can drop as low as minus 40C. The 'idiosyncrasies' of operating in this harsh environment meant that regular exposure was a must for the entire squadron, and so, up until the late 1990s, 41 (F) Squadron could expect to deploy to Bardufoss several times a year.
>
> The Arctic Circle may seem a long way from the perceived Cold War battlefields of Germany, but it is worth noting that, at its closest point, Norway is only sixty-six miles from the Russian naval base at Murmansk and it is around the Norwegian coastline that the Russian Navy would have had to come to break into the Atlantic. The Russian strategic bombers bound for the UK would have, in all likelihood, followed a similar course.
>
> Operating in the Arctic is significantly different from operating in the temperate climes of Central Europe. During the winter months they do not get a lot of sun that far north, which manifests itself in two ways. Firstly, there are only a few hours of usable daylight each day, so some part of every sortie will be conducted at night. Daylight is also a bit of a misnomer in this context, as the sun barely gets above the horizon. Secondly it is flippin' cold, so any time spent outside a heated building has to be kept to a minimum. The weather can turn very quickly as well, and seems to only have two settings – clear blue skies or blizzards.

Sukhoi Su 22 M4 Fitter-K 9616 of 7 Eskadra Lotnictwa Taktycznego (7th Tactical Fighter Squadron) and Jaguars at Coltishall on 14 June 2005. (Author)

It takes a lot longer to go from 'outbrief' to airborne in these conditions, for a number of reasons. Firstly, it takes a good twenty minutes to get dressed as you tread the fine line between 'dressing to survive' and being able to move in the cockpit. Inevitably the pilots end up looking like green 'Michelin Men'. It is too cold for the jets to be kept outside and so each pilot has to be dropped off at the HAS containing his aircraft. Taxiing to the runway is not something you can rush when everything is covered in snow, and there are apocryphal stories of stationary Jaguars sliding off taxiways without any assistance from the pilot.

Take-off itself is something of a treat for Jaguar pilots. In the cold conditions the engines perform extremely well and the aircraft seems to leap airborne like a jet half its age. This is good because Bardufoss itself lies in a mountainous region of Norway and the standard Jaguar 'curvature of the earth departure' is not an option.

Jaguar GR.3A XZ112/FE of 54 Squadron taxies in past a Sukhoi Su 22 M4 Fitter-Ks of 7 Eskadra Lotnictwa Taktycznego (7th Tactical Fighter Squadron) at Coltishall on 14 June 2005. (Author)

GR.3A XX737/EE of 6 Squadron and XZ392 with the famous Saint markings on the black tail airborne from Coltishall on 15 June 2005. (Gary Parsons)

Once safely airborne, Norway delights with some of the most spectacular flying I have ever experienced. Flying in a north-easterly direction from Bardufoss one flies through a region of beautiful snow-covered mountains that are interspersed with huge fjords. There is little sign of human habitation although you have to be extremely vigilant for the high-tension cables that are strung across many of the valleys. Once through this area you come to the wide-open expanse of the Kautekeino Plain. This is classic Arctic tundra, miles and miles of snowy wasteland with little or no sign of life. The low sun casts an eerie glow over the whole landscape, which makes it extremely beautiful, at least from the warm cockpit of the Jag, though the fact that you are miles from anywhere and the temperature outside is probably below minus 20 never quite leaves the back of your mind. There is little doubt that anyone who has experienced low level in Norway counts it among the highlights of their flying careers.

The journey back from the operating area to Bardufoss is not the relaxing transit that concludes most sorties, as you know that you are going to have land the aircraft back on a potentially snow- and ice-covered runway. Also, in order to get to that point you have to make the approach down 'the hill'. Everyone who has been to Bardufoss will know what I am talking about. For the uninitiated, the last mile of the final approach to the recovery runway is actually down the side of a hill, hence the name. The recommended technique is to start at the top of the hill, fully configured at a radar height of 100 ft. You then fly down the hill, keeping the height between 50 and 100 ft. In the last few hundred yards the hill steepens slightly and the threshold appears. You have the option of a dirty dive to it or a more standard approach to the instrument touchdown point. A third option, known as the 'clatter of bits', is a combination of the two and is the one favoured by most virgins to Bardufoss.

Once back on terra firma you are faced with the problem of stopping ten tons of aircraft, travelling at 150 knots on an ice rink. The parachute is a must in these conditions, and the use of the cable is probably more common here than anywhere else. Once again, legends abound of Jaguars taking the cable backwards after particularly hairy landings. That said, the Jag was built in the days when aircraft were hewn from a solid piece of metal, so pulling them out of snowdrifts and putting them back on the line is not a major problem.

Norway seems to be a place of contradictions. It is hard to understand why people would get any enjoyment from flying operations in the Arctic Circle, where it is dark and cold all the time. Yet I have never met any member of 41 (F) Squadron, aircrew or ground crew, who did not look forward to a Bardufoss detachment. It may be because the snow and crisp, cold air gives the place a Christmas-card feel. It may be because of the beauty of the place or just maybe it is because of the pride that comes from knowing that, despite the conditions, 41 (F) Squadron, for two decades, 'came, saw and conquered'. Over many years they have earned the right to be known as 'Arctic Warriors'.

With the ending of the Cold War, Britain's forces, and in particular the RAF, were able to renew old traditions and exercise with former WarPac opponents. On Monday 18 October 1999 six Jaguars of 41 (F) Squadron left Coltishall bound for Miroslawiec Air Base, Poland, thus becoming the first RAF jet squadron to deploy behind the former Iron Curtain into what was previously a Warsaw Pact country but was NATO's newest member. The deployment was for Exercise *Jade Fusion* in support of the British Army UK 1 Division Exercise *Ulan Eagle 99*, as Flight Lieutenant Sion Hughes, a member of the 'team' recalls:

Not being quite sure what to expect at the other end in terms of weather, approach aids, or Polish ATC, it was nice to hear the welcoming tones of Michelle, our air trafficker, borrowed from the tower at Colt, along with Paul the 'tac' PAR bloke from Brize, as we found the airfield to be Blue and not fogged out as forecast. Following a suitably punchy arrival to show these Polish pilots how it was done (or so we thought), we were transported to the resident squadron's building known as the Pilots' House. The Poles had been very generous (a recurring theme) and given us their planning room to use as our own, which, despite the best efforts of the weekend's vodka, the advance team had set up in great style.

The next hurdle to overcome was getting to grips with the Polish flying system. Flight plans for the missions had to be in twenty-four hours in advance, and with no formalized NOTAM system that we could discover this caused a few problems when we were told, sometimes at the outbrief, that three out of the five low-flying areas we had planned through were closed due to a lone Colt dropping medicated animal feed. The Polish low-flying system consists of designated areas measuring roughly 30 km by 15 km, where you can fly to 100 ft. Outside of these we were limited to 1,000 ft. Around the airfield to 20 km you can also fly to 100 ft. Try that around Coltishall and the phone wouldn't stop ringing for a month. The rules for the airfield, however, were much simpler: left-hand breaks to each runway, end of rules. When asked about what we could and could not do, the Polish chap in the tower replied with a cheery 'The airfield is yours, no problem.' SATCO take note! The more restrictive national rules then came into play, and 100 ft MSD breaks were

T.4 XX838/FZ of 41 Squadron, GR.3A EJ of 6 Squadron and FV taking off from Coltishall on 14 June 2005. (Author)

declared the order of the det, allowing the resident SU-22 *Fitters* to win the lowest fly-bys by some margin.

Throughout the det we were lucky with the weather, which generally proved to be somewhere in between the local forecaster (pessimistic) and our own 'tac met man' Neil (optimistic). This allowed us to fly well in excess of the RIC's most optimistic guess in the 'How many trips?' sweepstake. While doing this we also flew a great deal of CAS as both Red and Blue Air for the Army, and took the opportunity of flying as many of the *Fitter* pilots as we could in the T-bird to give

GR.3A XZ399/EJ of 6 Squadron and T.4 XX838/FZ of 41 Squadron taking off from Coltishall on 14 June 2005. (Author)

GR.3A XZ399/EJ of 6 Squadron and T.4 XX838/FZ of 41 Squadron taking off from Coltishall on 14 June 2005. (Author)

T.4 XX835/FY taxiing out at Coltishall on 14 June 2005. (Author)

them an idea of how we operate. They were all enthusiastic about the Jaguar's handling, which made us wonder what on earth a *Fitter* must be like: an opportunity experienced by the Boss, Exec, Gain and Quicky, who all agreed that the *Fitter* is not blessed with great handling but has LOTS of power. On further discussion with the Poles over tactics it seems that the *Fitter* suited their needs, as back when we would have been the target the plan was to send lots of aircraft, in a straight line, very fast to the DPI.

The area of Poland that we were operating over is akin to a slightly more rolling version of Norfolk but with more lakes and wooded areas. The woods are home to various wild animals, including deer and boar. These are hunted by the local populace, including some of the Polish pilots, who very kindly invited along three of our det to go hunting on the middle Sunday . . . . Throughout the detachment the Poles were always friendly, eager to help and very keen to learn about how we operated with regard to their integration into NATO.

Given RAF Coltishall's Polish history during the Second World War it proved timely to host a reciprocal visit in June 2000 during the 60th Anniversary of operations at RAF Coltishall, the last Battle of Britain fighter station to have been continuously used for fighter operations. Among the visitors were two Sukhoi Su 22 M4 *Fitter-Ks* of *8 Eskadra Lotnictwa Taktycznego* (8th Tactical Fighter Squadron) at Miroslawiec Air Base. It was the first time that the Polish Air Force had landed at Coltishall since February 1947. In August 2002 6 Squadron, led by Wing Commander Mike Seares, deployed six Jaguar GR.3/3A and two Jaguar T.4 aircraft and over 140 personnel to Graf Ignatievo Air Base, Bulgaria. The 'Flying Canopeners' would be the first RAF fast-jet squadron to operate with the *Bulgarski Voenno-Vazdushni Sili* (*BVVS*, or Bulgarian Air Force) since the end of the Cold War. Squadron Leader Johnny Stringer of 6 Squadron recalls:

The stimulus for deploying an RAF fast-jet squadron to Bulgaria and exercising with her air force came from the United Kingdom's 'Outreach' programme. The UK

GR.3A XZ114/EO landing at Coltishall on 14 June 2005. (Author)

GR.3A XX970/EH of 6 Squadron landing at Coltishall on 14 June 2005. This aircraft left Coltishall on 29 March 2006. (Author)

is actively committed to promoting peace and security in the new European countries that were created within Central and Eastern Europe in the aftermath of the end of the Cold War. The fundamental objective of this scheme is to assist in the development throughout the region of stable, sovereign and democratic states. The primary means used is bilateral development of stable, sovereign and democratic states throughout the region. The primary means used is a series of bilateral defence co-operation programmes organized by the MoD between the UK's Armed Forces

GR.3A XZ103/FP of 41 Squadron airborne from RAF Coltishall on 17 September 2005. (Gary Parsons)

and those of the Central European nations. Although a purely UK-generated programme, Outreach has similar goals to the NATO-sponsored 'Partnership for Peace (PfP) initiative – both programmes aim to help create a 21st-century Europe built on mutual trust and confidence. Within the RAF the Outreach programme is supported by HQ Strike Command, and it was the latter's exercise plans staff who were instrumental in the initial organization and planning for Exercise *Lonecat 02*. Once the overall exercise objectives had been agreed at governmental level, and the participation of 6 Squadron confirmed in April 2002, it was time to get on with the in-depth planning and organization required to deploy a Jaguar squadron to a foreign operating base.

Every exercise and operation brings new problems and challenges, and the deployment to Bulgaria was to prove no different. The RAF deployed additional elements of infrastructure and logistical support (such as fuel bowsers) by road across Europe, using the expertise of 2 MT Squadron, to augment Bulgarian assets. Extensive discussions were held to reach agreement on the tactical training objectives for both air forces, the airspace available to operate in and, importantly from 6 Squadron's perspective, the clearance to operate down to operational low flying (OLF) heights of 100 ft above ground level.

For the Jaguar pilots, the exercise promised much: OLF; electronic warfare training against real former Soviet Union equipment; Close Air Support (CAS) training and weaponeering against realistic tactical targets on an unfamiliar range; and perhaps most interestingly, the opportunity to fly with and against MiG-21 *Fishbed* and Sukhoi Su-25 *Frogfoot* aircraft operated by the Bulgarians. For its part, the *BVVS* would get to see how a NATO nation planned, briefed, flew and debriefed the whole gamut of air-to-ground missions, and all within a combined air operation (COMAO) framework, with *BVVS* and RAF pilots flying alongside each other in multi-aircraft packages. Jaguars and MiGs would also conduct offensive counter air

GR.3A XX738/ED of 6 Squadron at Coltishall on 29 March 2006. (Author)

GR.3A XZ398/FA of 41 Squadron taxies out at Coltishall on the afternoon of 29 March 2006 (but returned soon after as it went tech before take-off). (Author)

missions (the 'enemy', or aggressor fighter role) against attacking Jaguars and *Frogfoots* (or '*Frogfeet*', as two or more of them were soon labelled). Lastly but equally important was the opportunity for the engineers of 6 Squadron and the two Bulgarian squadrons to operate together and for the latter to see how the RAF maintains its aircraft and faces the engineering challenges posed by deployed operations.

The squadron's main party deployed to Graf Ignatievo Air Base by VC 10 on Sunday 18 August 2002 to ensure that the necessary engineering support was in

GR.3A XX748/EG of 6 Squadron taxies out at Coltishall on 29 March 2006. (Author)

GR.3A XZ399/EJ and XZ392/EM of 6 Squadron and XX723/FF and one other Jaguar of 41 Squadron prepare to leave Coltishall for the last time on Wednesday 29 March 2006. (Author)

place prior to the arrival of the Jaguars the following day. Following a refuelling stop at Prague, the eight Jaguars arrived in two waves of four aircraft as planned on the afternoon of 19 August, dodging the odd inconvenient thunderstorm *en route*. Graf Ignatievo is home to the *1/1 IAE* (fighter squadron), operating MiG-21s, and the *2/2 IAE* flying MiG-29s. Additionally, five Su-25s were deployed from Besmer Air Base for the duration of the exercise. The runway and operating surfaces were in excellent condition, the product of recent NATO investment prior to the base hosting Exercise *Co-operative Key*, a NATO-sponsored PfP flying exercise. The base also boasted a newly refurbished planning, briefing and debriefing suite and some first-class working accommodation for the squadrons' engineers.

As ever, no foreign country visited by an RAF squadron is complete without that statement of British military presence, the 12 ft x 12 ft tent, here used as a canvas hut. The Bulgarians had also thoughtfully arranged for one room to be turned into a pilots' crew room, complete with an enormous Italian espresso coffee machine; it

A wave from the Coltishall control tower and the Jaguars depart. (Author)

One by one, fifteen Jaguars leave Coltishall for the last time on Wednesday 29 March 2006, most of them flying to their new station at RAF Coningsby, Lincolnshire, while two aircraft head for St Athan to be used as spares. (Author)

A formation of three Jaguars airborne from Coltishall on 29 March 2006. (Author)

soon became the most used facility on base. The town of Graf Ignatievo is seven miles north of Plovdiv, Bulgaria's second city, famous for its rich architectural heritage and steeped in history. It was a delightful place to be.

Exercise *Lonecat 02* was the most significant Anglo-Bulgarian military exercise yet to be held in Bulgaria, so the event attracted considerable media interest. From the opening ceremony until our departure on 30 August, a day did not pass without a microphone- or camera-carrying journalist appearing (normally unannounced) at crew-in or in the crew room. There was even a coach-load of British aviation enthusiasts on the first flying day of the exercise, and by the time of our departure, most of the pilots had found themselves quoted or photographed in the Bulgarian press. However, once the arrival briefings had been completed, both the *BVVS* and the RAF pilots were eager to get airborne and start operating together. The Bulgarians were very keen to see how the RAF operated at the tactical level, and the various missions flown were characterized by full integration of *BVVS* and RAF pilots from the planning stage through to the debrief. Bulgaria has high hopes of being admitted to membership of NATO and is keen to develop standard operating procedures that are aligned to those of the current members.

Indeed, the current upgrade programme of her MiG-29s is designed to ease integration with NATO air forces. The RAF is held to have much to offer because of our recent operational experience and position at the heart of the Alliance. For 6 Squadron's part, we were keen to share as much knowledge as we could about the conduct of air-to-ground operations within general NATO operating standards.

Initial exercise flying on Day One was centred on in-country familiarization for the RAF pilots, including dry passes at the Koren weapons range. From the outset, the two Jaguar T.4 two-seaters were used to fly Bulgarian pilots on every mission, while 6 Squadron pilots were able to experience flying in the MiG-21 and Su-25. Each aircraft had differing characteristics, with the MiG-21 and Jaguar closest in performance, but with the Su-25 having a notably more modern cockpit than the *Fishbed*. Jaguar pilots qualified to operate and instruct from the rear seat of the Jaguar T4 are used to a somewhat limited view from the rear cockpit, but this seemed positively panoramic compared to the view from the MiG-21. Visibility at

GR.3A XZ112/GW (left) and XZ117/FB (right) after a downpour at Coltishall on 1 April 2006. (Author)

41 Squadron disbandment parade at RAF Coltishall on 1 April 2006, with XZ103/FP behind. No. 41 (F) Squadron handed over the squadron numberplate to the Fast Jet and Weapons Operational Evaluation Unit at RAF Coningsby, and 6 Squadron left for Coningsby to continue flying the Jaguar until late 2007, when the aircraft will be replaced by the Typhoon. (Author)

GR.3A XZ103/FP of 41 Squadron at RAF Coltishall on 1 April 2006. (Gary Parsons)

low speed from the back seat of the MiG is augmented by a periscope; at high speed – well, 'stow the sight Luke and may the force be with you'. The cockpit ergonomics belonged to an earlier age, too, and although the addition of a cockpit-mounted GPS assisted navigation enormously, operating the MiG successfully undoubtedly required a fair of skill and application. An obvious advantage of its small and streamlined shape was the aircraft's small visual signature – it was very difficult to see until it was almost at or within weapons employment range, and we often saw the MiG's smoke trail before getting a 'tally' on the jet itself. Turning

T.4 XX847/EZ of 6 Squadron at Coltishall on 1 April 2006. (Author)

performance for a first-generation delta-winged aircraft was surprisingly impressive, and the *Fishbed* accelerated briskly even without the use of afterburner.

By comparison, the *Frogfoot* cockpit was everything the MiG was not – roomy, comparatively well laid out and providing an excellent outside view, befitting its role as a close-air-support aircraft. However, its survivability against a high-performance air threat was debatable; the *Frogfoot* pilot's best chance of survival lay in seeing an opponent early and turning rapidly towards the threat while defeating an infra-red missile through throttling back to reduce the aircraft's heat signature. Interestingly, and most rewardingly from the *BVVS*'s perspective, was the success that the *Frogfoots* enjoyed in the second week of the exercise in defeating attempted missile shots from the Jaguars. The collective and honest mission debriefs that were a feature of the exercise, augmented by the head-up-display video tapes from the Jaguar and debriefs from 6 Squadron pilots flying in the aggressor role, were instrumental in changing the *Frogfoot*'s operating tactics.

Although the Jaguar was not in the first flush of youth, the Bulgarian pilots who flew in the T.4s were struck by two things – the accuracy of the navigation kit and the relative comfort of the ride at low level and high speed. In equipment terms the 'front third' of the Jaguar represents pretty much the cutting edge of current fast-jet technology, if one allows for the lack of a radar. The accuracy is a function of an integrated inertial navigation system, profile-matching navigation solution, accurate to within a few feet in three dimensions. The Jaguars TIALD laser designation pod and AIM-9L air-to-air missiles can be cued to their respective targets by a helmet-mounted sight, while a ground proximity warning system and audio voice alerting device aids flight safety by warning the pilot of any potential controlled flight into terrain. Alongside an internal and external lighting suite fully compatible with night-vision goggles is the first tactical data link yet fitted to the RAF 'mud moving' fast-jet – the improved data modem (IDM). The Jaguar's IDM allows the burst transmission of target data to the pilot from a suitably radio-equipped forward air controller and has huge growth potential in a multitude of roles and scenarios. The comfort of the ride at low level is simply down to the Jaguar's high wing loading; the aircraft was designed to be as stable as possible in the low-level strike/attack role envisaged during the Cold War. The trade-off is a turn rate that is often unkindly referred to as requiring measurement using a calendar.

By the end of Week One, the RAF and *BVVS* were operating mixed attack formations of MiGs, Frogfoots and Jaguars in COMAO-type missions, with both Jaguars and MiGs acting as aggressor aircraft. A typical mission profile involved an ingress at medium level (15,000–20,000 ft) against fighters supported by ground-based early warning radars and associated fighter controllers; after descending to low level, deployed SA-8 surface-to-air missile systems would attempt to engage the attack package as it routed towards the Koran weapons range. Our two deployed RAF Regiment officers (swiftly labelled 'Pinky 2' and 'Perky' . . . it's a long story) provided an excellent service as forward air controllers and used laser target marking to illuminate targets for the incoming Jaguars. Weapons dropped included 3 kg and 14 kg practice bombs and 1,000 lb inert bombs, all from a variety of low- and medium-level delivery profiles. The targets were particularly challenging, with positive identification often achieved only seconds before weapon release. Having fought our way through to the range and dropped our bombs, we then had to counter successfully the threat posed by further MiG and Jaguar aggressors before recovering to Graf Ignatievo. Although the average sortie was only an hour long, the training value gained from such intensive missions was exceptional, and was well in excess of our expectations prior to leaving the UK. The quality and application of the *BVVS* pilots was impressive and contributed greatly to the success of the exercise. The prospect of Bulgarian membership of NATO in the near term has provided a powerful incentive to the development of modern tactics along Western lines.

Lonecat 02 was an outstanding success for all of its participants, both *BVVS* and RAF, and proved the value of the Outreach Programme. Until recently, the deployment of an entire RAF fast-jet squadron to a former Warsaw Pact country would have been unthinkable. The reality in the new Europe, forged from the ending of the Cold War and the collapse of the Soviet Union, is that the old certainties no longer apply. For Bulgaria and the UK, *Lonecat 02* was a powerful statement of the renewed trust and co-operation that now exists between both countries. At the tactical level it afforded 6 Squadron some extremely high-quality training against equipment still operated by other potential adversaries around the world. It also demonstrated to us the professionalism and pride of the pilots of the *BVVS*, and that – regardless of uniform or country – fast-jet pilots are, at heart, the same the world over. 6 Squadron left Bulgaria genuinely touched by the warmth shown to us by everyone we met during our stay.

In August 2004 four Sukhoi Su-22 M4 *Fitter-K*s and fifty personnel of 7 *Eskadra Lotnictwa Taktycznego* (7th Tactical Fighter Squadron) of the Polish Air Force at Powidz Air Base arrived at RAF Coltishall on a ten-day exchange with 41 (F) Squadron to practise ground-attack missions. The exchange also allowed aircrew and ground personnel to share ideas and become familiar with each other's operating procedures, enabling them to work efficiently as NATO allies. In September 2004 41 (F) Squadron paid a return visit to *7 Eskadra Lotnictwa Taktycznego* at Powidz, where full use was made of the different terrain and less restrictive airspace. On 11 November 2005 six Jaguars of 41 (F) Squadron deployed to Miroslawiec Air Base, Poland, to provide fast air support to British Army artillery units from 1 Armoured Division in Exercise *Uhlan Barbara 05*. This mainly involved the conduct of close air support, with forward air controllers deployed to the Droskow Promorski Training Area, as well as some valuable electronic warfare training against Rapiers of 32 Battery Royal Artillery at Miroslawiec Air Base. The squadron was also tasked by the Army to conduct some reconnaissance against deployed artillery units. However, the exercise proved to be frustrating due to the kind of weather one would expect in Poland in November. Two days' flying were lost, and on one occasion two jets had to divert to Powidz due to snowstorms at Miroslawiec.

From 20 September to 1 October 2004, 6 Squadron took part in exercise *Lone Cheetah*, the first chance the Jaguar force had to fly with the Romanian Air Force. Flying from Constanta, the Jaguars flew daily missions with the units of MiG-21 *Lancers*. The *Lancer*, a reworked version of the MiG-21 *Fishbed*, boasting a new radar and upgraded avionics, proved to be a worthy platform.

The final line up at RAF Coltishall on 1 April 2006, shortly before the heavens opened and the Jaguars left for Coningsby. Nearest aircraft is T.4 XX847/EZ of 6 Squadron. Behind are GR.3As XZ117/FB, XZ391/ET, XZ103/FP, T.4 XX847/EZ and GR.3A XZ112/GW, which went tech just prior to take-off and was flown out in the morning of Monday 3 April by Flight Lieutenant Jim Luke. (Author)

In the winter of 2005/6 the main training focus of the Jaguar force at RAF Coltishall was a joint US/UK venture, in late January 2006 at Nellis AFB. Maps of the Nevada desert lined the walls in the planning room and strange American-produced documents lay around, while each pilot had some aspect of the *Red Flag* programme or electronic warfare to read up on and brief the rest of 41 Squadron. The night team was no different,

Pilots strap in as the skies darken overhead. (Author)

and the planners attempted to get the pairs of pilots who would operate together as constituted units to fly together on ever more demanding training sorties. The poor weather of winter only served to frustrate plans, create delays and increase tension as the squadron geared up for its last major exercise. No. 41 Squadron expended a huge amount of energy to ensure that its performance would live up to that demanded by the reputation of the Jaguar force. Nowhere was this more so than among the night team; a group of highly experienced, dedicated Jaguar pilots who wanted 41's performance in its last major exercise to be remembered for all the right reasons as the aircraft retired from service and its proud operators took their skills to other aircraft.

As the evenings started to draw in with the approach of winter 2005/6, the leaves began falling on Coltishall's main drag [recalls Flight Lieutenant John Davy]. The 10C isotherm moved southwards down the North Sea and the Squippers hung immersion suits ominously on pilots' pegs, and thoughts turned towards the approaching night season. Flying night sorties ceased to require wholesale destruction of the day-wave and became a case of just moving the day slightly to the right. For the more junior pilots this normally meant picking up the night convex sortie they missed out on on the now defunct OCU, and it was a relatively tame affair. What can you do at night apart

Time to walk to the aircraft. (Dick Jeeves)

from a singleton practice diversion, a few instrument approaches at base, then a few circuits to finish off with? The more experienced knew exactly what this entailed. It was the chance to take part in some of the most demanding flying the Jaguar force could offer in a regime where safety margins are eroded and basic skills become even more demanding. It would certainly banish any complacency that experience might have brought during the long days of summer. It would also let squadron members expand their competence and self-satisfaction by becoming part of the *Red Flag* night team. Although 'OLF-ing' through the Nevada desert during the day, then enjoying Las Vegas's delights at night has many attractions, many saw flying as part of a large *Red Flag* night COMAO as the high point of their Jaguar flying.

The first part of joining the night team is, in many ways, one of the most alarming. Close-formation flying is a skill that tests many student pilots during their flying training, but by the time they arrive on a front-line Jaguar squadron, it is an assumed skill during the day. Remove all visual clues except a few pinpoints of light and it takes on a new, disorientating aspect. On a dark night, concentrating on the leader takes all one's capacity. Minor chores such as changing radio frequencies become extremely taxing and 'the Leans' set in with great ease. Another mundane activity, air-to-air refuelling, also becomes far more challenging, as you are now trying to collide, in a controlled manner, with an aeroplane you can hardly see. However, as with all challenges, practice helps and, although never an easy task, night conventional flying becomes another skill.

Flying a fast-jet at low level at night is one of the most demanding skills a pilot can undertake. Virtually every other platform at low level at night has at least one other sensor to enhance the image given by the 'gogs': the Harrier has forward-looking infra-red (FLIR); the Tornado has FLIR and terrain-following radar (TFR). We have none. Colour and depth perception are both non-existent. This can, obtusely, give the pilot a sensation of 'unreality': that he is playing a computer game and is thus not risking his life. Nothing could be further from the truth: visual

Goodbye to the Jaguars. (Author)

illusions, rare by day, become common at night, 'blooming' of the tubes hides and distorts obstacles, and deteriorating weather is hard to anticipate. Having said that, using the NVGs opens a large part of the 24-hour clock to tactical operations, denying any enemy time for respite and retaining the element of surprise. It is also an exhilarating experience to fly in good conditions, when, with a high, full moon, night becomes day – until one 'sneaks-a-peek' under the gogs and realizes it is nearly pitch-black outside. The NVG work-up follows the RAF's standard 'building block' approach: ground school and theory at CAM, a simulator sortie, a dual sortie, singleton solo, and pairs-work, before attempting affiliation training and CAS. Pilots are selected for the training on the basis of their experience and reliability: it is by no means certain that all Jaguar pilots will become NVG combat ready. NVG skills are even more perishable than day skills, so the requirement to complete sorties within certain time limits can make progress painfully slow.

Having just one sensor makes the standard Jaguar low- or medium-level 'dumb bomb' deliveries very difficult to employ, certainly with anything but the most relaxed of rules of engagement (ROE). The need to see a DM14 to commit an attack is made extremely difficult by the poor resolution at night. Employing forward-based troops to mark the target with a covert but NVG-visible infra-red marking torch eases the task considerably, and that, in conjunction with an LTM, would be necessary for precision strikes, especially in a CAS environment. Any explosion would cause severe 'blooming' problems for following aircraft, so less compression over the target may be required. This brings its own problems, with aircraft not being able to provide visual support for extended periods. TIALD provides a useful means of hitting point targets, but weather and threat scenarios may preclude a medium-level attack plan. Repeatedly, the main lesson identified after night tactical leadership training (TLT) exercises is that a precision weapon that can function independently of the launch aircraft, such as the GPS-guided enhanced Paveway, is necessary for a viable Jaguar night-attack role. The low-level recce pod, however, does provide the aeroplane with a significant role in the future air war. Its horizon-to-horizon IRLS allows commanders to get up-to-date imagery of future targets, or to assess the effects earlier strikes have achieved. The Jaguar's intra-flight data link allows formations to keep situational awareness among the formation high, although the difficulties with lack of peripheral vision means that pairs fly in a fighting wing/trail formation, rather than the standard Jaguar wide battle.

Following the announcement that RAF Coltishall was to close as part of the 2004 Defence Review, the first tangible evidence of the drawdown was witnessed on Friday 11 March 2005, when 16 (R) Squadron (and 54 (F) Squadron) disbanded at the Norfolk station following 170 years' combined service. On 1 April 2006, 41 (F) Squadron handed over the squadron numberplate to the Fast-jet and Weapons Operational Evaluation Unit at RAF Coningsby, and the squadron's illustrious history continues as 41 (R) Squadron. The same day, 6 Squadron moved back to RAF Coningsby, to continue flying the Jaguar until October 2007, when the aircraft will be replaced by the Typhoon.

Jaguars fly the Missing Man formation over rain-lashed Coltishall on 1 April 2006. (Author)

SPECIFICATIONS

Jaguar A

Type:

Single-seat tactical strike and ground attack fighter/bomber.

Accommodation:

Pilot only. Originally, a French-built ejection seat with zero altitude operation but only at speeds below 104 mph; later replaced by a Martin-Baker JRM4/FB9E with 'zero-zero' capability.

Power plant:

Two Rolls-Royce/Turboméca Adour Mk.102 afterburning turbofans subsequently upgraded to Mk.104 standard.

Performance:

Max speed 1,056 mph (1690km/h). Initial climb 30,000ft (9100m) in 90 seconds. Service ceiling 45,930ft (13,920m). Range 870 miles (1,392km) tactical. For roles overseas, up to three RP36 264gal (1,200 litre) tanks, giving a range of 2,485 miles (4,000km) and with in-flight refuelling, an endurance of ten hours.

Weights:

Empty 15,432lb (7000kg); normal 24,149lb (11,000kg); max 34,612lb (15,700kg).

Dimensions:

Length 55ft 2½ in (16.73m); span 28ft 6in (8.64m); height: 16ft 10½ in (5.1lm).

Internal equipment:

SFIM 250-1 twin-gyro inertial platform; Jaguar ELIDA air data computer system; Thomson-CSF 121 fire-control sighting unit/weapons selector with adapter/sighting camera. (From February 1977, a Thomson/CSF CILAS TAV-38 laser rangefinder in an undernose blister fairing). Decca RDN 72 EMD Doppler radar; Crouzet Type 90 navigation computer and target selector; fin-mounted Thomson-CSF passive radar warning receiver; Thomson-CSF 31 weapons aiming computer; Thomson-CSF RL50PJ incidence probe with angle-of-attack indicator; Thomson-CSF HUD, Dassault fire control computer for launch control of the Matra Martel anti-radar missile. Omera strike camera and a retractable IFR probe. VHF/UHF radios, VOR/ILS IFF and Tacan.

Defensive Systems:

Phimat chaff or Bofors BOZ-103 chaff/flare pod. Dassault Electronique Barracudaor ECM pod. Thomson-CSF TVM-015 Barem or Remora wide-band ECM detector/jammer pod. 56-cartridge Alkan 5020/5021 conformal chaff and flare launcher beneath each wing root. Sometimes an 18-cartridge Lactoix flare in the tailcone in place of the drag-chute. CF-TH RWR with tailfin leading edge mounted receiver aerial. Thomson-CSF Caiman or Basilisk pods could also be carried for EW support. The CT51J communication jamming pod saw limited use with EC/211.

Offensive Weapons: Typical war loads: 8 750kg; 11 450kg or 15 250kg bombs for close support; two Matra 550 Magic AAMs for low- or medium-level air superiority; AS.37 Martel for low-altitude anti-radar penetration with two 264 gallon (1200 litre) tanks. Two DEFA-550 30mm cannon with 300 rounds of ammunition. Five external hardpoints for a total of 10,000lb (4545 kg) of nuclear or non-nuclear stores: Thomson-CSF ATLIS I or II targeting pod for use with the Aérospatiale AS.30L guided missile or for stand off/self-designation of laser guided weapons including the 400kg and 1,000kg bombs. Matra 550 Magic AAMs, Matra Durandal runway denial rocket propelled bombs, 125 kg GP bombs; Matra SAMP 250-, 450- or 750 kg slick or retarded weapons; 400kg and 1,000kg laser guided bombs; Matra F1 pods containing 36 68mm rockets or F2 containing six 68mm rockets; Matra F3 pods containing four 100mm rockets; Matra-Brandt Belouga 640lb (290kg) BLG 66 grenade dispensers; Brandt BAP-100 anti-runway bomblets; BAT-120 anti-armour bomblets.

Jaguar E

Type: Two-seat advanced and operational conversion trainer.

Accommodation: Pilot (front seat) and instructor (rear seat) in tandem on Martin-Baker JRM4/FB9 ejection seats.

Power plant: Two Rolls-Royce/Turboméca Adour Mk.102 afterburning turbofans later uprated to the Mk.104.

Performance: Max speed 1,056mph (1,690km/h).

Weights: Empty 15,432lb (7,000kg); maximum 34,612lb (15,700kg).

Dimensions: Span 28ft 6in (8.64m); length 57ft 6¼ in (17.43m); height 16ft 0.5 in (4.86m).

Armament: Two 30mm DEFA cannons with 300 rounds of ammunition. Thomson CSE-121 fire control/sighting unit/weapons selector.

Jaguar GR.1/1A

Type: Single-seat tactical strike and ground attack fighter/bomber with secondary reconnaissance capability.

Accommodation: Pilot only, on a Martin-Baker Mk.9B zero/zero ejection seat.

Power plant:	(GR.1) two Rolls-Royce/Turboméca Adour Mk.102 afterburning turbofans rated at 5,115lb (2,325kg) of dry thrust and 7,305lb (3,320kg) with afterburner later replaced by Adour Mk.104 afterburning turbofans rated at 5,320lb (2,418kg) dry and 8,040lb (3,655kg) with afterburner.
Performance:	Max speed 1,056mph (1,690km/h). Climb rate 30,000ft (9,100m) in 90 seconds. Ceiling 45,930ft (13,920m).
Range:	334 miles (534km) lo-lo-lo, 875 miles (1,400km) hi-lo-hi and 2,190 miles (3,504km) ferry.
Weights:	Empty 15,432lb (7,000kg); normal 24,149lb (11,000kg); max 34,612lb (15,700kg).
Dimensions:	Length 55ft 2½ in (16.73m); span 28ft 6in (8.64m); height: 16ft 10½ in (5.11m).
Armament:	Twin 30mm Aden cannon with 150 rounds per gun, plus 5 external hardpoints for a total of 10,000lb (4,545kg) of stores, including CRV-7 air-to-surface rockets, over/under wing Sidewinder AAMs, CBUs, and standard and laser guided bombs, non-nuclear.

Jaguar T.2A/B

Type:	Two-seat operational conversion trainer with secondary strike and ground attack capabilities.
Accommodation:	Pilot (front seat) and instructor (rear seat) in tandem Martin-Baker Mk.9B zero/zero ejection seats.
Power plant:	Two Rolls Royce/Turboméca Adour Mk.104 afterburning turbofans rated at 5,320lb (2,418kg) dry and 8,040lb (3,655kg) with afterburner.
Performance:	Max speed 1,056 mph (1,690km/h). Climb rate 30,000fr (9100m) in 90 seconds. Ceiling 45,930ft (13,920m). Range 334 miles (534km) lo-lo-lo, 875 miles (1,400km) hi-lo-hi and 2,190 miles (3,504km) ferry.
Weights:	Empty 15,432lb (7,000kg); max 34,612 lb (15,700kg).
Dimensions:	Span 28ft 6in (8.64m); length 57ft 6½ in (17.43m). Height 16ft 1½ in (4.92m).
Armament:	One 30mm Aden cannon with 150 rounds of ammunition, plus five external hardpoints for 10,000lb (4545kg) of stores.

Jaguar International

Type:	Single-seat tactical support aircraft; reconnaissance capable.

Accommodation:	Pilot only, on Martin-Baker E9B (Ecuador), 09B (Oman), IN9B (India), or N9B (Nigeria) ejection seat.
Power plant:	Two Rolls-Royce/Turboméca Adour Mk.811 afterburning turbofans rated at 5,520lb (2,509kg) dry and 9,270lb (4,213kg) with afterburner.
Performance:	Max speed 1,056 mph (1,690km/h). Climb rate 30,000ft (9,100m) in 90 seconds. Ceiling 45,930ft (13,920m). Range 334 miles (534km) lo-lo-lo, 875 miles (1,400km) hi-lo-hi and 2,190 miles (3,504km) ferry.
Weights:	Empty 16,975lb (7,716kg); max 34,612 lb (15,700kg).
Dimensions:	Span: 28ft 6in (8.64m); length 55ft 2½ in (16.73m); height: 16ft 0.5in (4.86m).
Armament:	Two 30mm DEFA or Aden cannon with 130/150 rounds of ammunition per gun, plus 5 external hardpoints for 10,000lb (4,545kg) of stores and two overwing points for Sidewinder or Matra 550 Magic AAMs.

Jaguar IM/IS/IT *Shamsher*

Type:	IM (Anti-shipping version of the Jaguar International built by HAL fitted with Agave radar); IS (Deep Penetration Strike Aircraft version supplied by BAe and HAL); IT (conversion trainer version supplied by BAe and HAL.
Accommodation:	IM and IS; pilot only, IT (pilot and instructor) on Martin-Baker IN9B Mk.2 zero-zero ejection seat.
Power plant:	Two licence-built HAL Adour Mk.811 afterburning turbofans rated at 5,520lb (2,509 kg) dry and 9,270b (4213kg) with afterburner.
Performance:	Max speed 1,056 mph (1,690km/h). Climb rate 30,000ft (9,100m) in 90 seconds. Ceiling 45,930ft (13,920m). Range 334 miles (534km) lo-lo-lo, 875 miles (1,400km) hi-lo-hi and 2,190 miles (3,504km) ferry.
Internal equipment:	Early batches fitted with NAVWASS, later changed on HAL-built aircraft to Smiths Industries DARIN (Display, Avionics, Ranging and Inertial Navigation) integrated avionics suite which included: a French SAGEM Uliss 82 inertial navigation system; Smiths Industries/GEC-Marconi dual-mode Type 1301 HUDWAS (Head Up Display and Weapons Aiming System) showing raster and stroke symbology; Mil-Std-1553B databus; Collins UHF/VHF and IFF-400; GEC-Marconi COMED 2045 combined map and electronic display and a HAL IFF 400AM. (IM) Agave radar replaced by ELTA EL/M-2022 maritime radar system.

Weights:	Empty 16,975lb (7,716kg); max 34,612lb (15,700kg).

Dimensions:	Span: 28ft 6in (8.64m); length 55ft 2½in (16.73m); height: 16ft 0.5in (4.86m).

Armament: Two 30mm DEFA or Aden cannon with 130/150 rounds of ammunition per gun, plus 5 external hardpoints for 10,000lb (4,545kg) of stores and two overwing points for Sidewinder or Matra 550 Magic AAMs. (IM) Single BAe Sea Eagle anti-shipping missile on underfuselage mounting.

Jaguar International Two-Seater

Type: Two-seat operational conversion trainer.

Accommodation: Pilot (front seat) and instructor (rear seat) in Martin-Baker E9B (Ecuador), 09B (Oman), IN9B (India), or N9B (Nigeria) ejection seats.

Power plant: Two Rolls-Royce/Turboméca Adour Mk.811 afterburning turbofans rated at 5,520lb (2,509kg) dry and 9,270lb (4,213kg) with afterburner.

Performance: Max speed 1,056 mph (1,690km/h). Climb rate 30,000ft (9,100m) in 90 seconds. Ceiling 45,930ft (13,920m). Range 334 miles (534km) lo-lo-lo, 875 miles (1,400 km) hi-lo-hi and 2,190 miles (3504 km) ferry.

Weights: Empty 15,432lb (7,000kg); max 34,612lb (15,700kg).

Dimensions: Span 28ft 6in (8.64m); length 57ft 6½in (17.43m).

Armament: One 30mm DEFA or Aden cannon with 130/150 rounds of ammunition per gun, plus five external hardpoints for 10,000lb (4545kg) of stores and two overwing hardpoints for Sidewinder or Matra 550 Magic AAMs.

Jaguar GR.1B/GR.3

Type: Single-seat tactical strike and ground attack fighter/bomber with secondary reconnaissance capability. Capable of self/stand-off laser designation of PGMs. New avionics fit.

Accommodation: Pilot only, in Martin-Baker Mk.9 zero-zero ejection seat.

Power plant: Two Rolls Royce Turboméca Adour Mk.104 afterburning turbofans rated at 5,320lb (2,418kg) dry and 8,040lb (3,655kg) with afterburner – Mk.106 in projected upgrade.

Performance: Max speed 1,056 mph (1690 km/h). Climb rate 30,000ft (9100m) in 90 seconds. Ceiling 45,930ft (13,920m).

Range: 334 miles (534km) lo-lo-lo, 875 miles (1,400km) hi-lo-hi and 2,190 miles (3504 km) ferry.

Weights: Empty 15,432lb (7,000kg); normal 24,149lb (11,000kg); max 34,612lb (15,700kg).

Dimensions: Length 55ft 2½ in (16.73m); span 28ft 6in (8.64m); height l6ft 10 in (5.11m).

Armament: Twin 30mm Aden cannon with 150 rounds per gun, plus 5 external hardpoints for a total of 10,000lb (4,545kg) of stores, including CRV-7 air-to-surface rockets, over/under wing Sidewinder AAMs, CBUs, and standard and laser-guided bombs, non-nuclear.

APPENDIX II

Worldwide Operators

Bharatiya Vayu Sena (Indian Air Force)

	Serials	
Jaguar T.2 (Interim)	J1001-J1002	2 aircraft on loan - returned
Jaguar GR.1 (Interim)	J1003-J1018	16 aircraft on loan - returned
Jaguar International IM (Maritime Strike)	JM251-JM262	12 aircraft manufactured by HAL
Jaguar International IS (Strike)	JS101-JS135	35 aircraft direct supplied by BAe
	JS136-JS204	79 aircraft manufactured by HAL
Jaguar International IB (two seater trainer)	JT051-JT05	3 aircraft direct supplied by BAe
Jaguar International IT	JT054-JT065	12 aircraft manufactured by HAL
Jaguar International IT DARIN II	JT066-JT082	17 aircraft manufactured by HAL
		Total 158 + 18 loan/returned

Units	Date	Base	Role
5 'Tuskers' Squadron	8/81-current	Ambala	strike/reconnaissance
6 'Dragons' Squadron	1981-current	Pune	maritime strike
14 'Bulls' Squadron	9/80-current	Ambala	strike
16 'Black Cobras' Squadron 10/86-	current	Gorakhpur	strike
27 'Flaming Arrows' Squadron	1/85-current	Gorakhpur	strike
Aircraft & Systems Testing Establishment		Bangalore	testing

Fuerza Aerea Ecuatoriana (Ecuadorian Air Force)

	Serials
Jaguar International EB (Two-seater)	FAE311 & FAE312
Jaguar International ES (single-seater)	FAE300-FAE310 (FAE303/308 & 310 lost in accidents, replaced in1991 by XX121, XX722 & XX744)

Unit	Date	Base	Role
E*scuadron de Combate 2111 'Aguilas'* ('Eagles') now Jaguares	1977-	Aérea Militar Taura	Strike

Nigerian Air Force

Jaguar International SN	705-717
Jaguar International BN	700-704

Armée de L'Air

Serials

Jaguar A	A03, A04, Al-A160
Jaguar E	E0l, E02, El-E40
Jaguar M	M05

Units	Date Formed	Disbanded	Role	Base
Escadron de Chasse 3/3 Ardennes	10/3/77	29/3/87	SEAD	Nancy
Escadron de Chasse 1/7 Provence	24/5/73-	7/05	Strike	Saint-Dizier
Escadron de Chasse 2/7 Argonne	1/5/74	30/6/01	OCU	Saint-Dizier
Escadron de Chasse3/7 Languedoc	14/3/74	30/6/01	Strike	Saint-Dizier
Escadron de Chasse 4/7 Limousin	1/4/80	31/7/89	Strike	Istres
Escadron de Chasse 1/11 Roussillon	1/3/76	31/7/94	Strike	Toul
Escadron de Chasse 2/11 Vosges	3/11/76	31/7/96	ECM/SEAD	Toul
Escadron de Chasse 3/11 Corse	7/2/75	31/7/97	Strike	Toul
Escadron de Chasse 4/11 Jura	1/1/79	30/6/92	Strike/recce	Bordeaux
Centre d'lnstruction Tactique 339	5/9/88	7/2001	Combat Training Test	Luxeuil
Escadron de Chasse 5/330 Côte d'Argent				

OCU- operational conversion unit

SEAD Suppression of enemy air defences

Armée de l'Air Jaguar Units' Histories, Duties and Aircraft Markings

A wing (*escadre*) is divided into three or four squadrons (*escadrons*), each of which has two flights (*escadrilles*). The individual squadrons are usually named after regions in

France, while bases are numbered, and since 1984 also named in honour of famous aviators.

11 Escadre de Chasse 'Res Non Verba'

The second wing to form on the Jaguar, and originally equipped with F-l00 Super Sabres, the last being phased out in 1973/4. Based at Adrienne 136 'Colonel Georges Phelut' at Toul-Rosiers, *EC 11* had a non-nuclear role. *EC 1/11* and *EC 3/11* were ATLIS equipped, with *EC 1/11* assigned to European operations, while *EC 3/11* was assigned to the *Force d'Action Exterieure* in the overseas intervention role. *EC 2/11* was defence suppression specialists armed with Martel anti-radar missiles, CT51 and Barracudaor jammer pods. *EC 4/11* was attached to *BA 106* at Bordeaux/Meringac with the additional role of tactical reconnaissance using the RP36P recce pod. *EC 11* was tasked with overseas support of French interests, direct Army support and anti-radar/ECM duties during its operation of the Jaguar. The Toul-based component of *EC 11* was involved with regular exercises with the 1st Armoured Division of the French Army, while before its disbandment *EC 4/11* was assigned to support the 11th Parachute Division.

EC 3/11 flew three Jaguars on a 'proving trip' to Djibouti in 1975, followed by a further sortie to Senegal and the Ivory Coast in 1976 as part of Exercises *N'Diambour* and *Abidjan*. *EC 3/11* undertook the first operational overseas Jaguar deployment in 1977, when aircraft operated out of Senegal against rebel forces in Mauritania in Operation *Lamentin*. Twelve Jaguars of *EC 2/11* '*Vosages*' arrived at Djibouti in April 1978. In April 1978, under Operation *Tacaud*, eight of the *EC 3/11* Operation *Lamentin* Jaguars, still based at Dakar in Senegal, were detached to N'Djamena to support the ailing Chadian regime under threat from Libyan-backed guerrillas.

EC 11 was the first French Jaguar unit to compete in the US-hosted *Red Flag* at Nellis AFB in Nevada in 1980 and 1982. On 19 January 1984 four Jaguars of *EC 11* flew a round trip from Solenzara, Corsica, to Beirut, refuelled on five occasions by C-135F tankers, as part of Operation *Chevesne*, the French contribution to the UN peacekeeping force in Lebanon.

Meanwhile, on 12 August 1983 four Jaguars of *EC 4/11* '*Jura*' were made ready for Operation *Manta* and stationed at Libreville in Gabon, with four other Jaguars, three KC-l35F tankers and two Breguet Atlantic aircraft being based at Bangui Airport, Djibouti. By 21 August, six other Jaguars from *EC 3/11* '*Corse*', four Mirage F1C-200s and a single C-135F were also operational from N'Djamena. The Jaguars went into action on 2 September 1983. On 19 January 1984 four fully-armed Jaguars of *EC 11* with tanker support flew a non-stop reconnaissance mission, Operation *Chevesne*, from Solenzara in Corsica to Beirut and return to demonstrate the French arm of the UN peacekeeping force's ability to call for a swift response when required. By mid-February 1986 twelve Jaguar As of *EC 2/11*, *EC 3/11* at their Djibouti base, and *EC 4/11* were in Chad. Operation *Épervier* ('Sparrowhawk') went ahead on 16 February when eight Jaguars of *EC 3/11* '*Corse*' attacked a rebel airfield in Chad. Ten Jaguars of *EC 4/11* armed with Martel anti-radar missiles attacked Libyan-operated radar installations at Ouadi-Doum airfield. *EC 4/7* and *4/11* were assigned to CATac until its absorption by 1ème CATac in 1987. As part of Operation Daguet, the French contribution to Desert Storm, 11 *Escadre de Chasse* was placed on a standby footing for Gulf duties on 16 September 1990. *EC*

1/11 'Roussilon', EC 2/11 'Vosages' and *EC 3/11 'Corse'*, together with elements of *EC 4/11 'Jura'* at Bordeaux, operated from Al Ahsa, south-west of Dhahran, during the Gulf War. *EC 11* also took part in Operation *Crécerelle* in Bosnia, taking part in the setting-up of the air exclusion zone from 6 April 1993. The first of *EC 11*'s Jaguar As deployed to Trevise Istrania Air Base in Italy with other elements of *EC 3/11* and *EC 3/7*, being based at Rivolto in January and July.

Escadron de Chasse 1/11 'Roussillon'

1ème Escadrille. Markings: African mask on port side of tail.

2ème Escadrille. Markings: mask of comedy starboard side of tail.

Aircraft coded 11-EA to 11-EZ.

The second squadron from the wing to convert to the Jaguar from the F-100, beginning on 10 October 1975, with its prime task of supporting the Army. *EC 1/11* was disbanded on 31 July 1994.

Escadron de Chasse 2/11 'Vosages'

1ème Escadrille. Markings: vulture clutching a skull on starboard side of tail.

2ème Escadrille. Markings: pennant charged with ermine on port side of tail.

Aircraft coded 11-MA to 11-MZ

The third squadron in the wing to convert to the Jaguar was fully equipped by June 1977 with Jaguar As fitted with the laser rangefinder nose. *EC 2/11* specialized in providing electronic countermeasures, and its Jaguars carried in addition to their Martel missiles two Caiman (or CT51) jammer pods on their inner wing pylons and two Barax deception/jammer pods on the outer wing pylons. From June 1987, with the disbandment of *EC 3/3* 'Ardennes', *EC 2/11* carried out defence-suppression duties using the AS.37 Martel missile before being disbanded on 31 July 1996.

Escadron de Chasse 3/11 'Corse'

1ème Escadrille. Markings: snake on port side of tail

2ème Escadrille. Markings: *rencontre de chat* (cat's face) on starboard side of tail.

Aircraft coded 11-RA to 11-RZ.

The first squadron in the wing to convert to the Jaguar, becoming operational by 1976. *EC 3/11* undertook the first operational overseas Jaguar deployment in 1977 when the aircraft operated from Senegal against insurgents in Mauritania in Operation *Lamentin*. *EC 3/11* also took part in the support of the UN in Beirut in 1984. *EC 3/11* disbanded on 31 July 1997.

Escadron de Chasse 4/11 'Jura'

1ème Escadrille. Markings: secretary bird on port side of tail.

2ème Escadrille. Markings: sphinx on starboard side of tail.

Aircraft coded 11-YA to 11 YZ.

EC 4/11 'Jura' was formed from Detachment Air 15/531 at BA106 Bordeaux/Merignac on 12 December 1978 to begin working-up on the Jaguar. It formed part of the French Rapid Reaction Force with *EC 4/7 'Limousin'*, and was assigned to the low-level nuclear strike role until 1 September 1991. *EC 4/11* disbanded on 30 June 1992.

3 Escadre de Chasse

The third and final wing to receive Jaguars was based at Nancy-Ochey 113 and was assigned to defence-suppression duties with the Martel missile. *EC 3* was unique in having a mixed force of two squadrons of Mirage IIIEs (*EC 1/3 'Navarre'* and *EC 2/3 'Champagne'*) and one squadron of Jaguars (*EC 3/3 'Ardennes'*), which re-formed with the Mirage 5 in January 1974 and re-equipped with the Jaguar on 10 March 1977.

Escadron de Chasse 3/3 'Ardennes'

1ème Escadrille. Markings: a wild boar and red bar on the starboard side of the tail.

Aircraft coded 3-XA to 3-XZ.

At the 1980 *Congrès de la Chasse* at Cazaux, *EC 3/3* won the *Coupe Tactique*. *EC 3/3* operated in Chad in 1987 but the Jaguars were withdrawn on 29 May 1987 and the unit converted to the Mirage IIIE in commonality with the two other squadrons of the wing, defence-suppression duties passing to *EC 2/11*.

7 Escadre de Chasse

The first and last operator of the Jaguar in the French Air Force at Aérienne 113 'Commandant Antoine de Saint-Exupery' St Dizier/Robinson consisted of four squadrons. *EC 1/7 'Provence'*, the first Jaguar unit to form, assumed responsibility for operations with the AS.37 Martel missile. *EC 2/7 'Argonne'*, which had been renumbered from EC 1/8 at Casaux, became the French Jaguar OCU responsible for peacetime training in addition to its wartime role of tactical support, while *EC 3/7 'Languedoc'* undertook the AS.30L and ATLIS II illumination mission. *EC 4/7* used the RP36P (*réservoir pendulaire*) pod in the tactical reconnaissance role until disbandment in July 1989. *EC 1/7*, *EC 3/7* and *EC 4/7 'Limousin'*, which joined the wing in April 1980 and was detached to Istres, were assigned the 'pre-strategic' nuclear strike role. Equipped with the tactical nuclear AN52 weapon, they were to 'clear the way' for the Mirage IVA strike aircraft. *EC 4/7* disbanded on 31 July 1989 and the two other squadrons' nuclear assignment ceased on 1 September 1991, when they reverted to conventional attack duties.

Escadron de Chasse 1/7 'Provence'

1ème Escadrille. Markings: Bayard's helmet on port side of tailfin.

2ème Escadrille. Markings: Cross of Jerusalem on starboard side of the nose.

Aircraft coded 7-HA to 7-HZ.

Pilots destined for *EC 1/7* were the first to operate the Jaguar, and they underwent training at CEAM at Mont de Mansan. Following re-equipment with the Jaguar, *EC 1/7* moved to St Dizer, being declared operational on 1 September 1974. *EC 1/7* operated the AS.37 Martel missile until disbandment in June 2005.

Escadron de Chasse 2/7 'Argonne'

1ème Escadrille. Markings: Greek archer on port side of tail.

2ème Escadrille. Markings: cock's head on starboard side of the tail.

Aircraft coded 7-PA to 7-PZ.

Third squadron of the EC 7 to form on 11 October 1974, which operated as the OCU until disbandment on 30 June 2001. At the 1980 *Congrès de la Chasse* at Cazaux, *EC 2/7* won the *Coupe Comète* for air-to-air firing.

Escadron de Chasse 3/7 'Languedoc'

1ème Escadrille. Markings: blue and gold shank on starboard side of tail, facing either direction.

2ème Escadrille. Markings: Lorraine thistle on port side of tail.

Aircraft coded 71-A-71-Z.

Became operational on 1 July 1975 and was tasked specifically with ground attack, rather than tactical support, until 30 June 2001, when it disbanded.

Escadron de Chasse 4/7 'Limousin'

1ème Escadrille. Markings: eagle on the port side of the tail.

2ème Escadrille. Markings: desert fox on the starboard side of the tail.

Aircraft coded 7-NA to 7-NZ.

The final Jaguar squadron to form, on 1 April 1980. Originally based at St Dizier, moving later to Istres/Le Tube. Together with *EC 4/11 'Jura'*, formed part of the French Rapid Reaction Force and was assigned to the low-level nuclear strike role. *EC 4/7* was disbanded on 31 July 1989 and converted to the Mirage 2000N.

Centre d'Instruction Tactique 339 (CITac 339)

Markings: a hat on a terrestrial globe.

Aircraft coded 339-WA to 339-WZ.

Based at 'Lt Colonel Papin' Luxil/St Saveaun, the *Centre Prediction et d'Instruction* was originally equipped with Dassault Mystère 20 (Falcon 20) executive jets modified with nose radars to duplicate the nav/attack systems of various types of Mirage. Its role was expanded to cover other types of training, which resulted in a change of name to CITac on 1 July 1988 and the addition of five Jaguar Es, to teach low-level all-weather penetration techniques, and two Fouga Magisters. The unit disbanded in July 2001.

Centre d'Experiences Aériennes Militaires (CEAM)

CEAM markings: figure throwing a thunderbolt, kneeling on gears below clouds and stars.

CEAM 330 was located at Base Aérienne 118 'Capitaine K.W. Roland' Mont de Marsan and tested air force equipment. CEAM trials involved Jaguar prototypes E02 and A04, as well as early production aircraft. E2 was the first production Jaguar to arrive at CEAM, on 4 May 1974. A Jaguar A from CEAM at Mont de Marsan, flown by Capitaine M. Gauthier, conducted the first live drop of the French AN52 free-fall nuclear weapon in Operation *Maquis* over the Mururoa Atoll in French Polynesia on 24 July 1974. All CEAM Jaguars were transferred to other units as the need for them receded. CEAM 330's aircraft were 'owned' by *Escadron de Chasse 24/118* until on 15 October 1987 they were designated *Escadron de Chasse 5/330 'Cote d'Argent'*. Markings consisted of a tiger on the port side of the tail. Aircraft codes 330-AA to 330-AZ.

Centre d'Essais en Vol (CEV)

Markings: none.

Operating from Bretigny-sur-Orge, CEV tested the airworthiness of equipment destined for the *Direction Technique des Constructions Aeronautiques* and conducted trials of the ATLIS and AS.30L missile using three Jaguars (E-01, A3 and A4). The unit disbanded in 2005.

Al Quwwat Al Jawwiya Al Malakiya As Omaniya (Royal Air Force of Oman)

Serials

Jaguar International DB	201, 203, 213, 214
Jaguar International OS	204-212/215-224
Jaguar GR.1	226
Jaguar GR.1 (Interim)	225
Jaguar T.2 (Interim)	200

Unit	Date	Base
6 Squadron	3/77–current	Thumrait
20 Squadron	1983-current	Thumrait

APPENDIX III

Royal Air Force Jaguars

RAF Jaguars

	Serials
Jaguar B	XW566
Jaguar S	XW560-XW563
Jaguar GR.1	XX108-XX122
	XX817-XX827
	XX955-XX979
	XZ101-XZ120
	XZ355-XZ378
	XZ381-XZ400
Jaguar T.2	XX828-XX847
	XX915-XX916
	ZB615

NB: aircraft are listed as built; some have been re-designated several times.

Jaguar Units	**From**	**To**	**Role**
II (AC) Squadron	February 1976	December 1988	Tactical Recce RAFG
6 Squadron	October 1974	to Eurofighter c2007	OAS
14 (F) Squadron	7 April 1975	14 October 1985	OAS RAFG
16 Squadron	November 1991	13 March 2005	OCU
17 Squadron	June 1975	1 March 1985	OAS RAFG
20 Squadron	1 March 1977	24 June 1984	OAS RAFG
31 Squadron	1 July 1976	31 October 1984	OAS RAFG
41 Squadron	April 1976	1 April 2006	Target Recce
54 (F) Squadron	March 1974	13 March 2005	OAS
226 OCU	October 1974	to 16 Squadron	OCU

(OAS offensive air support, OCU - Operational Conversion Unit)

Serial No.	Type	Notes
XW560	S	A&AEE. On 11 August 1972 XW560 the port engine exploded during the run-up for take-off from Boscombe Down, Wiltshire, due to disintegration of the third-stage disc on the high-pressure compressor. The pilot evacuated the aircraft, which was soon engulfed in flames after a fuel pipe was severed by the explosion. To ground instruction at Lossiemouth.
XW563	S	Selected to promote Jaguar International.
XW566	B	DRA Avionics & Sensors Farnborough.
XX108	GR.1	DRA Boscombe Down.
XX109	GR.1	Second British production aircraft and the first to have the LRMTS and full avionics package. It was used in field trials on the as yet unopened M55 motorway near Blackpool, where it demonstrated the aircraft's amazing STOL capabilities. Used at Coltishall for ground instruction as 8918M, it was painted pink with a Desert Cats motif on the nose.
XX110	GR.1	To RAF Cosford for ground instruction as 8955M.
XX111	GR.1	First Jaguar delivered to the RAF (without chisel nose). Later to Indian Air Force. Now stored at RAF Shawbury.
XX112	GR.1/A	6 Squadron. Part of the initial deployment to Oman, 12.8.91.
XX113	GR.1	226 OCU. On 17.7.81 during a test flight from Abingdon XX113/09 crashed after a loose article jammed the port spoiler powered flying control unit and caused the aircraft to roll uncontrollably to the left. The pilot ejected and the aircraft crashed one mile south of Malvern, Worcestershire.
XX114	GR.1	226 OCU. XX114/02 crashed 19.9.83. During finals to Lossiemouth, the pilot, Ian McLean, hit a flock of birds, which went down the air intakes and caused both engines to fail. The pilot ejected immediately and was uninjured. He was flying again within two weeks.
XX115	GR.1	Ex Indian AF loan. Part of the initial deployment to Oman, 12.8.91. To 1 SoTT Cosford as 8821 M.
XX116	GR.1/A	Ex-Indian AF loan. RAF St Athan.

XX117	GR.1/A	Ex-Indian AF loan. DTEO DRA Boscombe Down.
XX118	GR.1	Ex-Indian AF loan.
XX119	GR.1	226 OCU. Ground instruction with 16 (R) Squadron Lossiemouth as 8898M. Passed to FJTS DTEO as GR.1B 'GD'.
XX120	GR.1	54 Squadron. Crashed 17.9.76 into the Kattegat, off the Samsoe Islands, Denmark, during Exercise Teamwork 76, after possible loss of control while in cloud. Pilot killed.
XX121	GR.1	1 SoTT Cosford as 8892M. Refurbished and sold to Ecuador in 1991.
XX122	GR.1	54 Squadron. XX122/GA crashed 2.4.82 into the Wash, off the Holbeach range, killing the Norwegian pilot, who had become disorientated in the hazy weather.
XX136	T.2	A&AEE. Flew at 1974 Farnborough Show. Crashed 22.11.74. Control was lost and the aircraft entered a spin from which the pilot could not recover. Both crew ejected and the aircraft crashed at Wimborne St Giles, Dorset.
XX137	T.2	226 OCU. XX137/A. On 6.2.76 crashed into Moray Firth four miles off Milltown after both crew ejected following a fuel leak. Allocated to the P&EE at Shoeburyness.
XX138	T.2A	Ex-Indian AF loan. To Omani Air Force.
XX139	T.2A	16 (R) Squadron Lossiemouth.
XX140	T.2	1 SoTT Cosford as 9008M.
XX141	T2A	6 Squadron.
XX142	T.2	226 OCU. XX142/G crashed 22.6.79 after the pilot had been asked to fly inverted to check for a loose article. This was done first at 1,500 ft and then at 1,000 ft. On the second attempt the nose dropped due to the application of positive g and rudder, and it flew into the Moray Firth ten miles north of Lossiemouth, Grampian, killing both crew. The laid-down minimum for a loose article check is 5,000 ft.
XX143	T.2B	ex-Indian AF loan. 226 OCU, RAF Lossiemouth. XX143/X T2A 16 (R) Squadron crashed on 8.9.96. Flight Lieutenant

Jon Witte, a student on his third solo, lost an engine on take-off and ejected safely. The aircraft crashed into the sea 400 yards off the beach. A 202 Squadron Sea King quickly rescued the pilot from the water. Witte suffered compression fractures of the T7 and T8 vertebrae, was in hospital for two weeks, then six months in a back brace, receiving a medical discharge in early 2000.

XX144	T.2A	16 (R) Squadron Lossiemouth 'U'.
XX145	T.2	Empire Test Pilots School Boscombe Down.
XX146	T.2B	54 Squadron.
XX147	T.2	17 Squadron. XX147/BY crashed 26.3.79 at Sudlahn, West Germany after suffering a bird strike while at 250 ft, which entered the cockpit. The crew had initially attempted to recover the aircraft, but ejected when speed began to decay due to the airbrakes being extended.
XX148	T.2	226 OCU. XX148/M crashed 29.7.77 at Whittingham, Northumberland, after control was lost during a simulated attack. The aircraft had rolled inverted to begin its attack dive, but nosed down and crashed. Both crew were killed when they ejected moments before the aircraft struck the ground.
XX149	T.2	226 OCU. XX149/N crashed 27.4.78. Emerged from cloud in a steep inverted dive and crashed into a mountain at Cullen, Banff. The crew initiated ejection moments before the aircraft crashed but they were both killed.
XX150	T.2	16 (R) Squadron Lossiemouth.
XX719	GR.1/A	Part of the initial deployment to Oman, 12.8.91.
XX720	GR.1/A(T)	54 Squadron, ex-Indian AF loan.
XX721	GR.1	54 Squadron. XX721/GE crashed 22.6.83 when both engines flamed out almost immediately after take-off from Hahn, West Germany, due to fuel starvation. The Danish pilot was unable to relight the engines and attempted to return to base, but was forced to eject.
XX722	GR.1	Refurbished and sold to Ecuador in 1991.

XX723	GR.1B	54 Squadron.
XX724	GR.1/A	Stored at Shawbury.
XX725	GR.1/A	Operation *Granby* 'T' *Johnny Fartpants*. To SAOEU Boscombe Down September 1997.
XX726	GR.1	First aircraft to carry the production 'chisel nose'. 1 SoTT Cosford as 8947M.
XX727	GR.1	To RAF Cosford for ground instruction as 8951M.
XX728	GR.1	6 Squadron, ex-Indian AF loan. Crashed 7.10.85. It was one of three Jaguar GR.1s of 6 Squadron flying a low-level sortie, which consisted of attacks on the Holbeach and Cowden ranges, followed by low-level tactical flying training. The formation was west of the Pennine Ridge heading in a north-west direction. The No. 2 aircraft (XX731) was flying on the starboard side, slightly behind his leader, who was flying XX728. As the leader crossed in front of the No. 2 at a pre-planned point, the aircraft collided. The pilot of XX728 was incapacitated during the collision and was killed when his aircraft crashed into Hartside Pass, near Alston, Cumbria. The pilot of XX731 was able to initiate a successful ejection sequence, although by this time he was at a dangerously low level.
XX729	GR.1/A	XX729/07 of 226 OCU. To 6 Squadron. Ex-Indian AF loan.
XX730	GR.1	To RAF Cosford for ground instruction as 8952M.
XX731	GR.1/A	6 Squadron. Crashed 7.10.85 Three Jaguar GR.1s of 6 Squadron were flying a low-level sortie, which consisted of attacks on the Holbeach and Cowden ranges, followed by low-level tactical flying training. The formation was west of the Pennine Ridge heading in a north-west direction. The No. 2 aircraft (XX731) was flying on the starboard side, slightly behind his leader, who was flying XX728. As the leader crossed in front of the No. 2 at a pre-planned point, the aircraft collided. The pilot of XX728 was incapacitated during the collision and was killed when his aircraft hit the ground near Alston in Cumbria. The pilot of XX731 was able to initiate a successful ejection sequence, although by this time he was at a dangerously low level.
XX732	GR.1/A	226 OCU. XX732/03 crashed 27.11.86 onto Stock Hill in the

Craik Forest, eleven miles south-west of Hawick, Borders. The USAF exchange pilot did not eject and was killed, possibly due to disorientation in cloud and being preoccupied with trying to recover from a dive and being unaware of the proximity of the ground.

XX733	GR.1/A	Operation *Granby* 'R' *Baggers*. Crashed on take-off at Coltishall on 23.1.96. The 28-year-old pilot, Flight Lieutenant Greg Noble of 41 Squadron, was killed. He was one of three Jaguar GR.1s tasked to fly to RAF Lossiemouth on a regular training mission. The first two aircraft were airborne and on their way when XX733/FR started its take-off run just before 11.00 hours. Noble omitted to select afterburner, and after a long take-off roll failed to gain height. The undercarriage caught the barrier at the end of the runway, causing it to belly-land into a cornfield. The main fuel tanks were punctured and an intense fire engulfed the front of the aircraft and he was killed. Following a private funeral service at the Roman Catholic cathedral in Norwich, Noble was laid to rest with full military honours in the small cemetery at Scottow, within yards of where he lost his life.
XX734	GR.1	Ex-Indian AF loan.
XX735	GR.1	6 Squadron. Crashed 15.9.76 at Eggebeck, Germany, during Exercise Teamwork 76 after loss of control while climbing out from a bomb toss manoeuvre due to the selection of airbrakes instead of slats. The pilot was killed.
XX736	GR.1	Ex-Indian AF loan. Forward fuselage to BAe Brough as 911CM. Coltishall BDRT.
XX737	GR.1/A	54 & 6 Squadrons, ex-Indian AF loan.
XX738	GR.1B (T)	FJTS Boscombe Down, ex-Indian AF loan.
XX739	GR.1	1 SoTT Cosford.
XX740	GR.1	To Omani Air Force, ex-Indian AF loan.
XX741	GR.1/A	Part of the initial deployment to Oman, 12.8.91. Stored Shawbury.
XX742	GR.1	6 Squadron. XX742/EF crashed 19.4.83. During ACT the pilot was unable to recover the aircraft from a roll to starboard, possibly due to disconnection of the roll control

system. He ejected and the aircraft crashed into the North Sea, forty miles off Bacton, Norfolk. The aircraft was not recovered.

XX743	GR.1	1 SoTT Cosford as 8949M.
XX744	GR.1	1 SoTT Cosford as 8892M. Refurbished and sold to Ecuador in 1991.
XX745	GR.1/A	226 OCU. 16 (R) Squadron Lossiemouth. 54 Squadron, XX745/GV. Involved in a mid-air collision with XX832/EZ T.2A of 6 Squadron during a sortie over Scotland on 31.5.00, and both diverted into Leuchars, Fife. XX832 suffered only slight damage but XX745 received severe damage to the underside of the cockpit area. It was returned to Coltishall by road, where damage was assessed as CAT 4. Transferred to St Athan, where the feasibility of using the cockpit off the stored XZ375 was examined.
XX746	GR.1A	1 SoTT Cosford as 8895M.
XX747	GR.1	RAFC Cranwell AMIF as 89C3M.
XX748	GR.1B	Operation *Granby* 'U'. 54 Squadron.
XX749	GR.1	226 OCU. XX749/21 crashed 10.12.79, Lumsden, Aberdeenshire, colliding with XX755/08 on a low-level training exercise. The pilot of XX749 was killed.
XX750	GR.1	226 OCU. 14 Squadron. On 7.2.84 XX750/AL crashed inverted at *Red Flag* after loss of control while taking avoiding action after being picked up by ground radar. The USAF exchange pilot was killed.
XX751	GR.1	To RAF Cosford for ground instruction as 8937M.
XX752	GR.1/A	6 Squadron.
XX753	GR.1	RAF EP&TU St Athan as 9087M.
XX754	GR.1/A	54 Squadron. Crashed 13.11.90. During a formation join-up manoeuvre the aircraft flew into a low ridge 87 ft above ground level in the desert in Qatar, 100 miles south of Bahrain. Flight Lieutenant Keith Collister did not eject and was killed. The Jaguars were on a low-level training sortie as part of the work-up for Operation *Granby*.

XX755	GR.1	226 OCU. Crashed 10.12.79, Lumsden, Aberdeenshire, colliding with XX749.
XX756	GR.1	1 SoTT Cosford as 8899M.
XX757	GR.1	1 SoTT Cosford as 8948M.
XX758	GR.1	226 OCU. XX758/18 crashed 18.11.81 when it flew into a hillside in the Grudie Valley, Dingwall, Highland, during a snowstorm. The pilot was killed.
XX759	GR.1	226 OCU. XX759/l9 Crashed 1.11.78. Entered cloud in a gentle climb but emerged in a near-vertical dive. It did not recover and crashed at Selkirk, Borders, killing the Ecuadorian pilot.
XX760	GR.1	14 Squadron. On 13.9.82 XX760/AA crashed onto moorland on the Dalreavoch Estate, Rogart, near Braegrudie, Sutherland, after the pilot ejected due to an engine fire caused by a fracture in the combustion chamber, which burnt through the casing and ignited fuel in the fuselage tanks.
XX761	GR.1	226 OCU. On 6.6.78 XX761/11 was destroyed in a ground fire during engine runs at Lossiemouth, Grampian. Cockpit salvaged for ground instruction as 8600M.
XX762	GR.1	226 OCU & 14 Squadron. XX762/28 crashed on the summit of Beinn-A-Chleibh, near Dalmally, Argyllshire, 23.11.79 in bad weather while acting as a chase aircraft. During the 'pull-up' the pilot ejected, possibly in the belief that the aircraft was about to strike the side of a hill. The pilot was killed after suffering a severe blow to the head.
XX763	GR.1	RAF CTTS St Athan as 9009M.
XX764	GR.1	RAF CTTS St Athan as 901CM.
XX765	GR.1	Converted to ACT. Now on display at Cosford Aerospace Museum.
XX766	GR.1/A	6 & 14 Squadrons.
XX767	GR.1/A	54 Squadron.
XX768	GR.1	17 Squadron. On 29.9.82 XX768/BA suffered an engine fire on approach to Brüggen, due to fatigue failure of a low-

pressure compressor, which ruptured several fuel system components. The pilot ejected before XX768 crashed at Heinsberg-Rauderath.

XX817	GR.1	17 Squadron. XX817/BB crashed 17.7.80 at Mönchengladbach, Germany. Shortly after take-off from Brüggen the port engine lost power. The pilot attempted to return to base but ejected when both engines caught fire due to a fuel leak. It crashed into woods seven miles from the airfield.
XX818	GR.1	1 SoTT Cosford as 8923M.
XX819	GR.1	1 SoTT Cosford as 8923M.
XX820	GR.1	31 Squadron. 17 Squadron. XX820/BD crashed 11.6.82. The left-hand engine failed during a circuit to land at Brüggen, after it ingested a bolt that had not been fitted correctly during servicing. The pilot ejected after levelling the aircraft to avoid some buildings.
XX821	GR.1	AMIF RAF Cranwell as 8896M.
XX822	GR.1	14 Squadron. XX822/AA. Crashed 2.7.76 fifteen miles (24 km) west of Alhorn, Germany, during air-to-ground firing practice. The pilot was killed – the first Jaguar fatality.
XX823	GR.1	17 Squadron. Crashed 25.7.78, Cagliari, Sardinia, flying into a hill during an APC sortie from Decimomannu.
XX824	GR.1	1 SoTT Cosford as 9019M 'AD'.
XX825	GR.1	1 SoTT Cosford as 9020M 'BM'.
XX826	GR.1	1 SoTT Cosford as 9021M.
XX827	GR.1	17 Squadron. XX827/BM crashed 12.2.81, Nellis Ranges, USA. The pilot pulled up sharply during a *Red Flag* exercise and rolled to starboard until inverted after being picked up on radar. The aircraft then stopped climbing but continued to roll until it struck the ground with both engines in reheat. The pilot did not eject and was killed.
XX828	T.2	226 OCU. XX828/P crashed on 1.6.81. The crew ejected after a black-headed gull struck and shattered the canopy while flying at 500 ft. Fragments of the canopy were

ingested by both engines, causing a double engine failure. It crashed eight miles E of Kirriemuir, Tayside.

XX829   T.2A   6 Squadron. 16 (R) Squadron Lossiemouth.

XX830   T.2   Empire Test Pilots School. The aircraft arrived at St Athan on 15.10.96 for overhaul. Either prior to or during the work the main fuel tank was punctured. Attempts to rectify the problem failed and the aircraft was deemed to be damaged beyond economical repair. The fuselage was put into store there before moving to Shawbury and later to Warton for use in trials for the fitment of a new engine to the Jaguar fleet.

XX831   T.2   226 OCU. 30 April 1975 XX831/W crashed at Lossiemouth, Grampian, after loss of control during an inverted run over the airfield during a display practice. Caused by a fouled control column. The pilot ejected at 500 ft and was slightly injured.

XX832   T.2/A   16 (R) Squadron Lossiemouth. XX832/EZ 6 Squadron. Involved in a mid-air collision with GR.1A XX745/GV of 54 Squadron during a sortie over Scotland 31.5.00, and both diverted to Leuchars, Fife. XX832 suffered only slight damage.

XX833   T.2B   SAOEU Boscombe Down.

XX834   T.2A   6 Squadron. Lost 7.9.88 close to the town of Claw near Stuttgart, West Germany. Flown by Coltishall-based pilot, 27-year-old Flight Lieutenant Paul Nelson, with his passenger, a USAF F-16 pilot, when the Jaguar was seen to hit a high-voltage power line prior to crashing. The passenger ejected just after the collision and landed safely with minor injuries. Nelson died in the impact. The pilot was flying below the minimum briefed height when the aircraft struck HT cables in a valley and crashed near Wilbad-Kreuth. He was killed when his ejection seat struck the side of the valley. Although the wires were erected in 1966, they did not appear on any maps.

XX835   T.2B   41 Squadron.

XX836   T.2   6 Squadron. Stored Shawbury.

XX837   T.2   1 SoTT Cosford 8978M.

XX838	T.2A	Stored Shawbury.
XX839	T.2A	226 OCU. To RAF CTTS St Athan as 9255M.
XX840	T.2A	226 OCU. Stored Shawbury.
XX841	T.2A	6 Squadron.
XX842	T.2A(T)	41 Squadron.
XX843	T.2A	Lost 29.8.91 in collision with Cessna 152 G-BMHL at between 300 and 400 ft near Carno in Powys, Wales. The pilot, Wing Commander William Pixton DFC AFC, ejected to safety seconds after the collision and suffered a broken arm. His front-seat passenger, Wing Commander John Mardon MBE, was killed. Mardon had had a double transplant operation at Papworth Hospital, Cambridgeshire, after five long years of illness. He carried on working for as long as possible at a desk job at Coltishall while waiting for the operation. During the operation itself, his heart, which was perfectly healthy, was used in a separate transplant operation to give a desperately ill man a new lease of life. The Cessna pilot, who had taken off from Halfpenny Green on an aerial photography flight, but was operating in a military low-flying area without authorization, was killed instantly. Earlier in the month Mardon had cycled the ninety miles from Coltishall to Papworth Hospital to raise over £26,500 for the hospital and the donor family's chosen charity.
XX844	T.2	St Athan as 9C23M.
XX845	T.2A	6 Squadron.
XX846	T.2A	41 & 54 Squadrons.
XX847	T.2A	Stored St Athan.
XX915	T.2	Empire Test Pilots School. Crashed 17.1.84.
XX916	T.2	Empire Test Pilots School. Crashed 24.7.81.
XX955	GR.1A	Stored Shawbury.
XX956	GR.1	1 SoTT Cosford at 8950M.

XX957	GR.1	XX957/CG of 20 Squadron was struck by lightning shortly after take-off from Brüggen, 21.10.81, which caused the left-hand engine to surge and shut down. The right-hand engine failed while making an emergency landing at Brüggen, and the pilot ejected before the aircraft crashed into open farmland.
XX958	GR.1	1 SoTT Cosford as 9022M.
XX959	GR.1	To RAF Cosford for Ground instruction as 8953M.
XX960	GR.1	14 Squadron. On 18.7.89 XX960/AY struck a TV mast and crashed at Iserlohn, West Germany, while attempting to rejoin its formation. The pilot safely ejected.
XX961	GR.1	17 Squadron. Crashed 25.5.80 during run and break for landing at Brüggen after the No. 2 aircraft (XX964) broke too early and collided with XX961. The pilot of XX964 ejected, but the pilot of XX961 did not and he was killed.
XX962	GR.1B	Operation *Granby* 'X *Fat Slags/St Georgina*. AMIF Cranwell.
XX963	GR.1	14 Squadron. XX963/AL 25.5.82 shot down thirty-five miles north-east of Brüggen, by a Sidewinder missile accidentally fired by 92 Squadron FGR.2 Phantom XV422. Steve Griggs, the pilot of XX963, ejected safely. The master armament switch in the Phantom had not been taped in the 'safe' position and the pilot inadvertently rendered 'live' one of the two main safety switches. The pilot and navigator were court martialled and found guilty of offences of neglect.
XX964	GR.1	17 Squadron. Crashed RAF Brüggen 28.5.80 after colliding with XX961.
XX965	GR.1A	Damaged Coltishall, 11.96. AMIF Cranwell.
XX966	GR.1A	1 SoTT Cosford as 8904M.
XX967	GR.1A	1 SoTT Cosford as 9006M.
XX968	GR.1A	31 Squadron, now 1 SoTT Cosford as 9007M.
XX969	GR.1A	1 SoTT Cosford as 8897M.
XX970	GR1/A/B	Part of the initial deployment to Oman 12.8.91, the first Jaguar to leave UK.

XX971	GR.1	31 Squadron. XX971/DE crashed on 21.3.78 after the No. 2 engine failed on take-off from Lahr, Germany. The pilot jettisoned the external stores and attempted an emergency landing on one engine. He allowed speed and height to decay and ejected when he considered that he would not reach the airfield.
XX972	GR.1	31 Squadron. XX972/DF crashed 6.8.81 into a house two miles south of Barnard Castle, Co. Durham, injuring the family and killing the pilot. Disorientation in the bad weather was the likely cause.
XX973	GR.1	31 Squadron. On 14.4.81 the pilot lost control of XX973/DG during ACT when he was flying at a high angle of attack and encountered the slipstream of one of the other aircraft. He ejected and the aircraft crashed into a field four miles (16.5 km) north-west of Gutersloh.
XX974	GR.1A	Part of the initial deployment to Oman, 12.8.91. 54 Squadron.
XX975	GR1	1 SoTT Cosford as 8905M.
XX976	GR.1	1 SoTT Cosford as 8906M.
XX977	GR.1	St Athan EDRT as 9132M.
XX978	GR.1	31 Squadron. XX978/DM. Crashed 14.6.77, at Verden, Germany, after loss of control during a low-level sortie, killing the pilot. Wreckage from the aircraft damaged a house.
XX979	GR.1A	FJTS Boscombe Down.
XZ101	GR.1A	First reconnaissance Jaguar issued to II (AC) Squadron.
XZ102	GR.1	II (AC) Squadron. XZ102/H. Crashed 14.12.76 ten miles (116 km) north-east of Laarbruch, immediately after take-off for a test flight. The pilot had difficulty controlling the aircraft. He managed to climb to 800 ft but it entered an uncontrollable roll, forcing him to eject. It crashed ten miles north-east of the base. The tailplane-powered control units had not been reconnected following the refitting of No. 2 engine.
XZ103	GR.1A	41 Squadron.

XZ104	GR.1A	41 Squadron.
XZ105	GR.1	II (AC) Squadron. On 16.6.83 XZ105/25 and XZ110/30 collided during a three-aircraft echelon break to port while approaching Goose Bay, Canada. Both pilots ejected, the aircraft crashing into water surrounding the airfield.
XZ106	GR1B	Operation *Granby* 'O' *Rule Britannia*. 41 Squadron.
XZ107	GR.1A	41 Squadron.
XZ108	GR.1A	II (AC) & 54 Squadron. On 9.1.90 the port wing of XZI08/GD struck the tailfin of Tornado GR.1A ZA394/11 of II (AC) Squadron after they approached each other head on at the Spadeadam weapons range, Northumberland, each pilot being unaware of the other's presence. The Tornado crew ejected after being unable to control the violently rolling aircraft, and it crashed near Hexham. The Jaguar pilot managed to correct his rolling aircraft and made an emergency landed at Leeming. On 3.9.98 Flight Lieutenant Whittaker of XZ108 lost control of the aircraft when acting as a singleton during a 2-v-1 air combat sortie over the North Sea with two other Jaguars. He ejected and the aircraft crashed into the sea thirteen miles north-east of Cromer, Norfolk.
XZ109	GR.1A	II (AC) Squadron, Brüggen.54 Squadron.
XZ110	GR.1	II (AC) Squadron. On 16.6.83 XZ110/30 and XZ105/25 collided during a three-aircraft echelon break to port while approaching Goose Bay, Canada. Both pilots ejected, the aircraft crashing into water surrounding the airfield.
XZ111	GR.1A	54 Squadron XZ111/GO. On 27.10.00 it suffered a bird strike and crashed five miles north-east of Dumfries, on open hillside between the town and Lockerbie, after the pilot, Flight Lieutenant 'Torch' Clarke RNZAF, ejected. The aircraft was flying with another Jaguar, which circled the crash site until a rescue helicopter arrived to pick up the pilot, who was not seriously injured.
XZ112	GR.1B	54 Squadron.
XZ113	GR.1A	41 Squadron.
XZ114	GR.1A	41 & 6 Squadrons.

XZ115	GR.1B	41 Squadron.
XZ116	GR.1	41 Squadron. On 17.4.87 Flight Lieutenant Andy Mannheim of 41 Squadron was killed on a low-level training exercise in the Lake District when XZ116/D was involved in a collision with Tornado GR.1 ZA493/G of 20 Squadron from Laarbruch. The Tornado, No. 1 in a two-aircraft formation, was in a left-hand turn around Dod Grag in the Borrowdale Valley near Keswick, Cumbria. The starboard wing struck the cockpit area of the Jaguar, which was flying in the opposite direction, killing the pilot instantly. The second Tornado had to pull up hard to avoid the subsequent fireball. The two-man crew of the Tornado ejected and escaped with minor cuts and burns to their faces. An extensive search of the crash scene was made, using two Sea Kings, a Wessex, mountain rescue teams and many local volunteers, but in vain. Mannheim had no time to initiate his ejection sequence and he died in the impact.
XZ117	GR.1A	St Athan.
XZ118	GR.1A	Operation *Granby* 'Y'. *Buster Gonad and his Unfeasibly Large Testicles*.
XZ119	GR.1A	41 Squadron. Operation *Granby* 'Z' *Katrina Jane*. AMIF Cranwell.
XZ120	GR.1	41 Squadron. Crashed into sea 25.2.77, Nordhorn, Denmark, after loss of contact in a formation join-up. The pilot was killed.
XZ355	GR.1	41 Squadron. SAOEU Boscombe Down.
XZ356	GR.1A	6 Squadron. Operation *Granby* 'N' *Mary Rose*. During Operation *Warden, Marshall Connolly*.
XZ357	GR.1A	Part of the initial deployment to Oman, 12.8.91. 41 Squadron.
XZ358	GR.1A	Operation *Granby* 'W' *Diplomatic Service*. AMIF Cranwell.
XZ359	GR.1A	Crashed 13.4.89 north of Berwick-on-Tweed. Squadron Leader Paul 'PV' Lloyd of 54 Squadron lost contact with his No. 2 in dense fog while flying over the coast. Lloyd flew into 500 ft high fog-shrouded cliffs 100 ft below the summit above Lumsdaine Beach 1½ miles north-west of St Abbs

Head, near Wheatstock, Berwickshire. Shortly afterwards his No. 2 backtracked and spotted the wreckage on the cliff tops. A Wessex from RAF Leuchars and a Sea King from RAF Boulmer were scrambled to the crash site. Together with a mountain rescue team they scoured the area. Lloyd's body was found and recovered a short time later.

XZ360	GR.1A	41 Squadron.
XZ361	GR.1A	II (AC) Squadron & 41 Squadron.
XZ362	GR.1A	6 & 54 Squadrons. XZ362/GC crashed in Alaska 24.6.96. Flight Lieutenant Whittaker was leader of an eight-ship formation operating from Eielson AFB near Fairbanks, Alaska, during DACT with F-16s as part of Exercise *Cope Thunder*. While rolling out of a turn twenty miles from Eielson, the aircraft struck the tops of trees on a lightly wooded ridge. It remained controllable but the left engine was winding down. Being unable to relight it and with other warning captions illuminating, Whittaker ejected. (He also ejected from XZ108 on 3.9.98!) An Alaskan ANG rescue team picked him up.
XZ363	GR.1B	41 Squadron. Part of the initial deployment to Oman, 12.8.91. On 26.7.2001 XZ363 crashed during Exercise *Cope Thunder* at Eielson AFB, Alaska, during a simulated ground attack. Flight Lieutenant Jason Hayes was killed.
XZ364	GR.1A	Operation *Granby* 'Q' *Sadman*. 54 Squadron.
XZ365	GR.1A	II (AC) Squadron. XZ365/33 crashed 10.7.85 when it struck trees on the top of a 2,450 ft hill near Meschede, east of Dortmund, West Germany. The pilot maintained control of the aircraft but ejected when a fire started in the cockpit.
XZ366	GR.1A	41 Squadron.
XZ367	GR.1B	Operation *Granby* 'P' *Debbie*, later *White Rose*. 54 Squadron.
XZ368	GR.1	1 SoTT Cosford as 890CM.
XZ369	GR.1B	Part of the initial deployment to Oman, 12.8.91. 6 Squadron.
XZ370	GR.1	2 SoTT RAF Cosford as 9004M.
XZ371	GR.1	RAF Cosford for ground instruction.

XZ372	GR.1A/B	Part of the initial deployment to Oman, 12.8.91. FJTS Boscombe Down. To St Athan for conversion 9.97.
XZ373	GR.1A	17, 54 & 6 Squadrons. Crashed on 21 June 1995 during a training sortie while being flown by a USAF exchange pilot with 6 Squadron. Due to a fuel imbalance in the underwing tanks control was lost during ACT. The pilot could not regain control and he ejected at 5,000 ft over the Adriatic Sea. A Royal Navy Sea King from the NATO base at Split subsequently rescued him.
XZ374	GR.1	1 SoTT Cosford as 9005M.
XZ375	GR.1B	Operation *Granby* 'S' *The Guardian Reader*. To CTTS St Athan as 9255M.
XZ376	GR.1	17 Squadron. XZ376/BE crashed 7.3.83. During a bomb toss manoeuvre on the Tain range, Highland, the aircraft entered cloud after bomb release. It emerged from the cloud in an inverted dive. The pilot over-corrected the recovery and lost control. He ejected at 325 ft but was knocked unconscious when he struck the canopy.
XZ377	GR.1A	6 Squadron.
XZ378	GR.1A	Stored Shawbury.
XZ381	GR.1B	6 Squadron 'EC'. GR.3 XZ381/D 16(R) Squadron, crashed 20.10.99. Ditched into the Moray Firth six miles north of Lossiemouth, Grampian, after the pilot, who was the station commander at Lossiemouth, was forced to eject while attempting to recover the aircraft back to base after it had suffered hydraulic failure, resulting in his being unable to lower the undercarriage. Another Jaguar was shepherding the aircraft, but the pilot elected to eject rather than risk crashing in a populated area after control difficulties were also experienced. It sank in 200 ft of water, but a salvage operation was begun to recover the aircraft. The pilot was in the water for fifteen minutes before being rescued by a 202 Squadron Sea King HAR.3, and was taken to Nottingham hospital, although he was not seriously injured.
XZ382	GR.1	BDRT Coltishall.
XZ383	GR.1	1 SoTT Cosford as 8901M.
XZ384	GR.1	17 Squadron. RAF Cosford for ground instruction as 8954M.

XZ385   GR.1A   16 (R) Squadron Lossiemouth.

XZ386   GR.1A   226 OCU & 14 Squadron. XZ386/05 Crashed 24.6.87. The pilot had to bunt and roll to port to avoid a collision when acting as an aggressor with two other Jaguars while flying up the Wye Valley three miles south-east of Builth Wells, Powys. He then entered the slipstream of one of the other Jaguars and had to manoeuvre hard to avoid a collision with the ground. Control was lost but he ejected too late and he was killed when the aircraft crashed. The pilot had previously ejected from Canberra WD963 on 29 June 1967 and belly-landed in Canberra WT209 on 1.2.68.

XZ387   GR.1A   31 Squadron. XZ387/GG 54 Squadron. 12.9.90, flew into the sea in the Solway Firth five miles off Southerness Point, Dumfries & Galloway, killing the pilot. The aircraft was part of a four-ship formation preparing for Operation *Granby*.

XZ388   GR.1   17 & 14 Squadrons. XZ388/AH crashed 2.4.85. During the let-down to the Munsterlager range near Rebberlali, West Germany, with two other Jaguars, Gary Brough, the pilot, mis-selected the radio frequency and had to reselect. When he looked out the aircraft was in a banked turn and close to the ground. He rolled level and applied full power but ejected when it became clear that the aircraft would strike the ground. Brough was knocked unconscious when he struck the canopy.

XZ389   GR.1   20 Squadron. 1 SoTT Cosford as 8946M. 'EL'.

XZ390   GR.1   1 SoTT Cosford as 90003M.

XZ391   GR.1A   2 Squadron. 16 (R) Squadron Lossiemouth.

XZ392   GR.1A   Stored Shawbury.

XZ393   GR.1A   54 Squadron. Crashed 12.7.84. ATC warned the Jaguar formation about Tornado GR1 ZA408 of TWCU. No. 2 in the formation spotted the aircraft and transmitted his position to the rest of the group, unfortunately on the wrong frequency. The pilot of XZ393/GK saw ZA408 directly ahead of him, and both aircraft collided over Cromer, Norfolk. The Jaguar crashed into the North Sea, while the Tornado crashed near Hempstead, Norfolk. All three crew ejected safely.

XZ394	GR.1	17 ('BJ') and 54 (GN) Squadrons.
XZ395	GR.1A	54 Squadron. On 22.8.84 XZ395/GJ crashed into the North Sea thirty miles north of Coltishall after the pilot ejected following loss of control due to excessive rudder movement, the cause of which could not be established.
XZ396	GR.1A	Part of the initial deployment to Oman, 12.8.91. AMF Coltishall.
XZ397	GR.1	To Indian Air Force.
XZ398	GR.1A	41 Squadron, ex-Indian AF loan.
XZ399	GR.1B	6 Squadron 'EJ'.
XZ400	GR.1A	Stored Shawbury.
ZB615	T.2	Fast-jet Test Squadron Boscombe

RAF JAGUAR OPERATIONS DESERT STORM

Sorties and Missions Flown

Type	Sorties (%)	Missions (%)
SuCAP/CSAR*	48 (7.8)	23 (14.6)
Reconnaissance	31 (5.0)	21 (13.3)
BAI	538 (87.2)	114 (72.1)
Total	617	158

Ordnance Expended

Weapon	Quantity
1,000lb (454 kg) bomb	750
CBU-87 Rockeye II	385
BL755 CBU	8
CRV-7 2.75 inch rocket	608 (32 LAU-5003 pods)
30mm ammunition	9,600 rounds
AIM-9L Sidewinder	3 (1 accidentally launched)

Combat Flying Hours

920 hours 15 minutes
*Support Combat Air Patrol/Combat Search and Rescue

Notes

Chapter 1

1. Though it was claimed that a lack of funding was the reason, money was later made available for the indigenous Mirage G variable-geometry design. Variable-geometry design continued in Britain while the government sought a European partner to replace the French. Finally, in July 1968, a Memorandum of Understanding was signed between Britain, Canada, West Germany, Italy, Belgium and the Netherlands, and on 22 July 1970 the British and West German governments decided to proceed with the Multi-Role Combat Aircraft (MRCA), being joined in September by Italy. Aerospace companies in all three countries collaborated to produce the Panavia Tornado.

2. The Hawk T.Mk 1 2-seat trainer is powered by one Rolls-Royce/Turboméca Adour Mk 151-01 turbofan and the Mk 100 2-seat advanced flying and weapons trainer and the Mk 200 single-seat air superiority and ground-attack warplane are each powered by a single Adour Mk 871. The Goshawk is powered by one Rolls-Royce/Turboméca F405-RR-401 (Adour 871) turbofan.

3. The training team is multi-national and comprises a nucleus of permanent TACEVAL staff on the strength of the headquarters of the Allied Air Forces Central Europe (AAFCE) at Brunssom in the Netherlands. Its members are chosen from the ranks of those who have themselves served with distinction 'in the field', together with acknowledged experts co-opted from other wings. Group Captain J.R. Walker AFC, writing in 1978, said, 'To put TACEVAL in context, imagine British Leyland being examined in great detail and without warning, by a team from Mercedes-Benz, Volkswagen, DAF, Peugeot, Mazda, Toyota and General Motors!'

4. A rating of '2' on a four-point scale indicates all that SACEUR requires and is 'Satisfactory'. A '3' rating is 'Marginal', but a '4' is 'Unsatisfactory', and a unit that achieves this can expect another TACEVAL visit in the very near future, usually after just enough delay to allow the new executives to take some remedial action – the old executives would probably have been sacked.

Chapter 2

5. After a tour on Jaguars, Steve Hicks went on to Harriers, where he quickly became a QWI; he then left the service on completion of his eight-year Short Service Commission and went on to fly for British Airways on the Boeing 747-400.

6. At Tain the use of the aircraft's LRMTS is permitted. Much of the flying over Scotland is cleared down to 250 ft (75 m), with minimal airspace restrictions. One area in the west of Scotland, officially referred to as 14 Tango Tactical Training Area (known also as 'moon country') is cleared, with special permission, for flights down to l00 ft (30 m).

7. Like the DEFA series, the Aden owes much to the German Mauser MG 213c revolver cannon of the Second World War. The name is taken from the Armament Development Establishment and ENfield where it was built.

8. XZ376/BE. During the bomb toss manoeuvre on the Tain range the Jaguar entered cloud after bomb release. It emerged from the cloud in an inverted dive. The pilot over-corrected the recovery and lost control. He ejected at 325 ft but was knocked unconscious when he struck the canopy.

9. Often known as canister ballistic units (CBU), this dual-role weapon is designed for release from low level. Each individual bomblet arms itself as it falls, and detonates on impact with a shaped-charge war head able to penetrate armour at least 250 mm thick, as well as scattering a cloud of 2,000 lethal fragments.

10. GR.1 XX114/02

Chapter 3

11. The insignia of RAF Germany.

12. Equally important to the effectiveness of this force were the five squadrons of SAMs, a wing of the RAF Regiment providing ground defence, a maintenance unit and many ancillary services. In the last-mentioned category is the 230-bed RAF hospital at Wegberg, near Mönchengladbach, responsible for the welfare of all British personnel, with their wives and families, in the area. Overall RAFG comprised 1,200 officers, 9,500 airmen and more than 18,000 dependants.

13. RAF Jaguars first participated in *Red Flag* in 1976, when eight Jaguar GR.ls from RAF Germany (five from 31 Squadron and three from 17 Squadron, took part during 17 January to 28 February. During the period at Nellis, pilots of II (AC), 41 (F), 17, 31 and 6 Squadrons flew as part of the 'Blue' force, operating with F-4E Phantoms as part of the primary air-to-ground exercise, as well as taking part in large composite attack forces.

14. XX750/AL of 14 Squadron crashed inverted on 7.2.84 at *Red Flag* as a result of losing control while taking avoiding action after being picked up by ground radar. The USAF exchange pilot was killed.

15. The aircraft LRMTS should not be confused with laser target designators for laser-guided bombs (LGBs), which are quite different. The FAC laser target markers could, however, be used for this purpose if required. Kevin regularly practised using the full LRMTS on Nordhorn Range as the range tower had its own laser target designator pointing at a particular target. The pilots could then turn in towards the target and the target marker would appear in the HUD, so that they could adjust their attack to steer through the marker cross and release a 3 kg practice bomb; as an additional check, they sometimes used the aircraft laser ranger as well. The laser ranger could be used

in normal bombing without the marked target seeker, and would have been the primary mode of operation in war, but because of peacetime safety limitations the radar altimeter was the most commonly used weapons-aiming sensor, although it was not as accurate as the laser ranger, especially if the terrain on approach to the target was not flat.

16. No. 20 Squadron disbanded on 29 June 1984 and became a Tornado GR.1 squadron at Laarbruch, before again disbanding as part of 'Options For Change' and reappearing as 20 (Reserve) Squadron, the Harrier OCU at Wittering. No. 31 Squadron operated the Jaguar in RAF Germany until on 13 June 1984 the first Tornado GR.1 arrived at Brüggen. The squadron gave up the last of its Jaguars on 1 November 1984, when it became operational on the Tornado.

17. On 1 April 1985 GR.1 XZ388/AH of 14 Squadron crashed during the let-down to Munsterlager range near Rebberlali. Gary Brough, the pilot, was looking into the cockpit, changing radio frequencies, while in a turn at low level and attempting to catch up with his leader, when he inadvertently over-banked, so that when he looked up, he was almost upside down and the world was green. The aircraft ploughed through some saplings, which were only a few feet high, as he rolled and pulled to recover. At that point he wisely decided to leave. Fortunately the Martin-Baker ejection seat operated as advertised and he survived, although he was knocked unconscious when he struck the canopy.

18. Buccaneer S.2Bs made their combat debut on 1/2 February 1991, when a bridge over the River Euphrates was successfully marked for six Pave Way guided bombs dropped by two Tornado GR.1s. Additionally they dropped their own 1,000 lb (454 kg) LGBs during Tornado raids from 21 February. In all the twelve Buccaneers flew 218 sorties, dropping forty-eight bombs.

19 A modified version of the Hunter T.8 fitted with the same Ferranti Blue Fox airborne interception radar as the Sea Harrier FRS.Mk 1,

20. II (AC) Squadron, the second squadron of the Royal Flying Corps (RFC), was originally formed in 1912. The reason for the somewhat unusual squadron designation is not clear, but it would appear that the RFC had no firm rules on whether Roman or Arabic numerals should be used for squadron numbers, and about 25% of the early squadrons used Roman numerals. Then, in 1924 the Air Ministry introduced letters after the squadron number to signify its role: thus AC for Army Co-operation, B for Bomber and F for Fighter. Although this system was discontinued for security reasons in the Second World War, it was subsequently brought back into use by a number of squadrons.

21. Refurbished USN A-7A with Allison TF30-P-408 turbofan for export to Portugal where they equipped *302* and *304 Esquadra de Ataque* of the *Force Aïra Portuguesa*. 304 was only declared operational with the A-7/TA-7P late in 1985.

22. The 64th and 65th Fighter Weapons Squadrons equipped with F-5E Tiger IIs, selected for its similarity to the MiG-21 in size and performance, were known as the 'Aggressors'. The CAF (Canadian Armed Forces) also used CF-5As of the 433rd and 434th Squadrons in the Aggressor role.

23. During the Gulf War Flight Lieutenant Kevin Noble flew eleven TIALD missions on Tornadoes of 13 Squadron, two of which were aborted because of bad weather, although on two other occasions they had designated for the second pair of bombers in the formation when the original TIALD aircraft became unserviceable. Starting on 8 February, a total of ninety-five TIALD missions were carried out by Tornadoes in the nineteen days up to the cease-fire, 261 LGBs hit their targets and no aircraft were lost. Throughout this period, only the two original TIALD pods, which had been built for development purposes, were available, and these were shuffled between a maximum of five Tornado GR.1s, which had received the necessary modifications to accept them. In use these two pods proved to be both reliable and user-friendly. One pod registered 100% serviceability and the other 98.2%. On 1 July 1991 Chris Allam was promoted to squadron leader. He retired from the RAF in 1977 and joined British Airways as a Boeing 747 captain.

Chapter 5

24. In all, Boeing supplied twelve C-135F (KC-135A) tankers to France.

25. This three-seat trainer and light attack aircraft was exported to numerous African countries. It can carry 661 lb (300 kg) of ordnance on two or four underwing pylons.

26. Like the Aden, the DEFA owes much to the German Mauser MG 213c revolver cannon of the Second World War.

Chapter 6

27. Nos 6, 41 (F) and 54 (F) Squadrons provided four, nine and seven pilots respectively, with two from 226 OCU.

28. XX725/T, XX733/R, XZ119/Z, XZ358/W, XZ364/Q, XZ367/P and XZ375/S.

29. XX748/U, XX754, XX962/X, XZ118/Y and XZ356/N.

30. By 21 January, Day 5 of the war, three Tornadoes had been lost in low-level night operations and another crashed on take-off, and it was announced that to reduce losses the Tornado missions would be flown at higher level. On 22 January a fourth Tornado was lost to enemy action. On 23 January a fifth Tornado GR.1 was shot down during an evening airfield raid, and on 24 January another Tornado landed at Dhahran with serious damage from exploding SAMs. On 25 January it was officially revealed that RAF low flying had been suspended. A sixth and final Tornado was lost in enemy territory on 14 February while on a medium-level bombing raid.

31. The end of the war came suddenly and unexpectedly when a ceasefire was declared on 28 February 1991. Air operations had started on 17 January and had continued for a total of forty-two days, while the ground war, which began on 24 February, had lasted only for 100 hours. However, these operations resulted in the complete defeat of the Iraqi forces. Thousands of Iraqi soldiers abandoned their stockpiles of equipment, weapons and ammunition and surrendered. On 27 February Kuwait was liberated, although it was not until 11 April that the conflict was declared officially over.

32. Nine awards were made to Coltishall personnel at the end of hostilities. The

Distinguished Flying Cross was awarded to Wing Commander William Pixton, Squadron Leader Michael Gordon, both 41 (F) Squadron, and Flying Officer Mal Rainier, 54 (F) Squadron, who at the time was the youngest recipient of the DFC since the Second World War. The Air Force Cross was awarded to Wing Commander Jerry Connolly, OC 6 Squadron, and Squadron Leader Les Hendry and Flight Lieutenant Chris Boyce were appointed Members of the British Empire. Flight Lieutenants Toby Craig, Peter Tholen and Craig Hill were Mentioned In Dispatches.

Chapter 7

33. The Jaguars at Gioia were involved in two air strikes. The first, on 22 September 1994, was in support of French UN personnel who called for air support following a Bosnian Serb rocket attack. Subsequently, a static Serb T55 tank was destroyed near the village of Osijek in the Sarajevo exclusion zone by a pair of Jaguars, each dropping two 1,000 lb bombs.

34. SOKO/Iav Craiova J-22/IAR-93 lightweight close-support and ground-attack aircraft, the result of a collaborative Yugoslav and Romanian project, which emerged with a configuration reminiscent of the Jaguar and powered by two Turboméca/ORAO-built Rolls-Royce Viper turbojets.

35. Chris Carder flew the Jaguar with 54 (F) Squadron from 1992 to 1996. He then became a Jaguar QFI at RAF Lossiemouth and he was the Jaguar display pilot in 1999. Earlier in his career as a Hawk QFI at RAF Valley he was twice the winner of the No. 4 Flying Training School aerobatic competition. He was also the 1991 solo Hawk display pilot. In 2000 he joined the Red Arrows as Red 4.

36. When UNPROFOR changed its role to become the United Nations Implementation Force (IFOR), Operation *Deny Flight* became Operation *Decisive Endeavour*, and in December 1996 IFOR's role changed again to become the United Nations Stabilization Force (SFOR), and Operation *Decisive Edge* then became Operation *Deliberate Guard*.

Chapter 8

37. After the Gulf War, simulated Scud missiles were added to the target array, and UAVs are now an integral part of each exercise. Combat search and rescue is more commonly practised, as is the protection of peace-support-type operations, such as humanitarian aid airdrops. Not only will the scenario need to be updated continuously, but the technology to support these changes will also need upgrading. The Nellis Air Combat Training System (NACTS) has replaced RFMDS. NACTS more than doubles the number of aircraft that can be tracked, and allows the information to be displayed on desktop computers.

38. 101 Squadron was equipped with K.Mk 2 and K.Mk 3 flight refuelling tankers converted from nine commercial VC 10 Model 1101s and 1154s respectively. The K.Mk 2's total fuel capacity, including the aircraft's own fuel, is 94,270 litres, and the K.Mk 3 102,780 litres (total). Nine L-1011-500s were acquired by the MoD in 1982–4, and eight equipped 216 Squadron, four being converted to TriStar C.Mk 1 tanker/transport standard by having fuel tanks installed in the fore and aft baggage

compartments, providing an additional 100,000 lb (45,360 gallons) of fuel capacity. Two of the four K.Mk 1s remained in service in the mid-1990s, with the remaining two aircraft and two newly acquired TriStar aircraft having been further modified to the TriStar KC.Mk 1 tanker/freighter standard.

39. Sixteen Mirage 2000EM single-seat and four Mirage 2000BM 2-seat aircraft were delivered to Egypt in 1986–8.

Glossary

A&AEE	Aeroplane and Armament Evaluation Establishment
AAA	automatic anti-aircraft; the normal term for anti-aircraft gunfire/anti-aircraft artillery
AAM	air-to-air missile
ACM	advanced cruise missile
ACMI	air combat manoeuvring instrumentation
ACR	advanced capability radar
ACT	active control technology
AFB	air force base
AGL	above ground level
AGM	air-to-ground missile
AI	area interdiction
ALBM	air-launched ballistic missile
ALCM	air-launched cruise missile
Alpha	angle of attack
AMU	aircraft maintenance unit
ANG	Air National Guard
ARM	anti-radiation missile (also see Shrike, Standard ARM)
ARTEL	air portable reconnaissance exploitation laboratory
ARTF	alkaline removable temporary finish
ASTE	Armament and Systems Testing Establishment
ATAF	Allied Tactical Air Force
ATLANTIC	airborne targeting low altitude thermal imaging and cueing
ATLIS	automatic tracking laser illuminating system
ATM	air task message

AWACS	airborne warning and control system
BDA	bomb damage assessment
BLU	bomblet units
C-135F	four-engine military version of the Boeing 707, used by the French Air Force as an air refuelling tanker
CALCM	conventional air-launched cruise missile
CAP	combat air patrol
CAS	close air support
CATac	*Commandement Aérien Tactique*
CBLS	carrier bomb light stores
CBU	cluster-bomb unit
CEAM	*Centre d'Experiences Aériennes Militaires*
CEP	circular error probable
CEV	*Centre d'Essais en Vol*
CFS	Central Flying School
Chaff	Small pieces of tinfoil-like metal strips cut to a specified length to jam enemy radars
CITAC 339	*Centre d'Instruction Tactique 339*
CKD	completely knocked down
CRL	common rail launcher
DACT	dissimilar air combat training
DARIN	display, avionics, ranging and inertial navigation
DERA	Defence Evaluation and Research Agency
DPSA	deep penetration strike aircraft
DRA	Defence Research Agency
DTEO	Defence Test and Evaluation Organization
ECM	Generic name for electronic countermeasures, usually applied to systems carried by an aircraft
EFA	European Fighter Aircraft
ETPS	Empire Test Pilots School
FAC	forward air control
FAE	*Fuerza Aerea Ecuatoriona*

FATac	*Force Aérienne Tactique*
FBW	fly-by-wire
FEAR	folding-fin aerial rocket
FJTS	Fast-jet Test Squadron
Flak	*See* AAA
FLIR	forward-looking infra-red
FOD	foreign object damage
FRA	first-run attack
GCI	ground-controlled interception
GLO	ground liaison officer
GPF	general-purpose fragmentation
GPS	global positioning satellite (system)
HAL	Hindustan Aeronautics Limited
HAS	hardened aircraft shelter
HDD	head-down display
HEAT	high-explosive anti-tank
HMSS	helmet-mounted sighting system
HOTAS	hands on throttle and stick
HQ	headquarters
HSI	heading speed indicator
HUD	head-up display
HUDWAS	head-up display and weapons-aiming system
IAF	Indian Air Force
IAM	Institute of Aviation Medicine
ICBM	intercontinental ballistic missile
IFF	identification friend or foe
IFR	in-flight refuelling
IFREP	in-flight report
ILS	instrument landing system
INAS	inertial navigation and attack system
IP	initial point

IRBM	intermediate-range ballistic missile
IRLS	infra-red linescan system
JCT	Jaguar Conversion Team
JMU	Jaguar maintenance unit
JOCU	Jaguar operational conversion unit
JP	Jet Provost or junior pilot
JUPO	Jaguar upgrade project officer
KIA	killed in action
KTO	Kuwait theatre of (operations)
LGBG	laser-guided bomb. A highly accurate conventional bomb with a kit attached that allowed it to follow a laser beam to a ground target
LIR	low infra-red
LOROP	long-range oblique photography
LOX	liquid oxygen
LRMTS	laser rangefinder and marked target seeker
MARTEL	missile anti-radar television
MCDW	minimum collateral damage weapon
MFD	multi-function display
MIA	missing in action
MILES	multiple-laser engagement system
MPCD	multi-purpose colour display
MPS	mission planning system
MU	maintenance unit
NACTS	Nellis Air Combat Training System
NASA	National Aeronautics and Space Administration
NAVWASS	navigation and weapons-aiming sub-system
NBC	nuclear, biological and chemical
NVG	night-vision goggles
OLF	operational low flying
OCU	operational conversion unit
PBF	pilot-briefing facility

PGM	precision-guided munition
PMD	precision munitions delivery
PODS	portable data store
POW	prisoner of war
PI	photographic interpreter
QFI	qualified flying instructor
QRA	quick-reaction alert
QWI	qualified weapons instructor
RAE	Royal Aircraft Establishment
RAF	Royal Air Force
RAFG	Royal Air Force Germany
RAM	radar-absorbent material
REMDS	*Red Flag* measurement and debriefing system
RHWR	radar homing and warning receiver
RIC	reconnaissance intelligence centre
RNorAF	Royal Norwegian Air Force
RWR	radar warning receiver
s.t.	static thrust
SACEUR	Supreme Allied Commander Europe
SAM	surface-to-air missile
SAOEU	strike/attack operational evaluation unit
SAP	simulated attack profile
SARCAP	search and rescue combat air patrol
SEM	service engineering modifications
SEP	specific excess power
SEPECAT	*Société Européenne de Production de l'Avion d'École de Combat et d'Appui Tactique*
Shrike	Small anti-radiation missile carried by Wild Weasels
Smart bombs	Generally applied to laser-guided bombs but also applicable to other types of guided bombs
SOAF	Sultan of Oman's Air Force
SOP	standard operating procedure

SoTT	school of technical training
SRAM	short-range attack missile
STANEVAL	standards evaluation
SuCAP	support combat air patrol
SWAM	surface wave radar-absorbent material
TABS	total avionics briefing system
TACAN	tactical air navigation
TERPROM	terrain profile matching
TIALD	thermal imaging airborne laser designation
TOT	time on target
TRNS	terrain reference navigation system
UAV	unmanned aerial vehicles
UOR	urgent operational requirement
USAFE	United States Air Force Europe
VIGIL	Vinten integrated infra-red linescan
VOR	VHF omni-directional radio range
WAMS	weapons-aiming mode selector

Index

SEPECAT
JAGUAR

COLOUR PROFILES

created by Dave Windle

Jaguar GR.Mk.1A. XZ356 'N' 'Mary Rose'

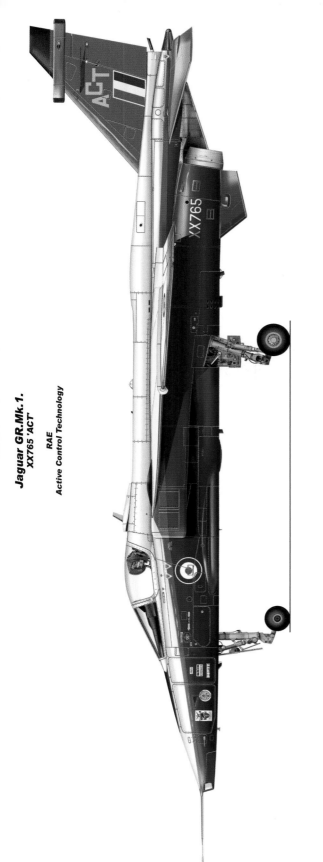

Jaguar GR.Mk.1.
XX765 'ACT'

RAE
Active Control Technology

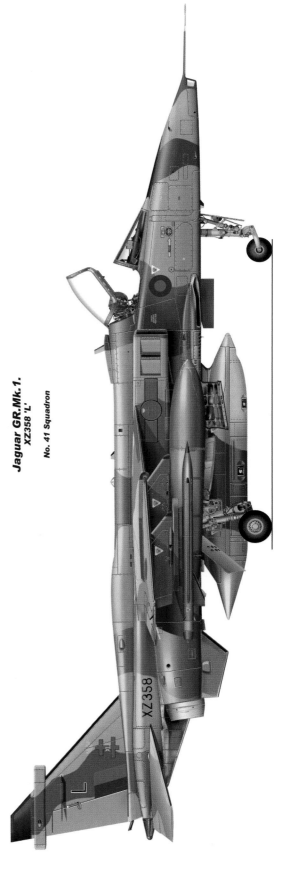

Jaguar GR.Mk.1.
XZ358 'L'

No. 41 Squadron

Jaguar T.Mk.2.
XX145

Empire Test Pilots School

Jaguar T.Mk.2.
XX834 'U'

No. 226 Operational Conversion Unit

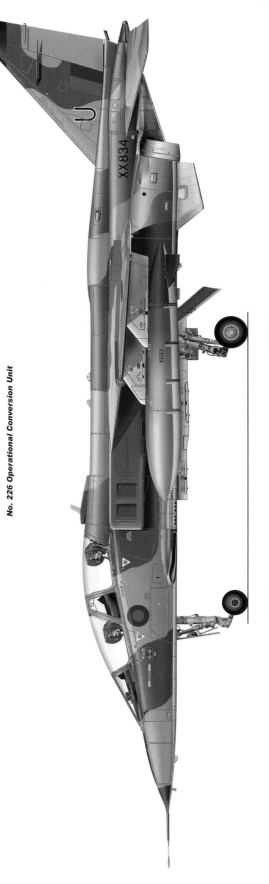

Jaguar GR.Mk.1A.
XZ362 'GC'

No. 54 Squadron

Jaguar GR.Mk.1A.
XZ364 'Q'
'SADMAN'

Jaguar Detachment
Muharraq, Bahrain 1991

Jaguar GR.Mk.1A.
XX733 'R'

Jaguar Detachment
Muharraq, Bahrain 1991
Sqn Ldr Dave Bagshaw

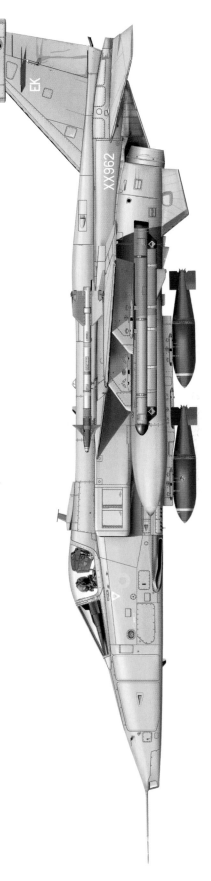

Jaguar GR.Mk.1A.
XX962 'EK'

No. 6 Squadron
Operation Volcano 1994

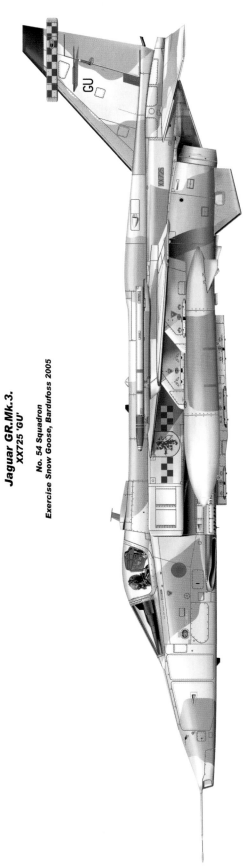

Jaguar GR.Mk.3.
XX725 'GU'

No. 54 Squadron
Exercise Snow Goose, Bardufoss 2005

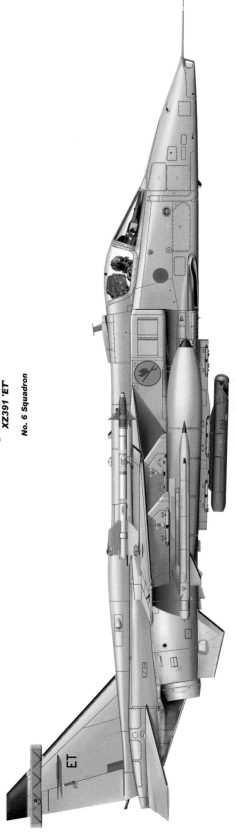

Jaguar GR.Mk.3A.
XZ391 'ET'

No. 6 Squadron

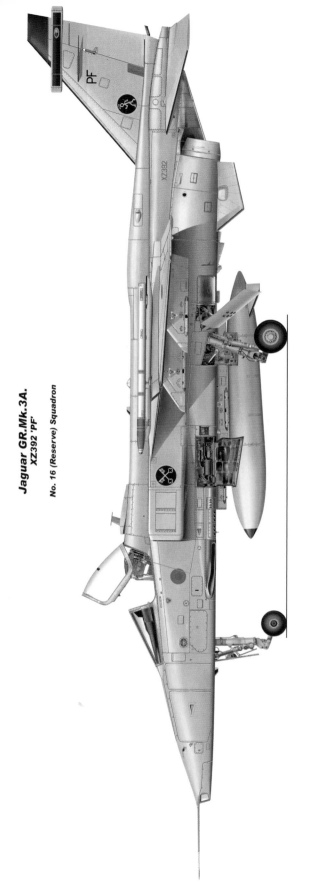

Jaguar GR.Mk.3A.
XZ392 'PF'

No. 16 (Reserve) Squadron

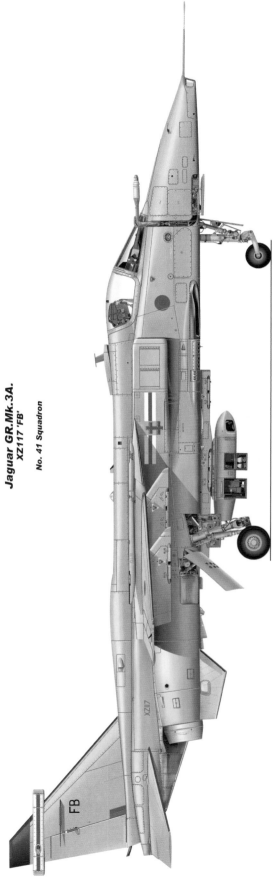

Jaguar GR.Mk.3A.
XZ117 'FB'

No. 41 Squadron

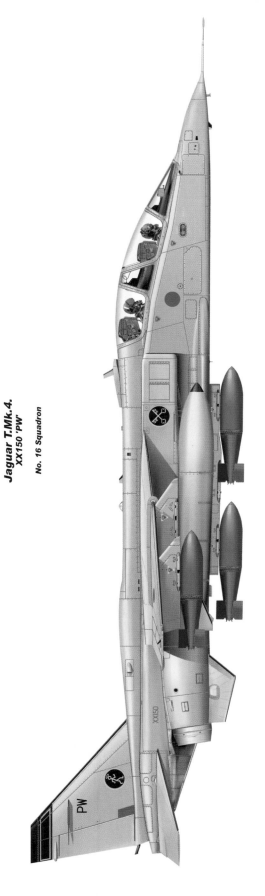

Jaguar T.Mk.4.
XX150 'PW'

No. 16 Squadron

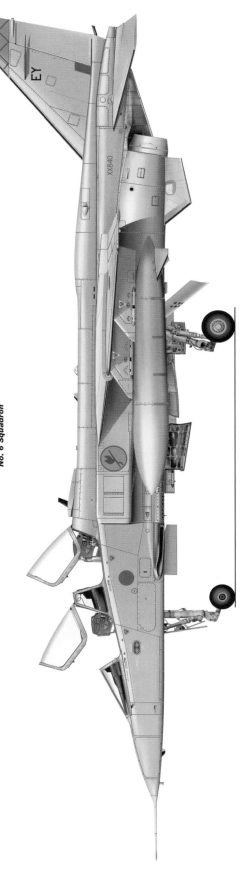

Jaguar T.Mk.4.
XX840 'EY'

No. 6 Squadron

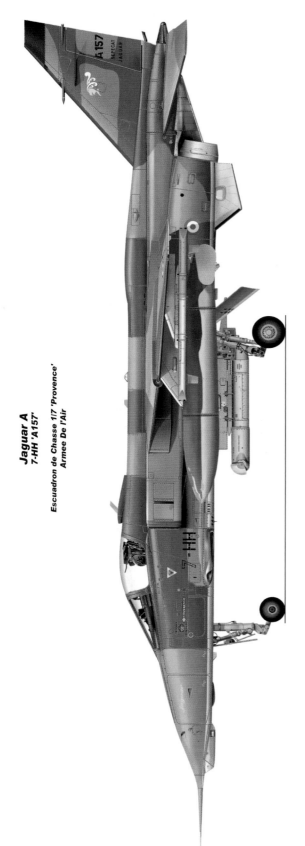

Jaguar A
7-HH 'A157'
Escuadron de Chasse 1/7 'Provence'
Armee De l'Air

Jaguar E
7-PP 'E15'
7 Escadre de Chasse
Armee De l'Air

Jaguar ES
G-27-272 'FAE327'

Fuerza Aerea Ecuatoriana
Escuadron de Combate 2111

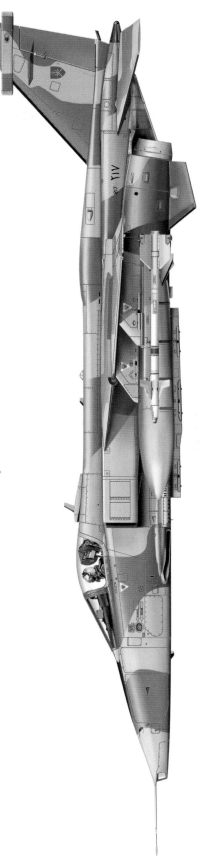

Jaguar OS
G-27-379 '217'

No. 20 Squadron
Royal Air Force of Oman

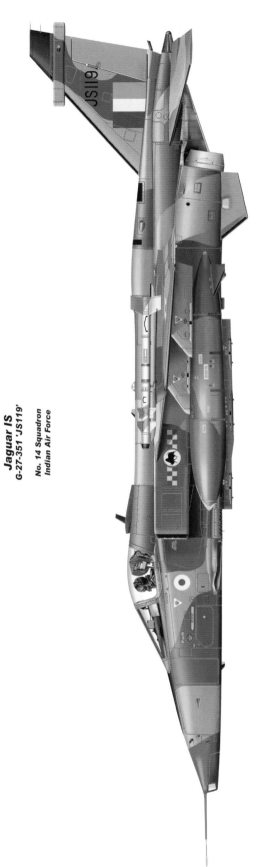

Jaguar IS
G-27-351 'JS119'

No. 14 Squadron
Indian Air Force

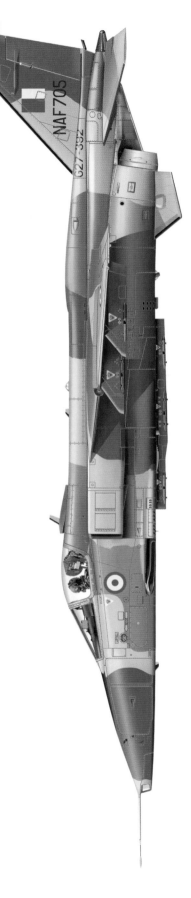

Jaguar SN
G-27-392 'NAF705'

Nigerian Air Force